DECORATIVE ART
IN AMERICA

DECORATIVE ART
IN AMERICA

A LECTURE BY
OSCAR WILDE

TOGETHER WITH LETTERS
REVIEWS AND INTERVIEWS
EDITED WITH AN INTRODUCTION
BY RICHARD BUTLER GLAENZER

NEW YORK

MCMVI

Copyright, 1906

CONTENTS

	PAGE
INTRODUCTION	vii
DECORATIVE ART IN AMERICA	1
JOAQUIN MILLER, THE GOOD SAMARITAN	17
MRS. LANGTRY AS HESTER GRAZEBROOK	23
"VERA" AND THE DRAMA	31
MR. WHISTLER'S "TEN O'CLOCK"	39
THE RELATION OF DRESS TO ART	47
THE TOMB OF KEATS	55
KEATS' SONNET ON BLUE	63
ENGLISH POETESSES	71
LONDON MODELS	87
"DORIAN GRAY" AND ITS CRITICS	101
RUDYARD KIPLING AND THE ANGLO-INDIANS	117
"A HOUSE OF POMEGRANATES"	121
THE RELATION OF THE ACTOR TO THE PLAY	127
THE CENSURE AND "SALOMÉ"	135
PARIS, THE ABODE OF ARTISTS	145
SARAH BERNHARDT AND "SALOMÉ"	149
THE ETHICS OF JOURNALISM	153
DRAMATIC CRITICS AND "AN IDEAL HUSBAND"	161
NOTES	
Introduction	175
Decorative Art in America	181
Joaquin Miller, the Good Samaritan	187

CONTENTS

	PAGE
Mrs. Langtry as Hester Grazebrook	193
"Vera" and the Drama	195
Mr. Whistler's "Ten O'Clock"	197
The Relation of Dress to Art	201
The Tomb of Keats	205
Keats' Sonnet on Blue	219
English Poetesses	229
London Models	241
"Dorian Gray" and its Critics	245
Mr. Kipling and the Anglo-Indians	251
"A House of Pomegranates"	253
The Relation of the Actor to the Play	255
The Censure and "Salomé"	257
Paris, the Abode of Artists	261
Sarah Bernhardt and "Salomé"	263
The Ethics of Journalism	265
Dramatic Critics and "An Ideal Husband"	269
INDEX	271

INTRODUCTION

If it took Labouchere three columns to prove that I was forgotten, then there is no difference between fame and obscurity.
            —*New York Herald, Sunday, August 12, 1883.*

INTRODUCTION

IF we are content to accept Oscar Wilde at his own final valuation and to judge him by the confession which he has left the world in *De Profundis*, we can apply to him no better epithet than *The Epicurean*. But confessions are at best misleading. They are tinctured by the exaggerations of humility. They are laden with self-abasement proportionate to the penitent's desire for absolution, rather than to the culpability of the malefactor. They confuse things material with things spiritual and the sins of the body with those of the intellect. Fearful of half-truths, they disclose monstrous untruths, until the spirit of self-immolation is glutted and the tortured soul satisfied that repentance has no further penance within reach. So, with Wilde, it is difficult to believe the whole of the "pitiless indictment which he brings against himself." *Flâneur* and dandy he accuses

INTRODUCTION

himself of being.[1] *Flâneur* and dandy he may have been. But, however profitless his *life*, must his *word* be wholly without purpose? Surely there was something more than mere dilettantism in talents so diverse, so brilliantly manifested, so exquisitely elusive. For elusive, perplexing, defiant of definition was he in all that he did—this man of genius, Oscar Wilde *par excellence* The Protean. The Protean—for we embrace the singer of songs to find that we have seized upon the cynic; we seek to learn the secret of worldly disdain and discover that we are communing with the prose poet; we are roused from the lulling charm of fable and delicate imagery by the mordant wit of the dramatist; with the smile still on our lips we are confronted by a soul in torment. Oscar Wilde, The Protean, the weaver of paradoxes—himself the great paradox! Try as we may, shall we ever understand him? "Be warned in time, James; and remain, as I do, incomprehensible. To be great is to be misunderstood."[2] At all events he remains unexplained and unexplainable, nor one, whom his most pitiless critics have been able to explain away.

Yet, if we are to approach him, as we must, with a small measure of understanding, let us begin where he ends in *The Truth of Masks* : "Not that I agree

INTRODUCTION

XI

with everything that I have said in this essay. There is much with which I entirely disagree. The essay simply represents an artistic standpoint. For in art there is no such thing as a universal truth. *A Truth in art is that whose contradictory is also true.*[3] Using this dogma as a basis for argument, Arthur Symons evolves the theory that Wilde was "an artist in attitudes."[4] "And it was precisely in his attitudes," he says, "that he was most sincere. They represented his intentions; they stood for the better, unrealized part of himself. Thus his attitude, towards life and towards art, was untouched by his conduct." There is a kernel of truth in the theory so long as emphasis be laid upon this sincerity; for with Wilde the attitude was not so much a pose assumed as a point of view accidentally encountered. Given the new point of view, with the change of perspective, new theories became not only admissible, but imperative.[5] Nor was inconsistency or insincerity possible to him, whose one fixed star was that "art never expresses anything but itself."[6] But not only was he sincere *in* his attitudes; he was sincere *concerning* his attitudes. "What people call insincerity," he says in *The Critic as Artist*, "is simply a method by which we can multiply our personalities." Were this example a random citation, it might carry little weight.

xii INTRODUCTION

But Wilde proceeds to say in the same essay, "To know anything about oneself, one must know all about others. There must be no mood with which one cannot sympathize, no dead mode of life that one cannot make alive. . . . Man is least himself when he talks in his own person. Give him a mask, and he will tell you the truth."[7] This, perhaps, is a key to the secret. That he intentionally adopted the shell of different personalities, is improbable. What seems unquestionable, however, is this assumption of certain quite distinct rôles, which coloured not only his life but his written word. And so a trait, unconscious at first, through mere repetition became self-conscious—deliberate, it may be— thereby substantiating the theory which he propounds. This much is certain. When he posed as an idealist, he was laughed at for a fool; when he posed as a cynic, he was applauded for a wit. But then the public could gain something from the pose of 1882, and had nothing to gain from that of 1892. "All art is quite useless,"[8] he says. Was it in consolation or self-justification? Again we find ourselves involved in a labyrinth of paradox. And so, inexplicable he remains. Yet, if a man be intelligent enough to simulate cleverness, or sufficiently gifted to exemplify genius, is he not cleverness intensified, may he not be genius magnified?

INTRODUCTION xiii

But this is by way of digression and bears only indirectly on Wilde's literary work. His better known essays, which were published in *The Nineteenth Century* and *The Fortnightly Review* at various intervals from 1885 to 1890, and which, after some revision, were reissued in a collected form under the characteristic title of *Intentions*, have received much of the attention which they deserve. Though comparatively unnoticed upon their individual appearance, as a collection they not only created a sensation, but received some serious consideration and appreciation at the hands of the more discriminating critics.[9] At present, their great merit is so generally accepted that it becomes almost platitudinous to insist upon the wit that characterizes their every phrase. Perhaps it is in these essays that we find Wilde in his most brilliant mood. Here we are given many of his ideas crystallized in the form of epigrams—dogmas so gracefully expressed that it seems as if such wealth of fancy could conceal no useful thought. Here is Wilde more truly *Protean* than ever. But here also much of potential utility has been polished into exquisitely arrayed abstractions so mellifluous that they do not invite serious interpretation.

But Wilde had another side: one extremely practical, in which wit was made secondary to wis-

xiv INTRODUCTION

dom, and form to fact; and though this side is emphasized more especially in his unpublished personal correspondence, evidence of it may be detected in his lecture on decorative art, his specific criticisms, and in the majority of the letters included in the following collection. Furthermore, to obtain an insight into the true significance of *Intentions*, it is essential to grasp the theories of the young man who lectured on art in 1882; who took issue with Whistler in 1885. For the dogmas of the New Æsthetics, set forth in *The Decay of Lying*, are in a measure visionary and not a little destructive, while the earlier doctrines are not only constructive, but practical. In the first instance, as an iconoclast, he laid bare much of the hypocrisy and smug complacency of the "literary gentleman" —the quasi-artist, creative and critical; in the second, as a teacher, he attempted to indicate certain means for improvement and to lead the way to truth by the path of his own ideals.

If we examine the files of *Punch* of a quarter of a century ago, we will find rather illuminating references to *Nincompoopiana*.[10] "Jellaby Postlethwaite" from that time became so prominent a personage in the world of cartoons, that in the year 1882, which discovers Oscar Wilde, the poet, lecturer, and soi-disant Æsthete approaching

INTRODUCTION xv

the port of New York,[11] it was difficult to scan any public sheet without finding some allusion to the æsthetic movement and its high-priest. In both Gilbert's *Patience*[12] and Burnand's *Colonel*,[13] he was held up to ridicule. *Puck*[14] led the van in this country. Cartoon followed upon cartoon, nor were there many reputable newspapers that did not engage some jealous scribe to parody the poems which he lacked the talent to write or the intelligence to emulate.[15]

It was under these conditions that Wilde delivered his lecture on *The English Renaissance*.[16] But alas, he committed the unpardonable offence of appearing in a pair of breeches which descended no further than his knees! Whereupon, the significance of his remarks was relegated to that level by an audience whose understanding could not surmount eccentricities of dress. His lecture, however fine and worthy and beautiful as a literary production, was known thenceforth as *Ruskin and Water*.

Wilde irritated England; disturbed British stolidity, conservatism and self-conceit. America he amused. American courtesy was too superficial to withstand America's sense of humour. The theories of a man with knickerbockers and long hair were *ipso facto* untenable. Said *The Sun* in a gen-

xvi INTRODUCTION

erous editorial: "Why rebuff a visitor simply because of the fashion of his clothes? . . . There is
no law, social or other, that compels a man to dress
like every other man you meet;"[17] and later of his
lecture in Boston, "It is not a performance so tri-
fling as to insult the intelligence of the audience,
but a carefully prepared essay which proves its
author to be a man of cultivation, taste, imagination, education and refinement."[18] But this attitude was the exception. The lecture remained
Ruskin and Water, and its author the mountebank.

So, the American public, which began by ridiculing his appearance, his clothes, and his manner-
isms, ended by ridiculing his opinions on art.
They attended his lectures, not to listen, but to
laugh; and though, at the time of his discourteous
reception by the students of Harvard,[19] he completely turned the tables on his tormentors and
earned the respect of his audience, this reaction in his
favour was of short duration. Once a buffoon,
always a buffoon. A clown, as every one knows,
must look to laughter for his highest reward. There
were dissenting voices; there were broad-minded
men and women who treated him as a gentleman
and not as a curiosity. One, indeed, John Paul,
had the courage to express his opinions in *The New-
York Tribune,*[20] to weigh fault against virtue, to

INTRODUCTION xvii

weigh carefully and judiciously. He alone seems to have appreciated what few people understood; for he saw that Wilde was in reality "suffering poignantly" from the attacks of the Press—in fact that it was because of these attacks and the attitude of the public, that he had, with a certain amount of quixotism, exaggerated the cut of his clothes and the dogmatism of those ideas which had proven ridiculous or offensive to his inartistic and ultra-conventional audiences.

Then came the tour in the West, which, he tells us, embraced some fifty or sixty cities.[21] When he returned, it was with a deeper knowledge of the needs of this country. And to suggest a remedy for those needs, he delivered his new lecture,[22] more simple in form than the first, more practical in its application to the requirements of the American people. As a plea for the encouragement of the handicraftsman; for the rejection of the hideously naturalistic tendency in house-furnishing; for the establishment of museums, enriched by the finest examples from the finest periods of decorative art; for beautiful surroundings for children, and for schools in which these children might develop their artistic proclivities under the guidance of artists and capable artisans—as a *plea* for all that is beautiful, noble and sane in art, this lecture falls little short

xviii INTRODUCTION

of being a masterpiece. As a *plea* only, for from
the standpoint of style—from Oscar Wilde's own
standpoint—it cannot compare with any one of the
Intentions. But from the standpoint of rational
criticism and of actual utility, it surpasses anything
that he has done. For once, at least, the artist
created something thoroughly useful, and if, according to his own dictum, "we can forgive a man
for making a useful thing as long as he does not
admire it,"[23] perhaps there are many of us who, with
equal consistency, now admire that useful thing as
long as we can never forgive the man who made it.
For at the time that he expressed these theories
his suggestions, his admonitions and his hopes were
received with indifference, if not altogether with
contempt, by both the public and the Press. But
the Press and the public, it must be admitted, were
almost synonymous, so much had the former
moulded the latter to its uses and blunted both its
perception and sense of justice. To insist that this
lecture has revolutionized art in America, would be
ridiculous. To deny that its precepts have been in
a large measure realized, would be preposterous.
Perhaps Wilde was no more than one of a number
of influences at work for the improvement of taste.
But the fact that public opinion at large was so
thoroughly antagonistic to his views, remains, in

INTRODUCTION xix

the light of succeeding events, proof positive that these views were just, inevitable, and well-timed. Whether they originated with him, is a matter of small importance. The one important fact is that he had the courage to express them. Now that we have sufficient culture to accept them—at least in principle—we should have the honesty, if not the generosity to acknowledge our error, if not our debt.

Wilde has expressed in a dozen ways the doctrine that all art should be self-conscious, conventional and decorative;[24] that to be Art, it must be these things; conversely, that the art which is unconscious, unstudied and merely imitative—that is to say, reproductive of objects in Nature—is not Art at all, but a hybrid, masquerading in the garments of Art. These tenets have now become postulates, at least in so far as they concern interior decoration. However unwelcome were the strictures he laid on the crude taste displayed in the homes of England and America, the justice of his criticisms may no longer be questioned. He not only objected to the "inane worship of Nature"[25] as exemplified in the decorative arts, more notably in tapestry and carpet, but explained wherein lay the futility of that worship. He both appreciated and taught the niceties and limitations of the mural and textile arts, the

INTRODUCTION

charm of restraint and simplicity, and the restfulness of pattern.[26]

As early as 1883, he remarked in an interview [27] with a New York journalist: "The French art imported into America is not suited here; it should be *costly* or it will not be pretty. The Americans are going back to the real, simple art that flourished in the Colonial days. This is the only genuine American art and will be the art of the Republic in the future." This was the prediction of no dreamer. Would indeed that it might have been more productive as a warning! For there remains to this day a majority that should be restrained from innocently indulging in the gilt abortions so commonly miscalled French furniture. But at that period all classes were equally barbarous in their want of artistic refinement. In spite of this, at the end of the decade a change for the better became so marked that Wilde could write, "Ugliness has had its day. Even in the houses of the rich there is taste;" [28] and again in 1891, "It would be quite impossible at the present moment to furnish a room as rooms were furnished a few years ago, without going for everything to an auction of second-hand furniture from some third-rate lodging-house. The things are no longer made." [29]

In many respects, Wilde was in accord with

INTRODUCTION
xxi

Whistler as regards the conditions of art. He has even been accused of borrowing his ideas from Whistler. That is absurd. It would be easier, if anything, to prove the reverse. In point of time, the exposition of Wilde's doctrines takes precedence over that of the painter. Said Whistler in *Ten O'Clock* (1885): "Humanity takes the place of Art, and God's creations are excused by their usefulness. Beauty is confounded with virtue, and, before a work of Art, it is asked, 'What good shall it do?'" Said Wilde in *L'Envoi to Rose Leaf and Apple Leaf*[30] (1882): "Nor, in its primary aspect has a painting, for instance, any more spiritual message or meaning for us than a blue tile from the wall of Damascus. . . . It is a beautifully-coloured surface, nothing more, and affects us by no suggestion stolen from philosophy, no pathos pilfered from literature, no feeling filched from a poet, but by its own incommunicable artistic essence."

In this elimination of all intellectual or ethical considerations, both Whistler and Wilde were opposed to Ruskin and his school. Accordingly, from the subjective point of view their beliefs were identical. It was from the objective point of view that they differed so materially. Whistler sought to isolate Art and the artist.[31] The sacred precinct of Beauty and its priest were, in his eyes, beyond the

xxii INTRODUCTION

ken of the vulgar; and beyond their reach should both remain. Wilde, on the other hand, deemed it praiseworthy and possible to educate the masses to an appreciation of the beautiful.[32] This very position was maintained and elaborated by Swinburne in his spirited reply[33] to *Ten O'Clock* in 1888.

Mr. H. W. Singer, in a recent monograph on Whistler,[34] refers to Wilde's attitude as "an artificial enthusiasm for art," which, he goes on to say, "is just as futile as its enforced exercise." Wilde himself would agree with the conclusion, if the premises were true. But they are indubitably false. He never exercised pressure; he never attempted to "drive his following to the love of art." So, when Mr. Singer adds, "For the conditions to be absolutely healthy, the people must come of their own accord," and says it presumably in confutation of the fabricated doctrines of a purely imaginary Wilde, he should make it impossible for the latter to have written, "The truths of art cannot be taught. They are revealed only—revealed to natures which have made themselves receptive of all beautiful impressions by the study and worship of all beautiful things."[35] And when Mr. Singer prefaces his argument by stating that "the movement inaugurated by the latter (Wilde) spent itself in an affected style of dress, and of necessity aroused the antip-

INTRODUCTION xxiii

athy of every honest man," he should remember that, according to the artist whom he champions, ethical problems are irrelevant to art, and that all expression of personal feeling merely stultifies the man who mistakes such expression for logic. Mr. Singer is, unfortunately, a fair example of popular ignorance as regards the real theories of Wilde; and his logic, typical of the logic applied to what little truth is known. But Swinburne established Wilde's position, however unconsciously, when he wrote, "Good intentions will not secure good results; but neither—strange as it may seem—will the absence of good intentions."[36] At any rate, Wilde refused to be deterred from the hope that Beauty would ultimately become "the national inheritance of all."[37] As he put it in 1890, "The Creeds are believed, not because they are rational, but because they are repeated."[38]

But although he hoped for a national, a universal acceptance of art, he demanded complete liberty for the artist. "The work of art," he insisted, "is to dominate the spectator; the spectator is not to dominate the work of art."[39] He claimed for literature the same license that is granted to the Press. He claimed for the stage the same freedom that is granted to art, whether verbal, plastic, or pictorial. He did not expect exemption from criticism, but he

xxiv INTRODUCTION

believed that all criticism should mean something more than mere approval or condemnation; that it should reflect the mood and the individuality of the critic, being an impression made *on* him and not merely an analysis made *by* him [40]—in short, that criticism should be as imaginative and creative as the subject-matter it criticizes.

As in painting, so in literature he opposed the authority of convention; and more especially in literature, he resented the restrictions placed upon subject-matter by an arbitrary standard of morals, and the Puritanism of a Press, which advocated these restrictions. Upon this, he dwells at some length in *"Dorian Gray" and its Critics.* So, in *The Censure and "Salomé,"* he arraigns in a masterly manner the inconsistencies by which the Anglo-Saxon discriminates between what is fit and unfit for stage-production.

In *"Vera" and the Drama* and *The Relation of the Actor to the Play,* he confines himself to an exposition of the canons of dramatic art and a discussion of the limitations of the actor. And in each and every instance, despite an occasional flippancy of tone, there is always a strong undercurrent of common sense, which, coupled with his inexhaustible wit, does much to atone for his native egotism and his imperturbable arrogance. On the other

INTRODUCTION   XXV

hand, *Joaquin Miller, the Good Samaritan; Paris, the Abode of Artists;* and *The Ethics of Journalism* seem at first glance to consist of very little save this arrogance and egotism in their most offensive form. This, however, is more apparent than real. On each occasion, Wilde had been provoked beyond human endurance. In the face of mere personal abuse, he had a thousand times remained silent, however malicious and unfounded the charges made against him. It was only when his reputation as an artist was attacked that he accepted a challenge. A little knowledge of the situation in America in 1882, a realization of the injustice of the Censure in 1892, and a mere glance at *The Shamrock* of 1894, will extenuate, if not altogether justify, the tone which he assumed.

The last article of this collection, *Dramatic Critics and "An Ideal Husband,"* which was not the direct product of his pen, may have been embellished with slight exaggerations by the chronicler, Mr. Burgess. Yet it is Wilde—Wilde in his most irritating mood. It actually bristles with startling impertinences, the most inconsequential dogmas, the most pitiful affectations. As if fearful of the future, Wilde seems to be demanding a final opportunity to exhibit his powers of verbal *coloratura;* an hour in which to vin-

INTRODUCTION

dicate his reputation as a juggler of ideas. And yet in this, as in almost everything that he wrote or did, there is something of the naive child. "People like myself, who have child-like, simple natures," is his way of putting it, in a letter[41] to Leonard Smithers. And Wilde knew. Perhaps, after all, it was this child-like attitude which subjected him to such universal misunderstanding. Certainly it was with the simplicity and impetuosity of a child that he first took the world into his confidence. A child does not question the interest of the veriest stranger. In much the same way, Wilde, delighted with new vistas of art, intoxicated by the beauty of the thoughts to which they gave occasion, did not hesitate to give these thoughts public expression nor to hang upon them all the jewels of his fancy. But the world looked upon the offering as an affectation, and upon his lack of reserve as an indelicacy, as a want of dignity and good breeding. Now, this attitude of the world rankled; for he saw that it was unjust, that it was hypocritical. Too late, he learned that a man cannot be himself, however much he may wish it; that he may think anything, but that he must say or do nothing that is unsanctioned by usage. Oscar Wilde was a dreamer and his dreams called forth laughter. So he cherished them in secret, till they lost much of their bloom

INTRODUCTION xxvii

and distilled the fatal poison that at last destroyed him. And so, he who had been an idealist with a loathing for the ugly, sordid things of life, became a cynic whose heart still throbbed in echo to all that was beautiful and good in the realm of fancy.

The most pitiful dreamer, the wittiest cynic and the most brilliant wit of his century he remains. But above all else, he will be known as the artist. Max Beerbohm[42] tells us that Pater, in one of his few book reviews, remarked that in Wilde's work there was always "the quality of the good talker." But he was more, far more than a mere talker. He was a verbal colourist, a great decorative artist, whose words make as direct an appeal to the eye as their sound does to the ear, or their sense to the intellect. They are suggestive in themselves. They are the very essence of Art. "If one loves Art at all," he says, "one must love it beyond all other things in the world, and against such love, the reason, if one listened to it, would cry out. There is nothing sane about the worship of beauty. It is too splendid to be sane. Those of whose lives it forms the dominant note will always seem to the world to be pure visionaries."[43] And with Wilde it was Art that formed the dominant note.

RICHARD BUTLER GLAENZER.

NEW YORK, February, 1906.

It will be a marvellous thing—the true personality of man—when we see it. It will grow naturally and simply, flower-like, or as a tree grows. It will not be at discord. It will never argue or dispute. It will not prove things. It will know everything. And yet it will not busy itself about knowledge. It will have wisdom. Its value will not be measured by material things. It will have nothing. And yet it will have everything; and whatever one takes from it, it will still have—so rich will it be. *It will not be always meddling with others, or asking them to be like itself. It will love them because they will be different.* And yet, while it will not meddle with others, it will help all, as a beautiful thing helps us by being what it is. The personality of man will be very wonderful. It will be as wonderful as the personality of a child.

— The Soul of Man Under Socialism.

There are artists of two sorts: the ones present answers; the others ask questions. It is essential to know if one is of the one sort or of the other, for he who asks the questions is never the one who answers them. There are certain works of art that wait long for interpretation for the reason that they answer questions that have not yet been asked; for often the question comes very long after the answer.—Translation from "*The Sayings of Oscar Wilde.*"

Prétextes by André Gide.

A dreamer is one who can only find his way by moonlight, and his punishment is that he sees the dawn before the rest of the world.

— The Critic as Artist. Part II.

And even the light of the sun will fade at the last,
  And the leaves will fall, and the birds will hasten away,
  And I will be left in the snow of a flowerless day
To think of the glories of Spring, and the joys long past.

—From '*Magdalen Walks.*'
Magdalen College, 1878.

I know that every forest tree
  By labour rises from the root;
  I know that none shall gather fruit
By sailing on the barren sea.

—From '*Lotus Leaves.*'
Oxford, 1877.

DECORATIVE ART IN AMERICA

Art should never try to be popular. The public should try to make themselves artistic. — *The Soul of Man Under Socialism.*

The whole history of the decorative arts in Europe is the record of the struggle between Orientalism with its frank rejection of imitation, its love of artistic convention, its dislike to the actual representation of any object of Nature, and our own imitative spirit. Wherever the former has been paramount, . . . we have had beautiful and imaginative work in which the visible things of life are transmuted into artistic conventions, and the things that Life has not, are invented and fashioned for her delight. But wherever we have returned to Life and Nature, our work has always become vulgar, common, and uninteresting. — *The Decay of Lying.*

The art that is frankly decorative is the art to live with. It is, of all our visible arts, the one art that creates in us both mood and temperament. Mere colour, unspoiled by meaning, and unallied with definite form, can speak to the soul in a thousand different ways. The harmony that resides in the delicate proportions of lines and masses becomes mirrored in the mind. The repetitions of pattern give us rest. — *The Critic as Artist. Part II.*

All good work aims at a purely artistic effect. But, as in your cities, so in your literature, it is an increased sensibility to beauty that is lacking. All noble work is not national merely, but universal. — *Lecture on the English Renaissance. 1882.*

DECORATIVE ART IN AMERICA: A LECTURE[1]

IN my first lecture,[2] I gave you something of the history of Art in England. I sought to trace the influence of the French Revolution upon its development. I said something of the song of Keats and the school of the Pre-Raphaelites. But I do not want to shelter the movement which I have called "The English Renaissance" under any palladium, however noble, or any name, however revered. The roots of it have indeed to be sought for in things that have long passed away, and not, as some suppose, in the fancy of a few young men—although I am not altogether sure that there is anything much better than the fancy of a few young men.

When I appeared before you on a previous occasion, I had seen nothing of American art save the Doric columns and Corinthian chimney-pots visible on your Broadway and Fifth Avenue. Since then

4   DECORATIVE ART IN AMERICA

I have been through your country to some fifty or sixty cities,[3] I think. I find what your people need is not so much high imaginative art, but that which hallows the vessels of every-day use. I suppose that the poet will sing and the artist will paint regardless whether the world praises or blames. He has his own world and is independent of his fellowmen. But the handicraftsman is dependent on your pleasure and opinion. He needs your encouragement and he must have beautiful surroundings. Your people love art, but do not sufficiently honour the handicraftsmen. Of course, those millionaires who can pillage Europe for their pleasure need have no care to encourage such; but I speak for those whose desire for beautiful things is larger than their means. I find that one great trouble all over is that your workmen are not given to noble designs. You cannot be indifferent to this, because art is not something which you can take or leave. It is a necessity of human life.

And what is the meaning of this beautiful decoration which we call art? In the first place, it means value to the workman, and it means the pleasure which he must necessarily take in making a beautiful thing. The mark of all good art is not that the thing done is done exactly or finely, for machinery may do as much, but that it is worked

DECORATIVE ART IN AMERICA 5

out with the head and the workman's heart. I cannot impress the point too frequently that beautiful and rational designs are necessary in all work. I did not imagine until I went into some of your simpler cities that there was so much bad work done. I found where I went bad wall-papers, horribly designed, and coloured carpets, and that old offender, the horse-hair sofa, whose stolid look of indifference is always so depressing. I found meaningless chandeliers and machine-made furniture, generally of rosewood, which creaked dismally under the weight of the ubiquitous interviewer. I came across the small iron stove[4] which they always persist in decorating with machine-made ornaments, and which is as great a bore as a wet day or any other particularly dreadful institution. When unusual extravagance was indulged in it was garnished with two funeral urns.

It must always be remembered that what is well and carefully made by an honest workman after a rational design, increases in beauty and value as the years go on. The old furniture brought over by the Pilgrims two hundred years ago, which I saw in New England, is just as good and as beautiful to-day as it was when it first came here. Now, what you must do is to bring artists and handicraftsmen together. Handicraftsmen cannot live,

6   DECORATIVE ART IN AMERICA

certainly cannot thrive, without such companionship. Separate these two, and you rob art of all spiritual motive. Having done this, you must place your workman in the midst of beautiful surroundings. The artist is not dependent on the visible and the tangible. He has his visions and his dreams to feed on. But the workman must see lovely forms and beautiful forms, as he goes to his work in the morning and returns at eventide. And, in connection with this, I want to assure you that noble and beautiful designs are never the result of idle fancy or purposeless day-dreaming. They only come as the accumulation of habits of long and delightful observation. And yet such things may not be taught.[5] Right ideas concerning them can certainly only be obtained by those who have been accustomed to rooms that are beautiful and colours that are satisfying.

Perhaps one of the most difficult things for us to do is to choose a notable and joyous dress for men. There would be more joy in life if we should accustom ourselves to use all the beautiful colours we can in fashioning our own clothes. The dress of the future, I think, will use drapery to a great extent and will abound with joyous colour. At present we have lost all nobility of dress, and in doing so, have almost annihilated the modern sculptor. And

DECORATIVE ART IN AMERICA

in looking around at the figures which adorn our parks, one could almost wish that we had completely killed the noble art. To see the frock coat of the drawing-room done in bronze or the double waistcoat perpetuated in marble, adds a new horror to death. But indeed, in looking through the history of costume, seeking an answer to the questions we have propounded, there is little that is either beautiful or appropriate. One of the earliest forms is the Greek drapery, which is so exquisite for young girls. And then, I think we may be pardoned a little enthusiasm over the dress of the time of Charles I, so beautiful indeed, that in spite of its invention being with the Cavaliers, it was copied by the Puritans. And the dress for the children at that time must not be passed over. It was a very golden age of the little ones. I do not think that they have ever looked so lovely as they do in the pictures of that time. The dress of the last century in England is also peculiarly gracious and graceful. There is nothing bizarre or strange about it, but it is full of harmony and beauty. In these days, when we have suffered so dreadfully from the incursions of the modern milliner, we hear ladies boast that they do not wear a dress more than once.[6] In the old days, when the dresses were decorated with beautiful designs and worked with

8 DECORATIVE ART IN AMERICA

exquisite embroidery, ladies rather took a pride in bringing out the garment and wearing it many times and handing it down to their daughters—a process which I think would be quite appreciated by modern husbands when called upon to settle their wives' bills.

And how shall men dress? Men say they don't particularly care how they dress, and that it is little matter. I am bound to reply that I do not believe them and do not think that you do. In all my journeys through the country, the only well-dressed men that I saw—and in saying this I earnestly deprecate the polished indignation of your Fifth Avenue dandies—were the Western miners. Their wide-brimmed hats,[7] which shaded their faces from the sun and protected them from the rain, and the cloak, which is by far the most beautiful piece of drapery ever invented, may well be dwelt on with admiration. Their high boots, too, were sensible and practical. They wore only what was comfortable and therefore beautiful. As I looked at them, I could not help thinking with regret of the time when these picturesque miners should have made their fortunes and would go East to assume again all the abominations of modern fashionable attire. Indeed, so concerned was I that I made some of them promise that when they again

DECORATIVE ART IN AMERICA 9

appeared in the more crowded scenes of Eastern civilization they would still continue to wear their lovely costume. But I don't believe they will.[8]
Now, what America wants to-day is a school of rational design. Bad art is a great deal worse than no art at all. You must show your workmen specimens of good work, so that they may come to know what is simple and true and beautiful. To that end I would have you have a museum attached to these schools—not one of those dreadful modern institutions where there are a stuffed and very dusty giraffe and a case or two of fossils, but a place where there are gathered examples of art decoration from various periods and countries. Such a place is the South Kensington Museum in London, whereon we build greater hopes for the future than on any other one thing. There I go every Saturday night, when the Museum is opened later than usual, to see the handicraftsman, the wood-worker, the glass-blower and the worker in metals. And it is here that the man of refinement and culture comes face to face with the workman who ministers to his joy. He comes to know more of the nobility of the workman, and the workman, feeling the appreciation, comes to know more of the nobility of his work.

You have too many white walls. More colour is

10   DECORATIVE ART IN AMERICA

wanted. You should have such men as Whistler among you to teach you the beauty and joy of colour. Take Mr. Whistler's "Symphony in White,"[9] which you no doubt have imagined to be something quite bizarre. It is nothing of the sort. Think of a cool grey sky, flecked here and there with white clouds, a grey ocean and three wonderfully beautiful figures robed in white, leaning over the water and dropping white flowers from their fingers. Here are no extensive intellectual scheme to trouble you and no metaphysics, of which we have had quite enough in art. But if the simple and unaided colour strikes the right keynote, the whole conception is made clear. I regard Mr. Whistler's famous "Peacock Room"[10] as the finest thing in colour and art decoration which the world has known since Correggio painted that wonderful room in Italy where the little children are dancing on the walls.[11] Mr. Whistler finished another room just before I came away—a breakfast room in blue and yellow. The ceiling was a light blue, the cabinetwork and furniture were of a yellow wood, the curtains at the windows were white and worked in yellow, and when the table was set for breakfast with dainty blue china, nothing can be conceived at once so simple and so joyous.

The fault which I have observed in most of your

DECORATIVE ART IN AMERICA 11

rooms is that there is apparent no definite scheme of colour. Everything is not attuned to a keynote as it should be. The apartments are crowded with pretty things which have no relation to one another. Again, your artists must decorate what is more simply useful. In your art schools I found no attempt to decorate such things as the vessels for water. I know of nothing uglier than the ordinary jug or pitcher. A museum could be filled with the different kinds of water vessels which are used in hot countries. Yet we continue to submit to the depressing jug with the handle all on one side. I do not see the wisdom of decorating dinner-plates with sunsets and soup-plates with moonlight scenes. I do not think it adds anything to the pleasure of the canvas-back duck to take it out of such glories. Besides, we do not want a soup-plate whose bottom seems to vanish in the distance. One feels neither safe nor comfortable under such conditions. In fact, I did not find in the art schools of the country that the difference was explained between decorative and imaginative art.

The conditions of art should be simple. A great deal more depends upon the heart than the head. Appreciation of art is not secured by any elaborate scheme of learning. Art requires a good healthy atmosphere. The motives for art are still around

12   DECORATIVE ART IN AMERICA

about us as they were around about the ancients. And the subjects are also easily found by the earnest sculptor and the painter. Nothing is more picturesque and graceful than a man at work. The artist who goes to the children's playground, watches them at their sport, and sees the boy stoop to tie his shoe, will find the same themes that engaged the attention of the ancient Greeks, and such observation and the illustrations which follow will do much to correct that foolish impression that mental and physical beauty are always divorced.

To you more than perhaps to any other country, has nature been generous in furnishing material for art-workers to work in. You have marble-quarries where the stone is more beautiful in colour than the Greeks ever had for their beautiful work, and yet day after day I am confronted with the great building of some stupid man who has used the beautiful material as if it were not precious almost beyond speech. Marble should not be used save by noble workmen. There is nothing which gave me a greater sense of barrenness in travelling through the country than the entire absence of wood-carving on your houses. Wood-carving is the simplest of the decorative arts. In Switzerland the little barefooted boy beautifies the porch of his father's house with examples of skill in this

DECORATIVE ART IN AMERICA 13

direction. Why should not American boys do a great deal more and better than Swiss boys?

There is nothing to my mind more coarse in conception and more vulgar in execution than modern jewelry. This is something that can be easily corrected. Something better should be made out of the beautiful gold which is stored up in your mountain hollows and strewn along your river beds. When I was at Leadville and reflected that all the shining silver I saw coming from the mines would be made into ugly dollars, it made me sad. It should be made into something more permanent. The golden gates at Florence are as beautiful to-day as when Michael Angelo saw them.

We should see more of the workman than we do. We should not be content to have the salesman stand between us—the salesman, who knows nothing of what he is selling save that he is charging a great deal too much for it. And watching the workmen, will teach that most important lesson, the nobility of all rational workmanship.

I said in my last lecture that art would create a new brotherhood[12] among men by furnishing a universal language. I said that under its beneficent influences war might pass away. Thinking this, what place can I ascribe to art in our education? If children grow up among all fair and lovely things,

14   DECORATIVE ART IN AMERICA

they will grow to love beauty and detest ugliness before they know the reason why. If you go into a house where everything is coarse, you find things chipped and broken and unsightly. Nobody exercises any care. If everything is dainty and delicate, gentleness and refinement of manner are unconsciously acquired. When I was in San Francisco I used to visit the Chinese Quarter frequently. There I used to watch a great hulking Chinese workman at his task of digging, and used to see him every day drink his tea from a little cup as delicate in texture as the petal of a flower, whereas in all the grand hotels of the land, where thousands of dollars have been lavished on great gilt mirrors and gaudy columns, I have been given my coffee or my chocolate in cups an inch and a quarter thick.[18] I think I have deserved something nicer.

The art systems of the past have been devised by philosophers who looked upon human beings as obstructions. They have tried to educate boys' minds before they had any. How much better it would be in these early years to teach children to use their hands in the rational service of mankind! I would have a workshop attached to every school, and one hour a day given up to the teaching of simple decorative arts. It would be a golden hour to the children. And you would soon raise up a

DECORATIVE ART IN AMERICA 15

race of handicraftsmen who would transform the face of your country. I have seen only one such school[14] in the United States, and this was in Philadelphia, and was founded by my friend Mr. Leland.[15] I stopped there yesterday and have brought some of the work here this afternoon to show you. Here[16] are two discs of beaten brass: the designs on them are beautiful, the workmanship is simple and the entire result is satisfactory. The work was done by a little boy twelve years old. This is a wooden bowl, decorated by a little girl of thirteen. The design is lovely, and the colouring delicate and pretty. Here you see a piece of beautiful woodcarving, accomplished by a little boy of nine. In such work as this children learn sincerity in art. They learn to abhor the liar in art—the man who paints wood to look like iron, or iron to look like stone. It is a practical school of morals. No better way is there to learn to love Nature than to understand Art. It dignifies every flower of the field. And the boy who sees the thing of beauty which a bird on the wing becomes when transferred to wood or canvas, will probably not throw the customary stone.[17] What we want is something spiritual added to life. Nothing is so ignoble that art cannot sanctify it.

JOAQUIN MILLER,
THE GOOD SAMARITAN

Satire paid the usual homage which mediocrity yields to genius.
—Lecture on the English Renaissance. 1882.

If you survive yellow journalism, you need not be afraid of yellow fever. *—Lecture on America. Current London Gossip.*
New York Times, July 23, 1883.

There is much to be said in favour of modern journalism. By giving us the opinions of the uneducated, it keeps us in touch with the ignorance of the community. By invariably discussing the unnecessary, it makes us understand what things are requisite for culture, and what are not. *— The Critic as Artist. Part II.*

In America the President reigns for four years, and journalism governs for ever and ever.*— The Soul of Man Under Socialism.*

The public is wonderfully tolerant. It forgives everything except genius. *— The Critic as Artist. Part I*

Society often forgives the criminal; it never forgives the dreamer.
— The Critic as Artist. Part II.

The meaning of any beautiful created thing is at least as much in the soul of him who looks at it, as it was in his soul who wrought it.
—The Critic as Artist. Part I.

JOAQUIN MILLER,
THE GOOD SAMARITAN[1]

109 West 33rd Street,
New York, February 9th, 1882.

MY DEAR OSCAR WILDE:—

I read with shame about the behaviour of those ruffians at Rochester at your lecture there.[2] When I see such things here in the civilized portion of my country and read the coarse comments of the Philistine Press, I feel like thanking God that my home lies three thousand miles further on, and in what is called the wilderness. Should you get as far as Oregon in your travels, go to my father's. You will find rest there and room, as much land as you can encompass in a day's ride, and I promise you there the respect due a stranger to our shores, to your attainments, your industry and your large, generous, and tranquil nature. Or should you

20 DECORATIVE ART IN AMERICA

decide to return here and not bear further abuse, come to my house-top and abide with me, where you will be welcome and loved as a brother.[3] And bear this in mind, my dear boy, the more you are abused the more welcome you will be. For I remember how kind your country[4] was to me, and at your age I had not done one-tenth your work. May my right hand fail me when I forget this. But don't you lose heart or come to dislike America. For whatever is said or done, the real heart of this strong young world demands and will have fair play for all. This sentiment is deep and substantial and will show itself when appealed to. So go ahead, my brave youth, and say your say if you choose. My heart is with you and so are the hearts of the best of America's millions. Thine for the Beautiful and True,

JOAQUIN MILLER.

II

St. Louis,[5] February 28th, 1882.

MY DEAR JOAQUIN MILLER:—

I thank you for your chivalrous and courteous letter. Believe me, I would as lief judge of the strength and splendour of sun and sea by the dust that dances in the beam and the bubble that breaks

JOAQUIN MILLER, THE GOOD SAMARITAN 21

on the wave,[6] as take the petty and profitless vulgarity of one or two insignificant towns[7] as any test or standard of the real spirit of a sane, strong, and simple people, or allow it to affect my respect for the many noble men or women[8] whom it has been my privilege in this great country to know.

For myself and the cause which I represent, I have no fears as regards the future. Slander and folly have their way for a season, but for a season only, while, as touching either the few provincial newspapers which have so vainly assailed me, or that ignorant and itinerant libeller of New England who goes lecturing from village to village in such open and ostentatious isolation, be sure I have no time to waste on them! Youth being so glorious, art so godlike, and the very world about us so full of beautiful things, and things worthy of reverence, and things honourable, how should one stop to listen to the lucubrations of a literary *gamin*, to the brawling and mouthing of a man whose praise would be as insolent as his slander is impotent, or to the irresponsible and irrepressible chatter of the professionally unproductive?

'T is a great advantage, I admit, to have done nothing, but one must not abuse even that advantage!

Who after all, that I should write of him, is this scribbling anonymuncule in grand old

22 DECORATIVE ART IN AMERICA

Massachusetts, who scrawls and screams so glibly about what he cannot understand? This apostle of inhospitality,[9] who delights to defile, to desecrate and to defame the gracious courtesies he is unworthy to enjoy? Who are these scribes,[10] who, passing with purposeless alacrity from the police news to the Parthenon, and from crime to criticism, sway with such serene incapacity the office which they so lately swept? "Narcissuses of imbecility,"[11] what should they see in the clear waters of Beauty and in the well undefiled of Truth but the shifting and shadowy image of their own substantial stupidity? Secure of that oblivion for which they toil so laboriously, and, I must acknowledge, with such success, let them peer at us through their telescopes and report what they like of us. But, my dear Joaquin, should we put them under the microscope there would be really nothing to be seen.

I look forward to passing another delightful evening with you on my return to New York, and I need not tell you that whenever you visit England you will be received with that courtesy with which it is our pleasure always to welcome all Americans, and that honour with which it is our privilege to greet all poets.

Most sincerely and affectionately yours,

OSCAR WILDE.

MRS. LANGTRY AS HESTER
GRAZEBROOK

Elle est comme une colombe qui s'est égarée . . . Elle est comme un narcisse agité du vent . . . Elle ressemble à une fleur d'argent.
—*Salomé.*

In the case of a very fascinating woman, sex is a challenge, not a defense. —*An Ideal Husband;*
also, *Phrases and Philosophies for the use of the Young.*

Beauty is a form of genius—is higher indeed, as it needs no explanation. —*The Picture of Dorian Gray.*

The critic reproduces the work that he criticizes in a mode that is never imitative, and part of whose charm may really consist in the rejection of resemblance, and shows us in this way not merely the meaning but also the mystery of Beauty, and, by transforming each art into literature, solves once for all the problem of Art's unity. —*The Critic as Artist. Part I.*

No great artist ever sees things as they really are. If he did, he would cease to be an artist. —*The Decay of Lying.*

A great work of dramatic art should . . . be presented to us in the form most suitable to the modern spirit . . . Perfect accuracy of detail, for the sake of perfect illusion, is necessary for us. What we have to see is that the details are not allowed to usurp the principal place. They must be subordinate always to the general motive of the play. But subordination in art does not mean disregard of truth; it means conversion of fact into effect, and the assigning to each detail its proper relative value.
—*The Truth of Masks.*

MRS. LANGTRY AS HESTER GRAZEBROOK[1]

IT is only in the best Greek gems, on the silver coins of Syracuse, or among the marble figures of the Parthenon frieze, that one can find the ideal representation of the marvellous beauty of that face which laughed through the leaves last night[2] as Hester Grazebrook.

Pure Greek it is, with the grave low forehead, the exquisitely arched brow; the noble chiselling of the mouth, shaped as if it were the mouthpiece of an instrument of music; the supreme and splendid curve of the cheek; the augustly pillared throat which bears it all: it is Greek because the lines which compose it are so definite and so strong, and yet so exquisitely harmonized that the effect is one of simple loveliness purely: Greek, because its essence and its quality, as is the quality of music and of architecture, is that of beauty based on absolutely mathematical laws.[3]

26   DECORATIVE ART IN AMERICA

But while art remains dumb and immobile in its passionless serenity, with the beauty of this face it is different: the grey eyes lighten into blue or deepen into violet as fancy succeeds fancy; the lips become flower-like in laughter or, tremulous as a bird's wing, mould themselves at last into the strong and bitter moulds of pain or scorn. And then motion comes, and the statue wakes into life. But the life is not the ordinary life of common days; it is life with a new value given to it, the value of art: and the charm to me of Hester Grazebrook's acting in the first scene of the play to-night was that mingling of classic grace with absolute reality which is the secret of all beautiful art, of the plastic work of the Greeks and of the pictures of Jean François Millet equally.

I do not think that the sovereignty and empire of women's beauty has at all passed away, though we may no longer go to war for them as the Greeks did for the daughter of Lēda.[4] The greatest empire still remains for them—the empire of art. And indeed this wonderful face, seen to-night for the first time in America, has filled and permeated with the pervading image of its type the whole of our modern art in England. Last century it was the romantic type which dominated in art, the type loved by Reynolds and Gainsborough, of wonder-

MRS. LANGTRY AS HESTER GRAZEBROOK   27

ful contrasts of colour, of exquisite and varying charm of expression, but without that definite plastic feeling which divides classic from romantic work. This type degenerated into mere facile prettiness in the hands of lesser masters, and in protest against it, was created by the hands of the Pre-Raphaelites a new type, with its rare combination of Greek form with Florentine mysticism. But this mysticism becomes overstrained and a burden, rather than an aid to expression, and a desire for the pure Hellenic joy and serenity came in its place; and in all our modern work, in the paintings of such men as Albert Moore[5] and Leighton[6] and Whistler, we can trace the influence of this single face giving fresh life and inspiration in the form of a new artistic ideal.

As regards Hester Grazebrook's dresses, the first was a dress whose grace depended entirely on the grace of the person who wore it. It was merely the simple dress of a village girl in England. The second was a lovely combination of blue and creamy lace. But the masterpiece was undoubtedly the last, a symphony in silver-grey and pink, a pure melody of colour which I feel sure Whistler would have called a *Scherzo*, and take as its visible motive the moonlight wandering in silver mist through a rose garden, unless indeed he saw this dress, in which

28   DECORATIVE ART IN AMERICA

case he would paint it and nothing else, for it is a dress such as Velasquez only could paint and Whistler very wisely always paints those things which are only within reach of Velasquez.

The scenery was, of course, prepared in a hurry.[7] Still much of it was very good indeed: the first scene especially, with its graceful trees and open forge and cottage porch, though the roses were dreadfully out of tone, and besides their crudity of colour, were curiously—badly grouped. The last scene was exceedingly clever and true to nature as well, being that combination of lovely scenery and execrable architecture which is so specially characteristic of a German spa. As for the drawing-room scene, I cannot regard it as in any way a success. The heavy ebony doors are entirely out of keeping with the satin panels; the silk hangings and festoons of black and yellow are quite meaningless in their position and consequently quite ugly; the carpet is out of all colour-relation with the rest of the room, and the table-cover is mauve. Still, to have decorated ever so bad a room in six days must, I suppose, be a subject of respectful wonder, though I should have fancied that Mr. Wallack had many very much better sets in his own stock.

But I am beginning to quarrel generally with most modern scene-painting. A scene is primarily

MRS. LANGTRY AS HESTER GRAZEBROOK   29

a decorative background for the actors, and should be kept always subordinate;[8] first, to the players, their dress, gesture, and action; and, secondly, to the fundamental principle of decorative art, which is not to imitate but to suggest nature. If the landscape is given its full realistic value, the value of the figures to which it serves as a background is impaired and often lost, and so the painted hangings of the Elizabethan age were a far more artistic, and so a far more rational form of scenery than most modern scene-painting is. From the same master-hand which designed the curtain at the Madison Square Theatre,[9] I would like very much to see a good decorative landscape in scene-painting; for I have seen no open-air scene in any theatre which did not really mar the value of the actors. One must either, like Titian, make the landscape subordinate to the figures, or like Claude, the figures subordinate to the landscape;[10] for if we desire realistic acting we cannot have realistic scene-painting.

I need not describe, however, how the beauty of Hester Grazebrook survived the crude roses and the mauve table-cloth triumphantly. That it is a beauty that will be appreciated to the full in America, I do not doubt for a moment, for it is only countries which possess great beauty that can appreciate beauty at all. It may also influence the art of

30   DECORATIVE ART IN AMERICA

America as it has influenced the art of England, for of the rare Greek type it is the most absolutely perfect example.

The Philistine may, of course, object that to be absolutely perfect is impossible. Well, that is so: but then it is only the impossible things that are worth doing nowadays!

"VERA" AND THE DRAMA

The drama is the meeting place of art and life; it deals, as Mazzini said, not merely with man, but with social man, with man in relation to God and to humanity.

—Lecture on the English Renaissance. 1882.

A good play is hardly ever finished. It must be fitted to the stage. It is not enough to make music; one must make music that the instruments can play. *—Interview with Oscar Wilde.*

New York World, August 12, 1883.

The actor is a critic of the drama. He shows the poet's work under new conditions and by a message special to himself. He takes the written word, and action, gesture, and voice become the media of revelation. *— The Critic as Artist. Part II.*

The play [*Vera*] is meant not to be read but to be acted, and the actor has always a right to object and to suggest.

—Letter to Mr. R. D'Oyly Carte. 1882.

"VERA" AND THE DRAMA

I

Charles Street, Grosvenor Square, July, 1883.

MY DEAR MISS PRESCOTT:—

It is with great pride and pleasure that I look forward to seeing you in the character of the heroine of my play[1]—a character which I entrust to you with the most absolute confidence,[2] for the first night I saw you act I recognized in you a great artist.

I do not only mean that there was strength and splendour in your acting, music and melody in your voice, and in every pose and gesture, as you walked the stage, the infinite grace of perfect expressiveness, but that behind all these things, which are merely the technique of acting, there lay the true artistic nature which alone can conceive a part, and the true artistic power which alone can create one.

As regards the play itself, I have tried in it to

34 DECORATIVE ART IN AMERICA

express within the limits of art that Titan cry of the peoples for liberty, which in the Europe of our day, is threatening thrones and making governments unstable from Spain to Russia, and from north to southern seas. But it is a play not of politics but of passion. It deals with no theories of government, but with men and women simply; and modern Nihilistic Russia, with all the terror of its tyranny and the marvel of its martyrdoms, is merely the fiery and fervent background in front of which the persons of my dream live and love. With this feeling was the play written, and with this aim should the play be acted.

I have to thank you for the list of your company which you have sent me; and congratulate you, as well as myself, on the names of the many well-known and tried actors which I see it includes.

I am very much pleased to know that my directions as regards scenery and costume have been carried out. The yellow satin council-chamber is sure to be a most artistic scene, and as you have been unable to match in New York the vermilion silk of which I sent you a pattern, I hope you will allow me to bring you over a piece large enough for your dress in the last act.

I look forward with much interest to a second visit to America, and to having the privilege of pre-

"VERA" AND THE DRAMA   35

senting to the American people *my first drama.*
There is, I think, no country in the world where
there are such appreciative theatrical audiences as
I saw in the United States.

I hope that by the time I arrive, the play will
be in good rehearsing order, and I remain, dear
Miss Prescott, your sincere friend and admirer,

OSCAR WILDE.

II

July, 1883.

MY DEAR MISS PRESCOTT:—

I have received the American papers and thank
you for sending them. I think we must remember
that no amount of advertising will make a bad
play succeed, if it is not a good play well acted. I
mean that one might patrol the streets of New
York with a procession of vermilion caravans twice
a day for six months to announce that *Vera*
was a great play, but if on the first night of its
production, the play was not a strong play, well
acted, well mounted, all the advertisements in the
world would avail nothing. My name signed to a
play will excite some interest in London and Amer-

36 DECORATIVE ART IN AMERICA

ica. Your name as the heroine carries great weight with it. What we want to do is to have *all* the real conditions of success in our hands. Success is a science; if you have the conditions, you get the result. Art is the mathematical result of the emotional desire for beauty. If it is not thought out, it is nothing.

As regards dialogue, you can produce tragic effects by introducing comedy. A laugh in the audience does not destroy terror, but, by relieving terror, aids it. Never be afraid that by raising a laugh you destroy tragedy. On the contrary, you intensify it. The canons of each art depend on what they appeal to. Painting appeals to the eye and is founded on the science of optics. Music appeals to the ear and is founded on the science of acoustics. The drama appeals to human nature, and must have as its ultimate basis the science of psychology and physiology. Now, one of the facts of physiology is the desire of any intensified emotion to be relieved by some emotion that is its opposite. Nature's example of the dramatic effect is the laughter of hysteria or the tears of joy. So, I cannot cut out my comedy lines. Besides, the essence of good dialogue is interruption. All good dialogue should give the effect of its being made by the reaction of the personages on one another. It should never seem to

"VERA" AND THE DRAMA 37

be ready-made by the author, and interruptions have not only their artistic effect but their physical value. They give the actors time to breathe and get new breath power.

I remain, dear Miss Prescott, your sincere friend,

OSCAR WILDE.

MR. WHISTLER'S "TEN O'CLOCK"

He who seems to stand most remote from his age is he who mirrors it best, because he has stripped life of that mist of familiarity which, as Shelley used to say, makes life obscure to us.

—Lecture on the English Renaissance. 1882.

A truly great artist cannot conceive of life being shown, or beauty fashioned, under any conditions other than those that he has selected. Creation employs all its critical faculty within its own sphere.

— The Critic as Artist. Part II.

All fine imaginative work is self-conscious and deliberate.

— The Critic as Artist. Part I.

In its primary aspect, a painting has no more spiritual message or meaning for us than a blue tile from the wall of Damascus, or a Hitzen vase. It is a beautifully-coloured surface, nothing more, and affects us by no suggestion stolen from philosophy, no pathos pilfered from literature, no feeling filched from a poet, but by its own incommunicable artistic essence.

—Rose Leaf and Apple Leaf: L'Envoi. 1882.

To the great painter there is only one manner of painting—that which he himself employs. The æsthetic critic, and the æsthetic critic alone, can appreciate all forms and modes. It is to him that Art makes her appeal. *— The Critic as Artist. Part II.*

MR. WHISTLER'S "TEN O'CLOCK" [1]

AT Princes' Hall Mr. Whistler made his first public appearance last Friday[2] as a lecturer on art, and spoke for more than an hour with really marvellous eloquence on the absolute uselessness of all lectures of the kind. He began with a very pretty *aria* on prehistoric history, describing how in early times hunter and warrior would go forth to chase and foray, while the artist sat at home making cup and bowl for their service. Rude imitations of nature they were first, like the gourd-bottle, till the sense of beauty and form developed, and, in all its exquisite proportions, the first vase was fashioned. Then came the higher civilization of architecture and arm-chairs, and with exquisite design, and dainty diaper, the useful things of life were made lovely; and the hunter and the warrior lay on the couch when they were tired, and, when they were thirsty, drank from the bowl, and never cared to love the exquisite proportions of the one, or the

42 DECORATIVE ART IN AMERICA

delightful ornament of the other; and this attitude
of the primitive anthropophagous Philistine formed
the text of the lecture, and was the attitude which
Mr. Whistler entreated his audience to adopt towards
art. Remembering, no doubt, many charming invi-
tations to wonderful private views, this fashionable
assemblage seemed somewhat aghast, and not a
little amused, at being told that the slightest appearance among a civilized people of any joy in beautiful things is a grave impertinence to all painters;
but Mr. Whistler was relentless, and with charming
ease, and much grace of manner, explained to the
public that the only thing they should cultivate was
ugliness, and that on their permanent stupidity
rested all the hopes of art in the future.

The scene was in every way delightful; he stood
there, a miniature Mephistopheles mocking the
majority! He was like a brilliant surgeon[3] lecturing
to a class composed of subjects destined ultimately
for dissection, and solemnly assuring them how
valuable to science their maladies were, and how
absolutely uninteresting the slightest symptoms of
health on their part should be. In fairness to the
audience, however, I must say they seemed extremely gratified at being rid of the dreadful responsibility of admiring anything, and nothing could
have exceeded their enthusiasm when they were

MR. WHISTLER'S "TEN O'CLOCK" 43

told by Mr. Whistler that no matter how vulgar their dresses were, or how hideous their surroundings at home, still it was possible that a great painter, if there was such a thing, could, by contemplating them in the twilight, and half closing his eyes, see them under really picturesque conditions, and produce a picture which they were not to attempt to understand, much less dare to enjoy. Then there were some arrows, barbed and brilliant, shot off, with all the speed and splendour of fireworks, at the archæologists, who spend their lives in verifying the birthplaces of nobodies, and estimate the value of a work of art by its date, or its decay; at the art critics who always treat a picture as if it were a novel, and try and find out the plot; at the dilettanti in general, and amateurs in particular, and (*O mea culpa!*) at dress reformers [4] most of all. "Did not Velasquez paint crinolines? What more do you want?"[5]

Having thus made a holocaust of humanity, Mr. Whistler turned to Nature, and in a few moments convicted her of the Crystal Palace, Bank holidays, and a general overcrowding of detail, both in omnibuses and in landscapes; and then, in a passage of singular beauty, spoke of the artistic value of dim dawns and dusks, when the mean facts of life are lost in exquisite and evanescent effects; when common

44 DECORATIVE ART IN AMERICA

things are touched with mystery, and transfigured with magic; when the warehouses become as palaces, and the tall chimneys of the factory seem like campaniles in the opal air—a passage of perfect prose, well worthy of him to whom alone among painters, has the moon revealed her silver secrets, and the rose of morning opened its petals of gold.

Finally, after making a strong protest against anybody but a painter judging of painting, and a pathetic appeal to the audience not to be lured by the æsthetic movement into having beautiful things about them,[6] Mr. Whistler concluded his lecture with a pretty passage about Fusiyama on a fan,[7] and made his bow to an audience which he had succeeded in completely fascinating by his wit, his brilliant paradoxes, and, at times, his real eloquence. Of course, with regard to the value of beautiful surroundings I differ entirely from Mr. Whistler. An artist is not an isolated eccentricity.[8] He is the resultant of a certain *milieu* and a certain entourage, and can no more be born of a nation that is devoid of any sense of beauty, than a fig can grow from a thorn, or a rose blossom from a thistle. That an artist will find beauty in ugliness, *le beau dans l'horrible*, is now a commonplace of the schools, the argot of the atelier, but I strongly deny that charm-

MR. WHISTLER'S "TEN O'CLOCK" 45

ing people should be condemned to live with magenta
ottomans, and Albert blue curtains, in their rooms,
in order that some painter may observe the side-
lights on the one and the values of the other. Nor
do I accept the dictum that only a painter is a judge
of painting.[9] I say that only an artist is a judge of
art; there is a wide difference. As long as a painter
is a painter merely, he should not be allowed to talk
of anything but mediums and megilp, and on those
subjects should be compelled to hold his tongue;
it is only when he becomes an artist that the secret
laws of artistic creation are revealed to him. For
there are not many arts, but one art merely: poem,
picture, and Parthenon, sonnet and statue—all are
in their essence the same, and he who knows one,
knows all.[10] But the poet is the supreme artist, for
he is the master of colour and of form, and the real
musician besides, and is lord over all life and all
arts; and so to the poet beyond others are these
mysteries known; to Edgar Allan Poe, and to
Baudelaire,[11] not to Benjamin West and Paul Delaroche.[12] However, I could not enjoy anybody else's
lectures unless I entirely disagreed with them, and
so I have no hesitation in describing Mr. Whistler's
effort of Friday night as a masterpiece. Not merely
for its clever satire and amusing jests will it be
remembered, but for the pure and perfect beauty

46   DECORATIVE ART IN AMERICA

of many of its passages—passages delivered with an earnestness which seemed to amaze those who had looked on Mr. Whistler as a master of persiflage merely, and had not known him, as we do, as a master of painting also.   For that he is indeed one of the very greatest masters of painting, is my opinion.   And I may add that in this opinion Mr. Whistler himself entirely concurs.

THE RELATION OF DRESS
TO ART

From a combination of the Greek principles of beauty with the German principles of health will come, I feel certain, the costume of the future. —*Letter on Woman's Dress.* *1884.*

The costume of the future in England, if it is founded on the true laws of freedom, comfort, and adaptability to circumstances, cannot fail to be most beautiful also, because beauty is the sign always of the rightness of principles, the mystical seal set upon what is perfect, and upon what is perfect only.
—*More Radical Ideas Upon Dress Reform.* *1884.*

Every single work of art is the fulfilment of a prophecy: for every work of art is the conversion of an idea into an image.
—*De Profundis.*

A work of art is the unique result of a unique temperament. Its beauty comes from the fact that the author is what he is. It has nothing to do with the fact that other people want what they want.
—*The Soul of Man Under Socialism.*

The meaning of joy in art—that incommunicable element of artistic delight . . . in painting is to be sought for, from the subject never, but from the pictorial charm only—the scheme and symphony of the colour, the satisfying beauty of the design: so that the ultimate expression of our artistic movement in painting has been, not in the spiritual visions of the Pre-Raphaelites for all their marvel of Greek legend and their mystery of Italian song, but in the work of such men as Whistler and Albert Moore, who have raised design and colour to the ideal level of poetry and music.
—*Rose Leaf and Apple Leaf: L'Envoi.* *1882.*

THE RELATION OF DRESS TO ART[1]

A NOTE IN BLACK AND WHITE
ON MR. WHISTLER'S LECTURE

"How can you possibly paint these ugly three-cornered hats?" asked a reckless art critic once of Sir Joshua Reynolds. "I see light and shade in them," answered the artist. "*Les grands coloristes*," says Baudelaire, in a charming article on the artistic value of frock coats, "*les grands coloristes savent faire de la couleur avec un habit noir, une cravate blanche, et un fond gris.*"

"Art seeks and finds the beautiful in all times, as did her high priest Rembrandt, when he saw the picturesque grandeur of the Jews' quarter of Amsterdam and lamented not that its inhabitants were not Greeks," were the fine and simple words used by Mr. Whistler in one of the most valuable passages of his lecture. The most valuable, that is,

49

50   DECORATIVE ART IN AMERICA

to the painter; for there is nothing of which the ordinary English painter more needs to be reminded, than that the true artist does not wait for life to be made picturesque for him, but sees life under picturesque conditions always—under conditions, that is to say, which are at once new and delightful. But between the attitude of a painter towards the public, and the attitude of a people towards art, there is a wide difference. That, under certain conditions of light and shade, what is ugly in fact may, in its effect,[2] become beautiful, is true: and this, indeed, is the real *modernité* of art: but these conditions are exactly what we cannot be always sure of, as we stroll down Piccadilly in the glaring vulgarity of the noonday, or lounge in the park with a foolish sunset[3] as a background. Were we able to carry our *chiaroscuro* about with us, as we do our umbrellas, all would be well; but, this being impossible, I hardly think that pretty and delightful people will continue to wear a style of dress, as ugly as it is useless, on the chance of Mr. Whistler spiritualizing them into a symphony, or refining them into a mist. To be etched is not the end of existence. The arts are made for life, and not life for the arts.

Nor do I feel quite sure that Mr. Whistler has been himself always true to the dogma he seems to lay down, that a painter should only paint the

THE RELATION OF DRESS TO ART   51

dress of his age, and of his actual surroundings. Far be it from me to burden a butterfly with the heavy responsibility of its past! I have always been of opinion that consistency is the last refuge of the unimaginative.   But have we not all seen, and most of us admired, a picture from his hand of exquisite English girls strolling by an opal sea in the fantastic dresses of Japan?[4] Has not Tite Street been thrilled with the tidings that the models of Chelsea were posing to the master, in peplums, for pastels?[5]

Whatever comes from Mr. Whistler's brush is far too perfect in its loveliness, to stand, or fall, by any intellectual dogmas on art, even by his own.   For Beauty is justified of all her children, and cares nothing for explanations.   But it is impossible to look through any collection of modern pictures in London, from Burlington House to the Grosvenor Gallery, without feeling that the professional model is ruining painting, and reducing it to a condi- tion of mere pose and *pastiche*.[6]

Are we not all weary of him, that venerable im- poster, fresh from the steps of the Piazza di Spagna, who, in the leisure moments that he can spare from his customary organ, makes the round of the studios, and is waited for in Holland Park?   Do we not all recognize him, when, with the gay *insouciance* of his

52 DECORATIVE ART IN AMERICA

nation, he reappears on the walls of our summer exhibitions, as everything that he is not, and as nothing that he is, glaring at us here as a patriarch of Canaan, here beaming as a brigand from the Abruzzi? Popular is he, this poor peripatetic professor of posing,[7] with those whose joy it is to paint the posthumous portrait of the last philanthropist, who, in his lifetime, had neglected to be photographed. Yet, he is the sign of the decadence, the symbol of decay.

For all costumes are caricatures. The basis of Art is not the Fancy Ball.[8] Where there is loveliness of dress, there is no dressing up. And so, were our national attire delightful in colour, and in construction simple and sincere; were dress the expression of the loveliness that it shields, and of the swiftness and motion that it does not impede; did its lines break from the shoulder,[9] instead of bulging from the waist; did the inverted wineglass cease to be the ideal of form[10]—were these things brought about, as brought about they will be, then would painting be no longer an artificial reaction against the ugliness of life, but become, as it should be, the natural expression of life's beauty. Nor would painting merely, but all the arts also, be the gainers by a change such as that which I propose; the gainers; I mean, through the increased atmos-

THE RELATION OF DRESS TO ART 53

phere of Beauty by which the artists would be surrounded, and in which they would grow up. For Art is not to be taught in Academies. It is what one looks at, not what one listens to, that makes the artist. The real schools are the streets. There is not, for instance, a single delicate line, or delightful proportion, in the dress of the Greeks, which is not echoed exquisitely in their architecture.[11] A nation arrayed in stove-pipe hats, and dress-improvers, might have built the Pantechnicon, possibly, but the Parthenon, never. And, finally, there is this to be said: Art, it is true, can never have any other aim but her own perfection, and it may be that the artist, desiring merely to contemplate and to create, is wise in not busying himself about change in others: yet wisdom is not always the best; there are times when she sinks to the level of common sense; and from the passionate folly of those, and there are many, who desire that Beauty shall be confined no longer to the bric-à-brac of the collector, and the dust of the museum, but shall be, as it should be, the natural and national inheritance of all[12]—from this noble unwisdom, I say, who knows what new loveliness shall be given to life, and, under these more exquisite conditions, what perfect artist born? *Le milieu se renouvelant, l'art se renouvelle.*

54   DECORATIVE ART IN AMERICA

Speaking, however, from his own passionless pedestal, Mr. Whistler in pointing out that the power of the painter is to be found in his power of vision, not in his cleverness of hand, has expressed a truth which needed expression, and which, coming from the lord of form and colour, cannot fail to have its influence. His lecture, the Apocrypha though it be for the people, yet remains from this time as the Bible for the painter, the masterpiece of masterpieces, the song of songs. It is true he has pronounced the panegyric of the Philistine, but I can fancy Ariel praising Caliban[13] for a jest: and, in that he has read the Commination Service over the critics, let all men thank him, the critics themselves indeed most of all, for he has now relieved them from the necessity of a tedious existence. Considered again, merely as a *littérateur*, Mr. Whistler seems to me to stand almost alone. Indeed, I know but few who can combine, so felicitously as he does, the mirth and malice of Puck with the style of the minor prophets.

THE TOMB OF KEATS

Spirit of Beauty! . . . . ●
Yet tarry! for the boy who loved thee best,
Whose very name should be a memory
To make thee linger, sleeps in silent rest
Beneath the Roman walls. . . . .

— The Garden of Eros.

ON THE RECENT SALE BY AUCTION OF KEATS' LOVE LETTERS [1]

These are the letters which Endymion wrote [2]
To one he loved in secret and apart,
And now the brawlers of the auction-mart [3]
Bargain and bid for each poor blotted note,
Aye! for each separate pulse of passion quote
The merchant's price! I think they love not art
Who break the crystal of a poet's heart
That small and sickly eyes may glare or gloat.

Is it not said, that many years ago,
In a far Eastern town some soldiers ran
With torches through the midnight, and began
To wrangle for mean raiment, and to throw [4]
Dice for the garments of a wretched man,
Not knowing the God's wonder, or His woe?

And out of the bronze of the image of THE SORROW THAT
ENDURETH FOREVER he fashioned an image of THE PLEASURE
THAT ABIDETH FOR A MOMENT. *— The Artist.*

THE TOMB OF KEATS[5]

As one enters Rome from the Via Ostiensis[6] by the Porta San Paolo, the first object that meets the eye is a marble pyramid[7] which stands close at hand on the left.

There are many Egyptian obelisks[8] in Rome, tall snake-like spires of red sandstone, mottled with strange writings, which remind us of the pillars of flame[9] which led the Children of Israel through the desert away from the land of the Pharaohs; but more wonderful than these to look upon is this gaunt, wedge-shaped pyramid standing here in this Italian city, unshattered amid the ruins and wrecks of time, looking older than the Eternal City itself, like terrible impassiveness turned to stone. And so in the middle ages men supposed this to be the sepulchre of Remus, who was slain by his own brother at the founding of the city, so ancient and mysterious it appears; but we have now, perhaps

58   DECORATIVE ART IN AMERICA

unfortunately, more accurate information about it, and know that it is the tomb of Caius Cestius, a Roman gentleman of small note, who died about 30 B. C.

Yet though we cannot care much for the dead man who lies in lonely state beneath it, and who is only known to the world through his sepulchre, still this pyramid will be ever dear to the eyes of all English-speaking people, because at evening its shadow falls on the tomb of one who walks with Spenser and Shakespeare and Byron and Shelley and Elizabeth Barrett Browning, in the great procession of the sweet singers of England.

For at its foot there is a green sunny slope, known as the Old Protestant cemetery,[10] and on this a common looking grave, which bears the following inscription :

"This grave contains all that was mortal of a young English poet, who, on his death-bed, in the bitterness of his heart, desired [11] these words to be engraved on his tomb-stone: 'Here lies one whose name was writ in water.' [12] February 24, 1821."

And the name of the young English poet is John Keats.

Lord Houghton[13] calls this cemetery "one of the most beautiful spots on which the eye and heart of man can rest," and Shelley speaks of it as "making

THE TOMB OF KEATS 59

one in love with death, to think one should be buried in so sweet a place;"[14] and indeed when I saw the violets and the daisies and the poppies that overgrow the tomb, I remembered how the dead poet had once told his friend that he thought the "intensest pleasure he had received iı life was in watching the growth of flowers," and how another time, after lying a while quite still, he murmured in some strange prescience of early death, "I feel the flowers growing over me."[15]

But this time-worn stone and these wild flowers are but poor memorials* of one so great as Keats: most of all, too, in this city of Rome, which pays such honor to her dead; where popes and emperors and saints and cardinals lie hidden in "porphyry wombs," or couched in baths of jasper and chalcedony and malachite, ablaze with precious stones and metals, and tended with continued service. For very noble is the site, and worthy of a noble monument.[16] Behind looms the grey pyramid, symbol of the world's age, and filled with

---

*Recently some well-meaning persons have placed a marble slab on the wall of the cemetery with a medallion-profile of Keats on it, and some mediocre lines of poetry.[17] The face is ugly and rather hatchet-shaped, with thick, sensual lips, and is utterly unlike the poet himself, who was very beautiful to look upon. "His countenance," says a lady[18] who saw him at one of Hazlitt's lectures, "lives in my mind as one of singular beauty and brightness; it had the ex-

60   DECORATIVE ART IN AMERICA

memories of the sphinx[19] and the lotus leaf and the glories of old Nile; in front is the Monte Testaccio,[20] built, it is said, with the broken fragments of the vessels in which all the nations of the East and the West brought their tribute to Rome; and a little distance off, along the slope of the hill under the Aurelian wall, some tall, gaunt cypresses rise, like burnt-out funeral torches,[21] to mark the spot where Shelley's heart (that "heart of hearts!")[22] lies in the earth; and above all, the soil on which we tread is very Rome!

As I stood beside the mean grave of this divine boy, I thought of him as of a Priest of Beauty slain before his time; and the vision of Guido's St. Sebastian[23] came before my eyes as I saw him at Genoa, a lovely brown boy, with crisp, clustering hair[24] and red lips, bound by his evil enemies to a tree, and though pierced by arrows, raising his eyes with divine, impassioned gaze toward the Eternal Beauty of the opening heavens. And thus my thoughts shaped themselves to rhyme:

pression as if he had been looking on some glorions sight." And this is the idea which Severn's picture[25] of him gives. Even Haydon's rough pen and ink sketch [26] of him is better than this "marble libel," which I hope will soon be taken down. I think the best representation of the poet would be a coloured bust, like that of the young Rajah of Koolapoor [27] at Florence, which is a lovely and life-like work of art.—*Author's Note.*

THE TOMB OF KEATS

61

HEU MISERANDE PUER[28]

Rid of the world's injustice and its pain,
He rests at last beneath God's veil of blue;[29]
Taken from life while life and love were new,
The youngest of the martyrs here is lain,
Fair as Sebastian and as foully slain.
No cypress shades his grave, nor funeral yew,
But red-lipped daisies, violets drenched with dew,
And sleepy poppies, catch the evening rain.

O proudest heart that broke for misery!
O saddest poet that the world hath seen!
O sweetest singer of the English land!
Thy name was writ in water on the sand,
But our tears shall keep thy memory green,
And make it flourish like a Basil-tree.[30]

Rome, 1877.

KEATS' SONNET ON BLUE

"Be happy," cried the Nightingale, "be happy; you shall have your red rose. I will build it out of music by moonlight and stain it with my own heart's-blood. All that I ask of you in return is that you will be a true lover, for Love is wiser than Philosophy, though she is wise, and mightier than Power, though he is mighty."

— *The Nightingale and the Rose.*

The most joyous poet is not he who sows the desolate highways of this world with the barren seed of laughter, but he who makes his sorrow most musical. — *Rose Leaf and Apple Leaf: L'Envoi.*

The joy of poetry comes never from the subject, but from an inventive handling of rhythmical language.

— *Lecture on the English Renaissance.*

Art finds her own perfection within, and not outside of, herself. . . . She is a veil, rather than a mirror. She has flowers that no forests know of, birds that no woodland possesses. She makes and unmakes many worlds, and can draw the moon from heaven with a scarlet thread. . . . She can bid the almond tree blossom in winter, and send the snow upon the ripe cornfield. At her word the frost lays its silver finger on the burning mouth of June.

— *The Decay of Lying.*

The world is made by the singer for the dreamer.

— *The Critic as Artist. Part I.*

KEATS' SONNET ON BLUE[1]

DURING my tour in America I happened one evening to find myself in Louisville,[2] Kentucky. The subject I had selected to speak on was *The Mission of Art in the Nineteenth Century*, and in the course of my lecture I had occasion to quote Keats' sonnet on Blue as an example of the poet's delicate sense of colour-harmonies. When my lecture was concluded there came round to see me a lady of middle age, with a sweet, gentle manner and a most musical voice. She introduced herself to me as Mrs. Speed,[3] the daughter of George Keats,[4] and invited me to come and examine the Keats manuscripts in her possession. I spent most of the next day with her, reading the letters of Keats to her father, some of which were at that time unpublished,[5] poring over torn yellow leaves and faded scraps of paper, and wondering at the little Dante in which Keats had written those marvellous notes on Milton.[6] Some months afterwards

66   DECORATIVE ART IN AMERICA

when I was in California, I received a letter from Mrs. Speed asking my acceptance of the original manuscript of the sonnet which I had quoted in my lecture. This manuscript I have had reproduced here,[7] as it seems to me to possess much psychological interest. It shows us the conditions that preceded the perfected form, the gradual growth, not of the conception but of the expression, and the workings of that spirit of selection which is the secret of style. In the case of poetry, as in the case of the other arts, what may appear to be simply technicalities of method are in their essence spiritual, not mechanical, and although, in all lovely work, what concerns us is the ultimate form, not the conditions that necessitate that form, yet the preference that precedes perfection, the evolution of the beauty, and the mere making of the music, have, if not their artistic value, at least their value to the artist.

It will be remembered that this sonnet was first published in 1848, by Lord Houghton[8] in his *Life, Letters, and Literary Remains of John Keats.* Lord Houghton does not definitely state where he found it, but it was probably among the Keats manuscripts belonging to Mr. Charles Brown.[9] It is evidently taken from a version later than that in my possession, as it accepts all the corrections, and makes three

KEATS' SONNET ON BLUE

67

variations. As in my manuscript the first line is torn away, I give the sonnet here as it appears in Lord Houghton's edition.[10]

ANSWER TO A SONNET ENDING THUS:—

"Dark eyes are dearer far [11]
Than those that make the hyacinthine bell." *
By J. H. REYNOLDS.[12]

Blue! 'Tis the life of heaven,—the domain
   Of Cynthia,—the wide palace of the sun,—
The tent of Hesperus and all his train,—
   The bosomer of clouds, gold, grey and dun.
Blue! 'Tis the life of waters—ocean
   And all its vassal streams: pools numberless
May rage, and foam, and fret, but never can
   Subside if not to dark-blue nativeness.
Blue! gentle cousin of the forest green,
   Married to green in all the sweetest flowers,
Forget-me-not,—the blue-bell,—and, that queen
   Of secrecy, the violet: what strange powers
Hast thou, as a mere shadow! But how great,
   When in an Eye thou art alive with fate!

Feb., 1818.[13]

In *The Athenæum* of the 3rd of June, 1876,[14] appeared a letter from Mr. A. J. Horwood, stating that he had in his possession a copy of *The Garden of Florence* in which this sonnet was transcribed.

* ' Make ' is of course a mere printer's error for ' mock,' and was subsequently corrected by Lord Honghton. The sonnet as given in *The Garden of Florence* reads ' orbs ' for ' those.'—*Author's Note.*

68   DECORATIVE ART IN AMERICA

Mr. Horwood, who was unaware that the sonnet had been already published by Lord Houghton, gives the transcript at length. His version reads *hue* for *life* in the first line, and *bright* for *wide* in the second, and gives the sixth line thus:

"With all his tributary streams, pools numberless,"

a foot too long: it also reads *to* for *of* in the ninth line. Mr. Buxton Forman is of the opinion that these variations are decidedly genuine,[15] but indicative of an earlier state of the poem than that adopted in Lord Houghton's edition. However, now that we have before us Keats' first draft of his sonnet, it is difficult to believe that the sixth line in Mr. Horwood's version is really a genuine variation.[16] Keats may have written,

"Ocean
His tributary streams, pools numberless,"

and the transcript may have been carelessly made, but having got his line right in his first draft, Keats probably did not spoil it in his second. The *Athenæum* version inserts a comma after *art* in the last line, which seems to me a decided improvement, and eminently characteristic of Keats' method.[17] I am glad to see that Mr. Buxton Forman has adopted it.

As for the corrections that Lord Houghton's

KEATS' SONNET ON BLUE

69

version shows Keats to have made in the eighth and ninth lines of this sonnet, it is evident that they sprang from Keats' reluctance to repeat the same word in consecutive lines, except in cases where a word's music or meaning was to be emphasized. The substitution of *its* for *his* in the sixth line is more difficult of explanation. It is due probably to a desire on Keats' part not to mar by any echo the fine personification of Hesperus.

It may be noticed that Keats' own eyes were brown, and not blue,[18] as stated by Mrs. Procter to Lord Houghton. Mrs. Speed showed me a note to that effect written by Mrs. George Keats on the margin of the page in Lord Houghton's Life (page 100, vol. i), where Mrs. Procter's description is given. Cowden Clarke[19] made a similar correction in his " Recollections; "[20] and in some of the later editions of Lord Houghton's book the word "blue" is struck out. In Severn's[21] portraits of Keats also the eyes are given as brown.

The exquisite sense of colour expressed in the ninth and tenth lines may be paralleled by

" The Ocean with its vastness, its blue green,"

of the sonnet to George Keats.[22]

ENGLISH POETESSES

Like the philosopher of the Platonic vision, the poet is the spectator of all time and all existence. For him no form is obsolete, no subject out of date; rather, whatever of life and passion the world has known in the desert of Judæa or in Arcadian valley, by the ruins of Troy or Damascus, in the crowded and hideous streets of the modern city, or by the pleasant ways of Camelot, all lies before him like an open scroll, all is still instinct with beautiful life.

—Lecture on the English Renaissance. 1882.

Lying and poetry are arts—arts, as Plato saw, not unconnected with each other—and they require the most careful study, the most disinterested devotion. *— The Decay of Lying.*

Rhyme, that exquisite echo which in the Muse's hollow hill creates and answers its own voice; rhyme, which in the hands of the real artist becomes not merely a material element of metrical beauty, but a spiritual element of thought and passion also, waking a new mood, it may be, or stirring a fresh train of ideas, or opening by mere sweetness and suggestion of sound some golden door at which the Imagination itself had knocked in vain !

— The Critic as Artist. Part I.

In the case of most of our modern poets, when we have analysed them down to an adjective, we can go no further, or, we care to go no further.

What English poetry has to fear is not the fascination of dainty meter or delicate form, but the predominance of the intellectual spirit over the spirit of beauty. *—A Note on Some Modern Poets.*

The Woman's World, December, 1888.

ENGLISH POETESSES[1]

ENGLAND has given to the world one great poetess[2]—Elizabeth Barrett Browning. By her side Mr. Swinburne would place Miss Christina Rossetti, whose New Year hymn[3] he describes[4] as so much the noblest of sacred poems in our language, that there is none which comes near it enough to stand second. "It is a hymn," he tells us, "touched as with the fire, and bathed as in the light of sunbeams, tuned as to chords and cadences of refluent sea-music beyond reach of harp and organ, large echoes of the serene and sonorous tides of heaven." Much as I admire Miss Rossetti's work, her subtle choice of words, her rich imagery, her artistic *naïveté*, wherein curious notes of strangeness and simplicity are fantastically blended together, I cannot but think that Mr. Swinburne has, with noble and natural loyalty, placed her on too lofty a pedestal. To me, she is simply a very delightful artist in poetry. This is indeed something so rare that

74   DECORATIVE ART IN AMERICA

when we meet it we cannot fail to love it, but it is
not everything. Beyond it and above it are higher
and more sunlit heights of song, a larger vision,
and an ampler air, a music at once more passionate
and more profound, a creative energy that is born
of the spirit, a winged rapture that is born of the
soul, a force and fervour of mere utterance that has
all the wonder of the prophet, and not a little of
the consecration of the priest. Mrs. Browning is
unapproachable by any woman who has ever
touched lyre or blown through reed since the days
of the great Æolian poetess.[5]   But Sappho, who,
to the antique world, was a pillar of flame, is to us
but a pillar of shadow.   Of her poems, burnt with
other most precious work by Byzantine Emperor
and by Roman Pope, only a few fragments remain.[6] Possibly they lie mouldering in the scented
darkness of an Egyptian tomb, clasped in the
withered hands of some long-dead lover.   Some
Greek monk at Athos[7] may even now be poring
over an ancient manuscript, whose crabbed characters conceal lyric or ode by her whom the Greeks
spoke of as "The Poetess," just as they termed
Homer "The Poet," who was to them the tenth
Muse, the flower of the Graces, the child of Erôs,
and the pride of Hellas—Sappho, with the sweet
voice, the bright, beautiful eyes, the dark hyacinth-

ENGLISH POETESSES

75

coloured hair. But, practically, the work of the marvellous singer of Lesbos [8] is entirely lost to us. We have a few rose leaves out of her garden. That is all. Literature nowadays survives marble and bronze, but in old days, in spite of the Roman poet's noble boast, it was not so. The fragile clay vases of the Greeks still keep for us pictures of Sappho, delicately painted in black and red and white; but of her song we have only the echo of an echo.

Of all the women of history, Mrs. Browning is the only one that we could name in any possible or remote conjunction with Sappho. Sappho was undoubtedly a far more flawless and perfect artist. She stirred the whole antique world more than Mrs. Browning ever stirred our modern age. Never had Love such a singer. Even in the few lines that remain to us, the passion seems to scorch and burn. But, as unjust Time, who has crowned her with the barren laurels of fame, has twined with them the dull poppies of oblivion, let us turn from the mere memory of a poetess to one whose song still remains to us as an imperishable glory of our literature; to her who heard the cry of the children from dark mine and crowded factory, and made England weep over its little ones; [9] who in the feigned sonnets from the Portuguese [10] sang of the spiritual mystery of Love, and of the intellectual gifts that Love

76 DECORATIVE ART IN AMERICA

brings to the soul; who had faith in all that is worthy, and enthusiasm for all that is great, and pity for all that suffers; who wrote the *Vision of Poets*, and *Casa Guidi Windows* and *Aurora Leigh*.[11] As one, to whom I owe my love of poetry no less than my love of country, has said of her:

> Still on our ears
> The clear "Excelsior" from a woman's lip
> Rings out across the Apennines, although
> The woman's brow lies pale and cold in death
> With all the mighty marble dead in Florence.
> For while great songs can stir the heart of men,
> Spreading their full vibrations through the world
> In ever-widening circles till they reach
> The Throne of God, and song becomes a prayer,
> And prayer brings down the liberating strength
> That kindles nations to heroic deeds,
> She lives—the great-souled poetess who saw
> From Casa Guidi[12] windows Freedom dawn
> On Italy, and gave the glory back
> In sunrise hymns to all Humanity!

She lives indeed, and not alone in the heart of Shakespeare's England, but in the heart of Dante's Italy also. To Greek literature she owed her scholarly culture,[13] but modern Italy created her passion for Liberty. When she crossed the Alps,[14] she became filled with a new ardour, and from that fine eloquent mouth, that we can still see in her portraits, broke forth such a noble and majestic

ENGLISH POETESSES

outburst of lyrical song as had not been heard from woman's lips for more than two thousand years. It is pleasant to think that an English poetess was to a certain extent a real factor in bringing about that unity of Italy that was Dante's dream, and if Florence drove her great singer into exile, she at least welcomed within her walls the later singer that England had sent to her.

If one were asked the chief qualities of Mrs. Browning's work, one would say, as Mr. Swinburne said of Byron's, its sincerity and its strength. Faults it, of course, possesses. " She would rhyme moon to table," used to be said of her in jest; and certainly no more monstrous rhymes are to be found in literature, than some of those we come across in Mrs. Browning's poems. But her ruggedness was never the result of carelessness. It was deliberate as her letters to Mr. Horne[15] show very clearly. She refused to sandpaper her Muse. She disliked facile smoothness and artificial polish. In her very rejection of art she was an artist. She intended to produce a certain effect by certain means, and she succeeded; and her indifference to complete assonance in rhyme often gives a splendid richness to her verse, and brings into it a pleasurable element of surprise.

In philosophy she was a Platonist, in politics an

78   DECORATIVE ART IN AMERICA

Opportunist. She attached herself to no particular party. She loved the people when they were king-like, and kings when they showed themselves to be men. Of the real value and motive of poetry she had a most exalted ideal. "Poetry," she says, in the preface to one of her volumes, "has been as serious a thing to me as life itself; and life has been a very serious thing. There has been no playing at skittles for me in either. I never mistook pleasure for the final cause of poetry, nor leisure for the hour of the poet. I have done my work[16] so far, not as mere hand and head work apart from the personal being, but as the completest expression of that being to which I could attain." It certainly is her completest expression, and through it she realizes her fullest perfection. "The poet," she says, elsewhere, "is at once richer and poorer than he used to be; he wears better broadcloth, but speaks no more oracles." These words give us the keynote of her view of the poet's mission. He was to utter Divine oracles, to be at once inspired prophet and holy priest; and as such we may, I think, without exaggeration, conceive her. She was a Sibyl delivering a message to the world, sometimes through stammering lips, and once at least with blinded eyes, yet always with the true fire and fervour of lofty and unshaken faith,

ENGLISH POETESSES

always with the great raptures of a spiritual nature, the high ardours of an impassioned soul. As we read her best poems we feel that, though Apollo's shrine be empty and the bronze tripod overthrown, and the vale of Delphi desolate, still the Pythia is not dead.[17] In our own age she has sung for us, and this land gave her new birth. Indeed, Mrs. Browning is the wisest of the Sibyls, wiser even than that mighty figure whom Michael Angelo has painted on the roof of the Sistine Chapel at Rome, poring over the scroll of mystery, and trying to decipher the secrets of Fate; for she realized that, while Knowledge is Power, Suffering is part of Knowledge.

To her influence, almost as much as to the higher education of women, I would be inclined to attribute the really remarkable awakening of woman's song that characterizes the latter half of our century in England. No country has ever had so many poetesses at once. Indeed, when one remembers that the Greeks had only nine muses, one is sometimes apt to fancy that we have too many. And yet the work done by women in the sphere of poetry is really of a very high standard of excellence. In England we have always been prone to underrate the value of tradition in literature. In our eagerness to find a new voice and a fresh mode

80   DECORATIVE ART IN AMERICA

of music, we have forgotten how beautiful Echo may be. We look first for individuality and personality, and these are, indeed, the chief characteristics of the masterpieces of our literature, either in prose or verse; but deliberate culture and a study of the best models, if united to an artistic temperament and a nature susceptible of exquisite impressions, may produce much that is admirable, much that is worthy of phrase. It would be quite impossible to give a complete catalogue of all the women who since Mrs. Browning's day have tried lute and lyre. Mrs. Pfeiffer, Mrs. Hamilton-King, Mrs. Augusta Webster, Graham Tomson, Miss Mary Robinson, Jean Ingelow, Miss May Kendall, Miss Nesbit, Miss May Probyn, Mrs. Craik, Mrs. Meynell, Miss Chapman,[18] and many others have done really good work in poetry, either in the grave Dorian mode of thoughtful and intellectual verse, or in the light and graceful forms of old French song, or in the romantic manner of antique ballad, or in that "moment's monument," as Rossetti called it, the intense and concentrated sonnet. Occasionally one is tempted to wish that the quick artistic faculty that women undoubtedly possess developed itself somewhat more in prose and somewhat less in verse. Poetry is for our highest moods, when we wish to be with the gods, and in poetry nothing but the very best

ENGLISH POETESSES

should satisfy us; but prose is our daily bread, and the lack of good prose is one of the chief blots on our culture. French prose, even in the hands of the most ordinary writers, is always readable, but English prose is detestable. We have a few, a very few masters, such as they are. We have Carlyle,[19] who should not be imitated; and Mr. Pater,[20] who, through the subtle perfection of his form, is inimitable absolutely; and Mr. Froude, who is useful; and Matthew Arnold, who is a model; and Mr. George Meredith,[21] who is a warning; and Mr. Lang, who is the divine amateur; and Mr. Stevenson,[22] who is the humane artist; and Mr. Ruskin,[23] whose rhythm and colour and fine rhetoric and marvellous music of words are entirely unattainable. But the general prose that one reads in magazines and in newspapers is terribly dull and cumbrous, heavy in movement and uncouth or exaggerated in expression. Possibly some day our women of letters will apply themselves more definitely to prose. Their light touch, and exquisite ear, and delicate sense of balance and proportion would be of no small service to us. I can fancy women bringing a new manner into our literature.[24]

However, we have to deal here with women as poetesses, and it is interesting to note that, though Mrs. Browning's influence undoubtedly contributed

82   DECORATIVE ART IN AMERICA

very largely to the development of this new song movement, if I may so term it, still there seems to have been never a time during the last three hundred years when the women of this kingdom did not cultivate, if not the art, at least the habit, of writing poetry. Who the first English poetess was, I cannot say. I believe it was the Abbess Juliana Berners,[25] who lived in the fifteenth century; but I have no doubt that Mr. Freeman would be able at a moment's notice to produce some wonderful Saxon or Norman poetess, whose works cannot be read without a glossary, and even with its aid are completely unintelligible. For my own part, I am content with the Abbess Juliana, who wrote enthusiastically about hawking; and after her I would mention Anne Askew,[26] who, in prison and on the eve of her fiery martyrdom, wrote a ballad that has, at any rate, a pathetic and historical interest. Queen Elizabeth's "most sweet and sententious ditty "[27] on Mary Stuart is highly praised by Puttenham, a contemporary critic, as an example of " Exargasia, or the Gorgeous in Literature," which somehow seems a very suitable epithet for a great Queen's poems. The term she applies to the unfortunate Queen of Scots, "the daughter of debate " has, of course, long since passed into literature. The Countess of Pembroke,[28] Sir Philip Sidney's sister, was much ad-

ENGLISH POETESSES

83

mired as a poetess in her day. In 1613 "the learned, virtuous, and truly noble ladie, Elizabeth Carew,"[29] published *A Tragedie of Mariam, the Faire Queene of Jewry*, and a few years later the "noble ladie Diana Primrose" wrote *A Chain of Pearl*, which is a panegyric on the "peerless graces" of Gloriana. Mary Morpeth, the friend and admirer of Drummond of Hawthornden; Lady Mary Wroth,[30] to whom Ben Jonson dedicated *The Alchemist*; and the Princess Elizabeth,[31] the sister of Charles I, should also be mentioned. After the Restoration, women applied themselves with still greater ardour to the study of literature and the practice of poetry. Margaret, Duchess of Newcastle,[32] was a true woman of letters, and some of her verses are extremely pretty and graceful. Mrs. Aphra Behn[33] was the first English woman who adopted literature as a regular profession. Mrs. Katherine Philips,[34] according to Mr. Gosse, invented sentimentality. As she was praised by Dryden and mourned by Cowley, let us hope that she may be forgiven. Keats came across her poems at Oxford when he was writing *Endymion* and found in one of them "a most delicate fancy of the Fletcher kind," but I fear that nobody reads "The Matchless Orinda" now. Of Lady Winchilsea's[35] *Nocturnal Reverie*, Wordsworth said that, with the

84   DECORATIVE ART IN AMERICA

exception of Pope's *Windsor Forest*, it was the only poem of the period intervening between *Paradise Lost* and Thomson's *Seasons* that contained a single new image of external nature. Lady Rachel Russell,[36] who may be said to have inaugurated the letter-writing literature of England; Eliza Haywood,[37] who is immortalized by the badness of her work, and has a niche in *The Dunciad;* and the Marchioness of Wharton,[38] whose poems Waller said he admired, are very remarkable types, the finest of them being, of course, the first named, who was a woman of heroic mould and of a most noble dignity of nature. Indeed, though the English poetesses up to the time of Mrs. Browning cannot be said to have produced any work of absolute genius, they are certainly interesting figures, fascinating subjects for study. Amongst them we find Lady Mary Wortley Montagu,[39] who had all the caprice of Cleopatra, and whose letters are delightful reading; Mrs. Centilivre,[40] who wrote one brilliant comedy; Lady Anne Barnard,[41] whose *Auld Robin Gray* was described by Sir Walter Scott as "worth all the dialogues Corydon and Phillis have together spoken from the days of Theocritus downwards," and is certainly a very beautiful and touching poem; Esther Vanhomrigh[42] and Hester Johnson,[43] the Vanessa and the Stella of Dean Swift's life; Mrs. Thrale[44] the friend of the great Lexicographer; the

ENGLISH POETESSES

worthy Mrs. Barbauld;[45] the excellent Mrs. Hannah More;[46] the industrious Joanna Baillie;[47] the admirable Mrs. Chapone,[48] whose *Ode to Solitude* always fills me with the wildest passion for society, and who will at least be remembered as the patroness of the establishment at which Becky Sharp was educated; Miss Anna Seward,[49] who was called the "Swan of Lichfield"; poor L. E. L.,[50] whom Disraeli described in one of his clever letters to his sister as "the personification of Brompton—pink satin dress, white satin shoes, red cheeks, snub nose, and her hair *à la* Sappho"; Mrs. Radcliffe,[51] who introduced the romantic novel, and has consequently much to answer for; the beautiful Duchess of Devonshire,[52] of whom Gibbon said that she was "made for something better than a Duchess"; the two wonderful sisters, Lady Dufferin and Mrs. Norton;[53] Mrs. Tighe,[54] whose *Psyche* Keats read with pleasure; Constantia Grierson,[55] a marvellous bluestocking in her time; Mrs. Hemans;[56] pretty, charming "Perdita,"[57] who flirted alternately with poetry and the Prince Regent, played divinely in *The Winter's Tale*, was brutally attacked by Gifford, and has left us a pathetic little poem on the snowdrop; and Emily Brontë,[58] whose poems are instinct with tragic power, and seem often on the verge of being great.

Old fashions in literature are not so pleasant as

86   DECORATIVE ART IN AMERICA

old fashions in dress. I like the costume of the age of powder better than the poetry of the age of Pope. But if one adopts the historical standpoint— and this is, indeed, the only standpoint from which we can ever form a fair estimate of work that is not absolutely of the highest order—we cannot fail to see that many of the English poetesses who preceded Mrs. Browning, were women of no ordinary talent, and that if the majority of them looked upon poetry simply as a department of belles lettres, so in most cases did their contemporaries. Since Mrs. Browning's day our woods have become full of singing birds, and if I venture to ask them to apply themselves more to prose and less to song, it is not that I like poetical prose, but that I love the prose of poets.

Most of our modern portrait painters are doomed to absolnte oblivion. They never paint what they see. They paint what the pnblic sees, and the public never sees anything.
— *The Decay of Lying.*

Not width but intensity is the true aim of modern art.
— *De Profundis.*

All beautiful things belong to the same age. . . . To those who are preoccupied with the beanty of form nothing else seems of much importance.
— *Pen, Pencil, and Poison.*

Art is a passion, and, in matters of art, Thought is inevitably coloured by emotion, and so is fluid rather than fixed, and, depending upon fine moods and exqnisite moments, cannot be narrowed into the rigidity of a scientific formula or a theological dogma.
— *The Critic as Artist. Part II.*

Whatever work we have in the nineteenth century mnst rest on the two poles of personality and perfection.
— *Rose Leaf and Apple Leaf: L'Envoi.*

While the poet can be pictorial or not, as he chooses, the painter must be pictorial always. For a painter is limited, not to what he sees in nature, but to what npon canvas may be seen.
— *The Critic as Artist. Part I.*

LONDON MODELS[1]

PROFESSIONAL models are a purely modern invention. To the Greeks, for instance, they were quite unknown. Mr. Mahaffy,[2] it is true, tells us that Perikles used to present peacocks to the great ladies of Athenian society in order to induce them to sit to his friend Pheidias,[3] and we know that Polygnotus[4] introduced into his picture of the Trojan women the face of Elpinike,[5] the celebrated sister of the great Conservative leader[6] of the day, but these *grandes dames* clearly do not come under our category. As for the old masters, they undoubtedly made constant studies from their pupils and apprentices, and even their religious pictures are full of the portraits of their friends and relations, but they do not seem to have had the inestimable advantage of the existence of a class of people whose sole profession is to pose. In fact the model, in our sense of the word, is the direct creation of Academic Schools.

90 DECORATIVE ART IN AMERICA

Every country now has its own models, except America. In New York, and even in Boston, a good model is so great a rarity that most of the artists are reduced to painting Niagara[7] and millionaires. In Europe, however, it is different. Here we have plenty of models, and of every nationality. The Italian models are the best. The natural grace of their attitudes, as well as the wonderful picturesqueness of their colouring, makes them facile—often too facile—subjects for the painter's brush. The French models, though not so beautiful as the Italian, possess a quickness of intellectual sympathy, a capacity in fact of understanding the artist, which is quite remarkable. They have also a great command over the varieties of facial expression, are peculiarly dramatic, and can chatter the argot of the atelier as cleverly as the critic of the *Gil Blas.* The English models form a class entirely by themselves. They are not so picturesque as the Italian, nor so clever as the French, and they have absolutely no tradition, so to speak, of their order. Now and then some old veteran knocks at a studio door, and proposes to sit as Ajax defying the lightning, or as King Lear upon the blasted heath. One of them some time ago called on a popular painter who, happening at the moment to require his services, engaged him, and told him to begin by

LONDON MODELS 91

kneeling down in the attitude of prayer. "Shall I be Biblical or Shakespearean, sir?" asked the veteran. "Well — Shakespearean," answered the artist, wondering by what subtle nuance of expression the model would convey the difference. "All right, sir," said the professor of posing,[8] and he solemnly knelt down and began to wink with his left eye! This class, however, is dying out. As a rule the model, nowadays, is a pretty girl, from about twelve to twenty-five years of age, who knows nothing about art, cares less, and is merely anxious to earn seven or eight shillings a day without much trouble. English models rarely look at a picture, and never venture on any æsthetic theories. In fact they realize very completely Mr. Whistler's idea of the function of an art-critic, for they pass no criticisms at all.[9] They accept all schools of art with the grand catholicity of the auctioneer,[10] and sit to a fantastic young impressionist as readily as to a learned and laborious academician. They are neither for the Whistlerites, nor against them; the quarrel between the school of facts and the school of effects[11] touches them not; idealistic and naturalistic are words that convey no meaning to their ears; they merely desire that the studio shall be warm, and the lunch hot, for all charming artists give their models lunch.

92 DECORATIVE ART IN AMERICA

As to what they are asked to do they are equally indifferent. On Monday they will don the rags of a beggar-girl for Mr. Pumper, whose pathetic pictures of modern life draw such tears from the public, and on Tuesday they will pose in a peplum for Mr. Phœbus, who thinks that all really artistic subjects are necessarily B.C. They career gaily through all centuries and through all costumes, and, like actors, are only interesting when they are not themselves. They are extremely good-natured, and very accommodating. "What do you sit for?" said a young artist to a model who had sent him in her card (all models by the way have cards and a small black bag). "Oh, for anything you like, sir," said the girl; "landscape if necessary!"

Intellectually, it must be acknowledged, they are Philistines, but physically they are perfect — at least some are. Though none of them can talk Greek, many can look Greek, which to a nineteenth-century painter is naturally of great importance. If they are allowed, they chatter a great deal, but they never say anything. Their observations are the only *banalités* heard in Bohemia. However, though they cannot appreciate the artist as an artist, they are quite ready to appreciate the artist as a man. They are very sensitive to kindness, respect, and generosity. A beautiful model who had sat

LONDON MODELS

93

for two years to one of our most distinguished English painters, got engaged to a street vendor of penny ices. On her marriage the painter sent her a pretty wedding present, and received in return a nice letter of thanks with the following remarkable postscript: " Never eat the green ices! "

When they are tired a wise artist gives them a rest. Then they sit in a chair and read penny dreadfuls, till they are roused from the tragedy of literature to take their place again in the tragedy of art. A few of them smoke cigarettes. This, however, is regarded by the other models as showing a want of seriousness, and is not generally approved of. They are engaged by the day and by the half day. The tariff is a shilling an hour, to which great artists usually add an omnibus fare. The two best things about them are their extraordinary prettiness and their extreme respectability. As a class they are very well-behaved, particularly those who sit for the figure, a fact which is curious or natural according to the view one takes of human nature. They usually marry well, and sometimes they marry the artist. In neither case do they ever sit again. For an artist to marry his model is as fatal as for a gourmet to marry his cook; the one gets no sittings, and the other gets no dinners.

On the whole the English female models are very

94 DECORATIVE ART IN AMERICA

naive, very natural, and very good-humoured. The virtues which the artist values most in them are prettiness and punctuality. Every sensible model consequently keeps a diary of her engagements and dresses neatly. The bad season is of course the summer, when the artists are out of town. However, of late years some artists have engaged their models to follow them, and the wife of one of our most charming painters has often had three or four models under her charge in the country, so that the work of her husband and his friends should not be interrupted. In France the models migrate *en masse* to the little seaport villages or forest hamlets where the painters congregate. The English models, however, wait patiently in London, as a rule, till the artists come back. Nearly all of them live with their parents, and help to support the house. They have every qualification for being immortalized in art except that of beautiful hands. The hands of the English model are nearly always coarse and red.

As for the male models, there is the veteran whom we have mentioned above. He has all the traditions of the grand style, and is rapidly disappearing with the school he represents. An old man who talks about Fuseli [12] is of course unendurable, and besides, patriarchs have ceased to be fashionable sub-

LONDON MODELS

jects. Then there is the true Academy model. He is usually a man of thirty, rarely good-looking, but a perfect miracle of muscles. In fact he is the apotheosis of anatomy, and is so conscious of his own splendour that he tells you of his tibia and his thorax, as if no one else had anything of the kind. Then come the Oriental models. The supply of these is limited, but there are always about a dozen in London. They are very much sought after, as they can remain immobile for hours, and generally possess lovely costumes. However, they have a poor opinion of English art, which they regard as something between a vulgar personality and a commonplace photograph. Next we have the Italian youth who has either come over specially to be a model, or takes to it when his organ is out of repair. He is often quite charming with his large melancholy eyes, his crisp hair, and his slim brown figure.[13] It is true he eats garlic, but then he can stand like a faun and couch[14] like a leopard, so he is forgiven. He is always full of pretty compliments, and has been known to have kind words of encouragement for even our greatest artists. As for the English lad of the same age, he never sits at all. Apparently he does not regard the career of a model as a serious profession. In any case he is rarely if ever to be got hold of. English boys too are difficult to

96 DECORATIVE ART IN AMERICA

find. Sometimes an ex-model who has a son, will curl his hair, and wash his face, and bring him the round of the studios, all soap and shininess. The young school don't like him, but the older school do, and when he appears on the walls of the ·Royal Academy he is called "The Infant Samuel." Occasionally also an artist catches a couple of *gamins* in the gutter and asks them to come to his studio. The first time they always appear, but after that they don't keep their appointments. They dislike sitting still, and have a strong and perhaps natural objection to looking pathetic. Besides they are always under the impression that the artist, is laughing at them. It is a sad fact, but there is no doubt that the poor are completely unconscious of their picturesqueness. Those of them who can be induced to sit do so with the idea that the artist is merely a benevolent philanthropist who has chosen an eccentric method of distributing alms to the undeserving. Perhaps the School Board will teach the London *gamin* his own artistic value, and then they will be better models than they are now. One remarkable privilege belongs to the Academy model, that of extorting a sovereign from any newly elected Associate or R. A. They wait at Burlington House till the announcement is made, and then race to the hapless artist's house. The one who

LONDON MODELS 97

arrives first receives the money. They have of late been much troubled at the long distances they have had to run, and they look with strong disfavour on the election of artists who live at Hampstead or at Bedford Park, for it is considered a point of honour not to employ the underground railway, omnibuses, or any artificial means of locomotion. The race is to the swift.

Besides the professional posers of the studio there are the posers of the Row, the posers at afternoon teas, the posers in politics, and the circus-posers. All four classes are delightful, but only the last class is ever really decorative. Acrobats and gymnasts can give the young painter infinite suggestions, for they bring into their art an element of swiftness, of motion, and of constant change that the studio model necessarily lacks. What is interesting in these "slaves of the ring" is that with them Beauty is an unconscious result, not a conscious aim, the result in fact of the mathematical calculation of curves and distances, of absolute precision of eye, of the scientific knowledge of the equilibrium of forces, and of perfect physical training. A good acrobat is always graceful, though grace is never his object; he is graceful because he does what he has to do in the best way in which it can be done — graceful because he is natural. If an

98 DECORATIVE ART IN AMERICA

ancient Greek were to come to life now, which, considering the probable severity of his criticism, would be rather trying to our conceit, he would be found far oftener at the circus than at the theatre. A good circus is an oasis of Hellenism in a world that reads too much to be wise, and thinks too much to be beautiful. If it were not for the running-ground at Eton, the towing-path at Oxford, the Thames swimming baths, and the yearly circuses, humanity would forget the plastic perfection of its own form, and degenerate into a race of short-sighted professors, and spectacled *précieuses!* Not that the circus-proprietors are, as a rule, conscious of their high mission. Do they not bore us with the *haute école*, and weary us with Shakespearean clowns? Still at least they give us acrobats, and the acrobat is an artist. The mere fact that he never speaks to the audience, shows how well he appreciates the great truth that the aim of art is not to reveal personality but to please. The clown may be blatant, but the acrobat is always beautiful. He is an interesting combination of the spirit of Greek sculpture with the spangles of the modern *costumier*.[15] He has even had his niche in the novels of our age, and if *Manette Salomon*[16] be the unmasking of the model, *Les Frères Zemganno*[17] is the apotheosis of the acrobat.

LONDON MODELS

99

As regards the influence of the ordinary model on our English school of painting, it cannot be said that it is altogether good. It is of course an advantage for the young artist sitting in his studio to be able to isolate "a little corner of life," as the French say, from disturbing surroundings, and to study it under certain effects of light and shade. But this very isolation leads often to mere mannerism in the painter, and robs him of that broad acceptance of the general facts of life which is the very essence of art. Model-painting, in a word, while it may be the condition of art, is not by any means its aim. It is simply practice, not perfection. Its use trains the eye and the hand of the painter. Its abuse produces in his work an effect of mere posing and prettiness. It is the secret of much of the artificiality of modern art, this constant posing of pretty people, and when art becomes artificial it becomes monotonous.[18] Outside the little world of the studio, with its draperies and its bric-à-brac, lies the world of life with its infinite, its Shakespearian variety. We must, however, distinguish between the two kinds of models, those who sit for the figure and those who sit for costume. The study of the first is always excellent, but the costume model is becoming rather wearisome in modern pictures. It is really of very

100 DECORATIVE ART IN AMERICA

little use to dress up a London girl in Greek draperies and to paint her as a goddess. The robe may be the robe of Athens, but the face is usually the face of Brompton. Now and then, it is true, one comes across a model whose face is an exquisite anachronism, and who looks lovely and natural in the dress of any country but her own. This, however, is rather rare. As a rule models are absolutely *de notre siècle,* and should be painted as such. Unfortunately they are not, and as a consequence we are shown every year a series of scenes from fancy dress balls which are called historical pictures, but are little more than mediocre representations of modern people masquerading.[19] In France they are wiser. The French painter uses the model simply for study; for the finished picture he goes to real life.

However, we must not blame the sitters for the shortcomings of the artists. The English models are a well-behaved and hard-working class, and if they are more interested in artists than they are in art, a large section of the public is in the same condition, and most of our modern exhibitions seem to justify its choice.

"DORIAN GRAY" AND ITS CRITICS

It is absurd to have a hard-and-fast rule about what one should read and what one shouldn't. More than half of modern culture depends on what one shonldn't read.

—Phrases and Philosophies for the use of the Young;
also, The Importance of Being Earnest.

Morality is simply the attitude we adopt toward people whom we personally dislike.

— Phrases and Philosophies for the use of the Young;
also, An Ideal Husband.

There is no such thing as a moral or an immoral book. Books are well written or badly written. That is all.

— The Preface to "The Picture of Dorian Gray."

"It is in working within limits that the master reveals himself," and the limitation, the very condition of any art is style.

— The Decay of Lying.

Start with the worship of form, and there is no secret in art that will not be revealed to you. *— The Critic as Artist. Part II.*

Art only begins where Imitation ends. *—De Profundis.*

Common sense is the enemy of romance. Leave us some unreality. Don't make us offensively sane.

—Letter to The Thirteen Club. 1894.

"DORIAN GRAY" AND ITS CRITICS[1]

I

To the Editor of the St. James Gazette.

Sir:—I have read your criticism[2] of my story *The Picture of Dorian Gray*,[3] and I need hardly say that I do not propose to discuss its merits or demerits, its personalities or its lack of personality. England is a free country, and ordinary English criticism is perfectly free and easy. Besides, I must admit that, either from temperament, or from taste, or from both, I am quite incapable of understanding how any work of art can be criticized from a moral standpoint. The sphere of art and the sphere of ethics are absolutely distinct and separate; and it is to the comparison between the two that we owe the appearance of Mrs. Grundy, that amusing old lady who represents the only original form of humour that the middle classes of this country have been able to produce. What I do object to most strongly is, that you should have placarded the

104   DECORATIVE ART IN AMERICA

town with posters on which was printed in large letters: Mr. Oscar Wilde's Latest Advertisement; A Bad Case.

Whether the expression "A Bad Case" refers to my book or to the present position of the Government, I cannot tell. What was silly and unnecessary was the use of the term "Advertisement."

I think I may say without vanity—though I do not wish to appear to run vanity down—that of all men in England, I am the one who requires least advertisement. I am tired to death of being advertised. I feel no thrill when I see my name in a paper.[5] The chronicler does not interest me any more. I wrote this book entirely for my own pleasure[6] and it gave me very great pleasure to write it. Whether it becomes popular or not is a matter of absolute indifference to me. I am afraid, Sir, that the real advertisement is your cleverly written article. The English public, as a mass, takes no interest in a work of art until it is told that the work in question is immoral, and your *réclame* will, I have no doubt, largely increase the sale of the magazine; in which sale, I may mention with some regret, I have no pecuniary interest. I remain, Sir, your obedient servant,

OSCAR WILDE.

16 TITE STREET, CHELSEA, June 25.

"DORIAN GRAY" AND ITS CRITICS   105

II [7]

June 26, 1890.

To THE EDITOR OF THE ST. JAMES GAZETTE.

Sir:—In your issue of to-day you state that my brief letter published in your columns is the "best reply" I can make to your article upon *Dorian Gray.* This is not so. I do not propose to fully discuss the matter here, but I feel bound to say that your article contains the most unjustifiable attack that has been made upon any man of letters for many years. The writer of it, who is quite incapable of concealing his personal malice, and so in some measure destroys the effect he wishes to produce, seems not to have the slightest idea of the temper in which a work of art should be approached. To say that such a book as mine should be "chucked into the fire" is silly. That is what one does with newspapers.

Of the value of pseudo-ethical criticism in dealing with artistic work I have spoken already. But as your writer has ventured into the perilous grounds of literary criticism, I ask you to allow me, in fairness not only to myself but to all men to whom literature is a fine art, to say a few words about his critical method.

He begins by assailing me with much ridiculous

106   DECORATIVE ART IN AMERICA

virulence because the chief personages in my stories are "puppies." They *are* puppies. Does he think that literature went to the dogs when Thackeray wrote about puppydom? I think that puppies are extremely interesting from an artistic as well as from a psychological point of view. They seem to me to be certainly more interesting than prigs; and I am of opinion that Lord Henry Wotton is an excellent corrective of the tedious ideal shadowed forth in the semi-theological novels of our age.[8]

He then makes vague and fearful insinuations about my grammar and my erudition. Now, as regards grammar, I hold that, in prose at any rate, correctness should always be subordinated to artistic effect and musical cadence; and any peculiarities of syntax that may occur in *Dorian Gray* are deliberately intended,[9] and are introduced simply to show the value of the artistic theory in question. Your writer gives no instance of any such peculiarity. This I regret, because I do not think any such instances occur.

As regards erudition, it is always difficult, even for the most modest of us, to remember that other people do not know quite as much as one does oneself. I myself frankly admit I cannot imagine how a casual reference to Suetonius and Petronius Arbiter can be construed into evidence of a desire

"DORIAN GRAY" AND ITS CRITICS 107

to impress an unoffending and ill-educated public by an assumption of superior knowledge. I should fancy that the most ordinary of scholars is perfectly well acquainted with the *Lives of the Cæsars* and with the *Satyricon*.[10] The *Lives of the Cæsars*, at any rate, form part of the ordinary curriculum at Oxford for those who take the Honour School of *Literæ Humaniores;*[11] and as for the *Satyricon*, it is popular even among passmen, though I suppose they are obliged to read it in translations.

The writer of the article then suggests that I, in common with that great and noble artist Count Tolstoi, take pleasure in a subject because it is dangerous. About such a suggestion there is this to be said. Romantic art deals with the exception and with the individual. Good people, belonging as they do to the normal, and so commonplace, type, are artistically uninteresting. But bad people are, from the point of view of art, fascinating studies. They represent colour, variety and strangeness. Good people exasperate one's reason; bad people stir one's imagination. Your critic, if I must give him so honourable a title, states that the people in my story have no counterpart in life; that they are, to use his vigorous if somewhat vulgar phrase, "mere catchpenny revelations of the non-existent." Quite so. If they existed they would not be worth

108 DECORATIVE ART IN AMERICA

writing about.[12] The function of the artist is to invent, not to chronicle. There are no such people. If there were, I would not write about them. Life by its realism is always spoiling the subject-matter of art.[13] The supreme pleasure in literature is to realize the non-existent. And, finally, let me say this. You have reproduced, in a journalistic form, the comedy of *Much Ado About Nothing*, and have, of course, spoiled it in your reproduction. The poor public, hearing from an authority as high as your own, that this is a wicked book that should be coerced and suppressed by a Tory Government, will, no doubt, rush to it and read it. But, alas! they will find that it is a story with a moral. And the moral is this: all excess, as well as all renunciation brings its own punishment. The painter, Basil Hallward, worshipping physical beauty far too much, as most painters do, dies by the hand of one in whose soul he has created a monstrous and absurd vanity. Dorian Gray having led a life of mere sensation and pleasure, tries to kill Conscience, and at that moment kills himself. Lord Henry Wotton seeks to be merely the spectator of life. He finds that those who reject the battle are more deeply wounded than those who take part in it. Yes: There is a terrible moral in *Dorian Gray*—a moral which the

"DORIAN GRAY" AND ITS CRITICS 109

prurient will not be able to find in it, but which will be revealed to all whose minds are healthy. Is this an artistic error? I fear it is. It is the only error in the book.

I remain, Sir, your obedient servant,

OSCAR WILDE.

III [14]

TO THE EDITOR OF THE ST. JAMES GAZETTE.

Sir:—As you still keep up, though in a somewhat milder form than before, your attacks on me and my book, you not merely confer on me the right, but you impose upon me the duty to reply.

You state, in your issue of to-day that I misrepresent you when I said that you suggested that a book so wicked as mine should be "suppressed and coerced by a Tory Government." Now you did not propose this, but you did suggest it. When you declare that you do not know whether or not the Government will take action about my book, and remark that the authors of books much less wicked have been proceeded against in law, the suggestion is quite obvious. In your complaint of misrepresentation you seem to me, Sir, to have been not quite candid. However, as far as I am

DECORATIVE ART IN AMERICA

concerned the suggestion is of no importance. What is of importance is that the editor of a paper like yours should appear to countenance the monstrous theory that the Government of a country should exercise a censorship over imaginative literature. This is a theory against which I, and all men of letters of my acquaintance, protest most strongly; and any critic who admits the reasonableness of such a theory shows at once that he is quite incapable of understanding what literature is, and what are the rights that literature possesses. A Government might just as well try to teach painters how to paint, or sculptors how to model,[15] as attempt to interfere with the style, treatment, and subject-matter of the literary artist; and no writer, however eminent or obscure, should ever give his sanction to a theory that would degrade literature far more than any didactic or so-called immoral book could possibly do.

You then express your surprise that "so experienced a literary gentleman" as myself should imagine that your critic was animated by any feeling of personal malice towards him. The phrase "literary gentleman" is a vile phrase; but let that pass. I accept quite readily your assurance that your critic was simply criticizing a work of art in the best way he could; but I feel that I was fully justified in forming the opinion of him I did. He

"DORIAN GRAY" AND ITS CRITICS 111

opened his article by a gross personal attack on myself. This, I need hardly say, was an absolutely unpardonable error of critical taste. There is no excuse for it, except personal malice; and you, Sir, should not have sanctioned it. A critic should be taught to criticize a work of art without making any reference to the personality of the author. This, in fact, is the beginning of criticism. However, it was not merely his personal attack on me that made me imagine that he was actuated by malice. What really confirmed me in my first impression was his reiterated assertion that my book was tedious and dull. Now, if I were criticizing my book, which I have some thoughts of doing, I think I would consider it my duty to point out that it is far too crowded with sensational incident and far too paradoxical in style, as far, at any rate, as the dialogue goes. I feel that from a standpoint of art these are the two great defects in the book. But tedious and dull the book is not. Your critic has cleared himself of the charge of personal malice, his denial and yours being quite sufficient in the matter; but he has only done so by a tacit admission that he has really no critical instinct about literature and literary work, which, in one who writes about literature, is, I need hardly say, a much graver fault than malice of any kind.

Finally, Sir, allow me to say this. Such an

112   DECORATIVE ART IN AMERICA

article as you have published really makes one despair of the possibility of any general culture in England.   Were I a French author, and my book brought out in Paris, there is not a single literary critic in France, on any paper of high standing, who would think for a moment of criticizing it from an ethical standpoint.   If he did so he would stultify himself, not merely in the eyes of all men of letters, but in the eyes of the majority of the public.   You have yourself often spoken against Puritanism. Believe me, Sir, Puritanism is never so offensive and destructive as when it deals with art matters. It is there that its influence is radically wrong.   It is this Puritanism, to which your critic has given expression, that is always marring the artistic instinct of the English.   So far from encouraging it, you should set yourself against it, and should try to teach your critics to recognize the essential difference between art and life.   The gentleman who criticized my book is in a perfectly hopeless confusion about it, and your attempt to help him out by proposing that the subject-matter of art should be limited does not help matters.   It is proper that limitations should be placed on actions.   It is not proper that limitations should be placed on art.   To art belong all things that are, and all things that are not, and even the editor of a London paper has no right to

"DORIAN GRAY" AND ITS CRITICS   113

restrain the freedom of art in the selection of subject-matter.

I now trust, Sir, that these attacks on me and on my book will cease. There are forms of advertisement that are unwarranted and unwarrantable.—I am, Sir, your obedient servant,

OSCAR WILDE.

16 TITE ST., S. W., June 27.

IV [16]

TO THE EDITOR OF THE ST. JAMES GAZETTE.

Sir:—In your issue of this evening you publish a letter from "A London Editor," [17] which clearly insinuates in the last paragraph that I have in some way sanctioned the circulation of an expression of opinion, on the part of the proprietors of *Lippincott's Magazine*, of the literary and artistic value of my story of *The Picture of Dorian Gray.*

Allow me, Sir, to state that there are no grounds for this insinuation. I was not aware that any such document was being circulated; and I have written to the agents, Messrs. Ward & Lock—who cannot, I feel sure, be primarily responsible for its appearance—to ask them to withdraw it at once. No publisher should ever express an opinion on the value

114   DECORATIVE ART IN AMERICA

of what he publishes. That is a matter entirely for the literary critic to decide. I must admit, as one to whom contemporary literature is constantly submitted for criticism, that the only thing that ever prejudices me against a book is the lack of literary style; but I can quite understand how any ordinary critic would be strongly prejudiced against a work that was accompanied by a premature and unnecessary panegyric from the publisher. A publisher is simply a useful middleman. It is not for him to anticipate the verdict of criticism.

I may, however, while expressing my thanks to the "London Editor" for drawing my attention to this, I trust, purely American method of procedure, venture to differ from him in one of his criticisms. He states that he regards the expression "complete" as applied to a story, as a specimen of the "adjectival exuberance of the puffer!" Here, it seems to me, he sadly exaggerates. What my story is, is an interesting problem. What my story is not, is a "novelette"[18]— a term which you have more than once applied to it. There is no such word in the English language as novelette. It should never be used. It is merely part of the slang of Fleet street.

In another part of your paper, Sir, you state that I received your assurance of the lack of malice in

"DORIAN GRAY" AND ITS CRITICS 115

your critic " somewhat grudgingly." This is not so. I frankly said that I accepted that assurance "quite readily," and that your own denial and that of your critic were " sufficient." Nothing more generous could have been said. What I did feel was that you saved your critic from the charge of malice by convicting him of the unpardonable crime of lack of literary instinct. I still feel that. To call my book an ineffective attempt at allegory that, in the hands of Mr. Anstey, might have been made striking, is absurd. Mr. Anstey's sphere in literature, and my sphere are different—very widely different.

You then gravely ask me what rights I imagine literature possesses. That is really an extraordinary question for the editor of a newspaper such as yours to ask. The rights of literature, Sir, are the rights of intellect.

I remember once hearing M. Renan say that he would sooner live under a military despotism than under the despotism of the church, because the former merely limited the freedom of the body while the latter limited the freedom of mind.[19] You say that a work of art is a form of action. It is not. It is the highest mode of thought.

In conclusion, Sir, let me ask you not to force on me this continued correspondence by daily attacks. It is a trouble and a nuisance. As you assailed

116   DECORATIVE ART IN AMERICA

me first, I have a right to the last word. Let that last word be the present letter, and leave my book, I beg you, to the immortality it deserves. I am, Sir, your obedient servant,

OSCAR WILDE.

16 TITE ST., S. W., June 28.

RUDYARD KIPLING AND THE ANGLO-INDIANS

From the point of view of literature, Mr. Kipling is a genius who drops his aspirates. From the point of view of life, he is a reporter who knows vulgarity better than any one has ever known it. Dickens knew its clothes and its comedy. Mr. Kipling knows its essence and its seriousness. He is our first authority on the second-rate, and has seen marvellous things through key-holes, and his back-grounds are real works of art.

— The Critic as Artist. Part II.

No doubt, everything that is worthy of existence, is worthy also of art—at least, one would like to think so—but while echo or mirror can repeat for us a beautiful thing, to artistically render a thing that is ugly requires the most exquisite alchemy of form, the most subtle magic of transformation.

—A Note on Some Modern Poets.
The Woman's World, December, 1888.

MR. KIPLING AND THE ANGLO-INDIANS [1]

September 25, 1891.

To the Editor of the Times.

Sir :—The writer of a letter signed "An Indian Civilian"[2] that appears in your issue of to-day makes a statement about me which I beg you to allow me to correct at once.

He says that I have described the Anglo-Indians as being vulgar. This is not the case. Indeed, I have never met a vulgar Anglo-Indian. There may be many, but those whom I have had the pleasure of meeting here have been chiefly scholars, men interested in art and thought, men of cultivation; nearly all of them have been exceedingly brilliant talkers; some of them have been exceedingly brilliant writers.

What I did say—I believe in the pages of *The Nineteenth Century* —was that vulgarity is the distinguishing note of those Anglo-Indians whom

120   DECORATIVE ART IN AMERICA

Rudyard Kipling loves to write about, and writes about so cleverly. This is quite true and there is no reason why Mr. Rudyard Kipling should not select vulgarity as his subject-matter, or as part of it. For a realistic artist, certainly, vulgarity is a most admirable subject. How far Mr. Kipling's stories really mirror Anglo-Indian society I have no idea at all, nor indeed, am I ever much interested in any correspondence between art and nature. It seems to me a matter of entirely secondary importance. I do not wish, however, that it should be supposed that I was passing a harsh judgment on an important and in many ways distinguished class, when I was merely pointing out the characteristic qualities of some puppets in a prose play.

I remain, Sir, your obedient servant,

OSCAR WILDE

"A HOUSE OF POMEGRANATES"

All bad art comes from returning to Life and Nature, and elevating them into ideals. Life and Nature may sometimes be used as part of Art's rough material, but before they are of any real service to art, they must be translated into artistic conventions. The moment Art surrenders its imaginative medium, it surrenders everything. — *The Decay of Lying.*

The marvels of design stir the imagiration. In the mere loveliness of the materials employed there are latent elements of culture. Nor is this all. By its deliberate rejection of Nature as the ideal of beauty, as well as of the imitative method of the ordinary painter, decorative art not merely prepares the soul for the reception of true imaginative work, but develops in it that sense of form which is the basis of creative no less than of critical achievement.
— *The Critic as Artist. Part II.*

There is a danger of modern illustration becoming too pictorial. What we need is good book-ornament—decorative ornament that will go with type and printing, and give to each page a harmony and unity of effect. — *Some Literary Notes.*
The Woman's World, January, 1889.

It is one thing to talk of the principles of art and quite another to create a piece of artistic work. — *Interview with Oscar Wilde.*
New York World, August 12, 1883.

"A HOUSE OF POMEGRANATES"[1]

TO THE EDITOR OF THE SPEAKER.

Sir:—I have just, at a price that for any other English sixpenny paper I would have considered exorbitant, purchased a copy of *The Speaker* at one of the charming kiosks that decorate Paris; institutions, by the way, that I think we should at once introduce into London. The kiosk is a delightful object, and when illuminated at night from within, as lovely as a fantastic Chinese lantern, especially when the transparent advertisements are from the clever pencil of M. Chéret. In London we have merely the ill-clad news-vendors, whose voice, in spite of the admirable efforts of the Royal College of Music to make England a really musical nation, is always out of tune, and whose rags, badly designed and badly worn, merely emphasize a painful note of uncomely misery, without conveying that impression of picturesqueness which is the only thing that makes the spectacle of the poverty of others at all bearable.

124 DECORATIVE ART IN AMERICA

It is not, however, about the establishment of kiosks in London that I wish to write you, though I am of the opinion that it is a thing that the County Council should at once take in hand. The object of my letter is to correct a statement made in a paragraph[2] of your interesting paper.

The writer of the paragraph in question, states that the decorative designs that make lovely my book *A House of Pomegranates*[3] are by the hand of Mr. Shannon,[4] while the delicate dreams that separate and herald each story are by Mr. Ricketts.[5] The contrary is the case. Mr. Shannon is the drawer of the dreams, and Mr. Ricketts is the subtle and fantastic decorator. Indeed, it is to Mr. Ricketts that the entire decorative scheme of the book is due, from the selection of the type and the placing of the ornamentation, to the completely beautiful cover that encloses the whole. The writer of the paragraph goes on to state that he does not "like the cover." This is, no doubt, to be regretted, though it is not a matter of much importance, as there are only two people in the world whom it is absolutely necessary that the cover should please. One is Mr. Ricketts who designed it; the other is myself whose book it binds. We both admire it immensely! The reason, however, that your critic gives for his failure to gain from the cover any im-

"A HOUSE OF POMEGRANATES" 125

pression of beauty, seems to me to show a lack of artistic instinct on his part, which I beg you will allow me to try to correct.

He complains that a portion of the design on the left-hand side of the cover reminds him of an Indian club with a house-painter's brush on top of it, while a portion of the design on the right-hand side suggests to him the idea of "a chimney-pot hat with a sponge in it." Now I do not for a moment dispute that these are the real impressions your critic received. It is the spectator, and the mind of the spectator, as I pointed out in the preface to *The Picture of Dorian Gray*, that art really mirrors. What I want to indicate is this; the artistic beauty of the cover of my book resides in the delicate tracing, arabesques, and massing of many coral-red lines on a ground of white ivory, the colour-effect culminating in certain high gilt notes, and being made still more pleasurable by the over-lapping band of moss-green cloth that holds the book together. What the gilt notes suggest, what imitative parallel may be found to them in that chaos that is termed Nature, is a matter of no importance.[6] They may suggest, as they do sometimes to me, peacocks and pomegranates and splashing fountains of gold water, or, as they do to your critic,[7] sponges and Indian clubs and chimney-pot hats. Such sug-

126   DECORATIVE ART IN AMERICA

gestions and evocations have nothing whatsoever to
do with the æsthetic quality and value of design.
A thing in Nature becomes much lovelier if it reminds
us of a thing of Art, but a thing of Art gains no
real beauty through reminding us of a thing in
Nature. The primary æsthetic impression of a work
of art borrows nothing from recognition or resemblance. These belong to a later and less perfect
stage of apprehension. Properly speaking, they are
not part of a real æsthetic impression at all, and the
constant preoccupation with subject-matter that
characterizes nearly all our English art criticism is,
what makes our art criticism, especially as regards
literature, so sterile, so profitless, so much beside
the mark, and of such curiously little account.
I remain, Sir, your obedient servant,

OSCAR WILDE.

BOULEVARD DES CAPUCINES, PARIS.

THE RELATION OF THE ACTOR
TO THE PLAY

From the point of view of form, the type of all the arts is the art of the musician. From the point of view of feeling, the actor's craft is the type. — *The Preface to "The Picture of Dorian Gray."*

The objective form is the most subjective in matter. Man is least himself when he talks in his own person. Give him a mask, and he will tell you the truth. — *The Critic as Artist. Part II.*

As the inevitable result of this substitution of an imitative for a creative medium, this surrender of an imaginative form, we have the modern English melodrama. The characters in these plays talk on the stage exactly as they would off it; . . . they present the gait, manner, costume, and accent of real people. . . . And yet how wearisome the plays are! They do not succeed in producing even that impression of reality at which they aim, and which is their only reason for existing. — *The Decay of Lying.*

THE RELATION OF THE ACTOR TO THE PLAY[1]

To the Editor of the Daily Telegraph.

Sir:—I have just been sent an article that seems to have appeared in your paper some days ago, in which it is stated that, in the course of some remarks addressed to the Playgoers' Club on the occasion of my taking the chair at their last meeting, I laid down as an axiom that the stage is only "a frame furnished with a set of puppets."

Now it is quite true that I hold that the stage is to a play no more than a picture frame is to a painting; and that the actable value of a play has nothing whatsoever to do with its value as a work of art. In this century in England, to take an obvious example, we have had only two great plays—one is Shelley's *Cenci*, the other, Mr. Swinburne's *Atalanta in Calydon*, and neither of them is in any sense of the word an actable play.

130   DECORATIVE ART IN AMERICA

Indeed, the mere suggestion that stage presentation is any test of a work of art is quite ridiculous. In the production of Browning's plays, for instance, in London and at Oxford, what was being tested was obviously the capacity of the modern stage to represent, in any adequate measure or degree, works of introspective method and strange or sterile psychology. But the artistic value of *Strafford* or *In a Balcony*, was settled when Robert Browning wrote their last lines. It is not, Sir, by the mimes that the Muses are to be judged.[2] So far, the writer of the article in question is right. Where he goes wrong is in saying that I described this frame—the stage—as being furnished "with a set of puppets." He admits that he speaks only by report; but he should have remembered, Sir, that report is not merely a lying jade, which I personally could readily forgive her, but a jade who lies without lovely inventions—a thing that I, at any rate can forgive her never.

What I really said was that the frame we call the stage was "peopled with either living actors or moving puppets," and I pointed out briefly, of necessity, that the personality of the actor is often a source of danger in the perfect presentation of a work of art. It may distort. It may lead astray. It may be a discord in the tone of symphony. For

RELATION OF THE ACTOR TO THE PLAY   131

anybody can act. Most people in England do nothing else. To be conventional is to be. a comedian. To act a particular part, however, is a very different thing and a very difficult thing as well. The actor's aim is, or should be, to convert his own accidental personality into the real and essential personality of the character he is called upon to impersonate, whatever that character may be;[3] or perhaps I should say that there are two schools of actors—the school of those who attain their effect by exaggeration of personality and the school of those who attain it by suppression. It would take too long to discuss these schools, or to decide which of them the dramatist loves best. Let me note the danger of personality, and pass on to my puppets. There are many advantages in puppets.[4] They never argue. They have no crude views about art. They have no private lives. We are never bothered by accounts of their virtues, or bored by recitals of their vices; and when they are out of an engagement they never do good in public or save people from drowning ! Nor do they speak more than is set down for them ! They recognize the presiding intellect of the dramatist and have never been known to ask for their parts to be written up. They are admirably docile, and have no personalities at all. I saw lately, in Paris, a per-

132   DECORATIVE ART IN AMERICA

formance by certain puppets of Shakespeare's *Tempest* in M. Maurice Boucher's translation. Miranda was the image of Miranda because an artist had so fashioned her; and Ariel was true Ariel, because so had she been made. Their gestures were quite sufficient, and the words that seemed to come from their little lips were spoken by poets who had beautiful voices. It was a delightful performance, and I remember it still with delight, though Miranda took no notice of the flowers I sent her after the curtain fell. For modern plays, however, perhaps we had better have living players, for in modern plays actuality is everything. The charm—the ineffable charm of the unreal is here denied us, and rightly.

Suffer me one more correction. Your writer describes the author of the brilliant fantastic lecture on *The Modern Actor* as "a protegé" of mine. Allow me to state that my acquaintance with Mr. John Gray [5] is, I regret to say, extremely recent, and that I sought it because he had already a perfected mode of expression both in prose and verse. All artists in this vulgar age need protection certainly. Perhaps they have always needed it. But the nineteenth century artist finds it not in Prince, or Pope, or patron, but in high indifference of temper; in the pleasure of the creation of beau-

RELATION OF THE ACTOR TO THE PLAY   133

tiful things and the long contemplation of them: in disdain of what in life is common and ignoble; and in such felicitous sense of humour as enables one to see how vain and foolish is all popular opinion, and popular judgment, upon the wonderful things of art. These qualities Mr. John Gray possesses in a marked degree. He needs no other protection, nor indeed would he accept it.

I remain, Sir, your obedient servant,

OSCAR WILDE.

LONDON, Feb. 19th.

THE CENSURE AND "SALOMÉ"

The mere artistic process of acting, the translation of literature back again into life, and the presentation of thought under the conditions of action, is in itself a critical method of a very high order. — *Literary and Other Notes.*

The Woman's World, January, 1888.

An educated person's ideas of art are drawn naturally from what art has been, whereas the new work of art is beautiful by being what art has never been; and to measure it by the standard of the past is to measure it by a standard on the rejection of which its real perfection depends. A temperament capable of receiving, through an imaginative medium, and under imaginative conditions, new and beautiful impressions, is the only temperament that can appreciate a work of art.

No spectator of art needs a more perfect mood of receptivity than the spectator of a play. — *The Soul of Man Under Socialism.*

To disagree with three-fourths of England on all points is one of the first elements of sanity, which is a deep source of consolation in all moments of spiritual doubt.

— *Lecture on the English Renaissance.*

England is the home of lost ideas. — *The Decay of Lying.*

THE CENSURE AND "SALOMÉ"[1]

AN INTERVIEW WITH OSCAR WILDE

THE Lord Chamberlain has declined to authorize the representation of Mr. Oscar Wilde's French play Salomé,[2] *so the* première *will probably be given in Paris instead of London. I should show (writes the interviewer) but small appreciation of Mr. Wilde's courtesy were I to describe the piece, or do more than refer incidentally to a conversation that would have appeared in this column on the eve of the first performance had* Salomé *been licensed for representation. I may, however, be permitted to say that judging from what I saw at rehearsal, art has suffered by the Lord Chamberlain's action; for with such interpreters as Madame Sarah Bernhardt and M. Albert Darmont there was no danger that the author's dignified treatment of the Biblical story would be degraded. I have had the advantage of reading a great many forbidden plays, for in Paris*

138 DECORATIVE ART IN AMERICA

the Censure is applied more frequently than in London, and I have no hesitation in saying that in nine cases out of ten the prohibitive measure is a mistaken policy. It is not pretended that there is any religious or moral gain to compensate for the wrong done to art. Diametrically opposed standards seem to be set up by the Censure in passing judgment on religious or social dramas. If Justice does not suffer every time some monstrous injustice is handled by the playwright, why should Religion suffer when the acts of its oppressors are made the subject of artistic treatment by the dramatic author? The public can be trusted to save Religion from insult.

This is of course the expression of my own opinion. It was with these thoughts running in my mind that I called on Mr. Oscar Wilde yesterday to beg him to modify an earlier interview he had given me in such particulars as might be important in view of the Lord Chamberlain's decision.

"Personally," *said Mr. Wilde,* "to have my *première* in Paris instead of in London is a great honour, and one that I appreciate sincerely. The pleasure and pride that I have experienced in the whole affair has been that Madame Sarah Bernhardt who is undoubtedly the greatest artist on any stage, should have been charmed and fascinated by my play and should have wished to act it."

THE CENSURE AND "SALOMÉ" 139

I could not help feeling that Mr. Wilde's pride was justified. It is the fashion of to-day to write single-rôle pieces for Madame Bernhardt. The talents of several authors have been almost exclusively devoted to the task of fitting the talents of the artist. Salomé *is not a one-rôle drama; it was not written for Madame Bernhardt; indeed, it had been in manuscript nearly six months before it was submitted to her.*

"Every rehearsal," *continued Mr. Wilde,* "has been a source of intense pleasure to me. To hear my own words spoken by the most beautiful voice in the world has been the greatest artistic joy that it is possible to experience.[3] So that you see, as far as I am concerned, I care very little about the refusal of the Lord Chamberlain's to allow my play to be produced. What I do care about is this—that the Censorship apparently regards the stage as the lowest of all the arts, and looks on acting as a vulgar thing. The painter is allowed to take his subjects where he chooses. He can go to the great Hebrew, and Hebrew-Greek literature of the Bible and can paint Salomé dancing, or Christ on the cross, or the Virgin with her child. Nobody interferes with the painter. Nobody says, ' Painting is such a vulgar art that you must not paint sacred things.' The sculptor is equally free. He can

140 DECORATIVE ART IN AMERICA

carve St. John the Baptist in his camel hair, and fashion the Madonna or Christ in bronze or in marble as he wills. Yet nobody says to him, 'Sculpture is such a vulgar art that you must not carve sacred things.' And the writer, the poet— he also is quite free. I can write about any subject I choose. For me there is no Censorship. I can take any incident I like out of sacred literature and treat it as I choose and there is no one to say to the poet, 'Poetry is such a vulgar art that you must not use it in treating sacred subjects.' But there is a Censorship over the stage and acting, and the basis of that Censorship is that, while vulgar subjects may be put on the stage and acted, while everything that is mean and low and shameful in life can be portrayed by actors, no actor is to be permitted to present under artistic conditions, the great and ennobling subjects taken from the Bible. The insult in the suppression of *Salomé*, is an insult to the stage as a form of art and not to me."

"*I understand that Madame Bernhardt's engagements will not allow her to play* Salomé *at an invitation performance. We shall not see your play in London, then?*"

" I shall publish *Salomé*. No one has the right to interfere with me, and no one shall interfere with me. The people who are injured are the actors; the

THE CENSURE AND "SALOMÉ"   141

art that is vilified is the art of acting. I hold that this is as fine as any other art and to refuse it the right to treat great and noble subjects is an insult to the stage. The action of the Censorship in England is odious and ridiculous. What can be said of a body that forbids Massenet's *Hérodiade*,[4] Gounod's *La Reine de Saba*,[5] Rubinstein's *Judas Maccabæus*,[6] and allows *Divorçons*[7] to be placed on any stage? The artistic treatment of moral and elevating subjects is discouraged, while a free course is given to the representation of disgusting and revolting subjects."

"*How came you to write* Salomé *in French?*"

"My idea of writing the play was simply this: I have one instrument that I know that I can command, and that is the English language. There was another instrument to which I had listened all my life, and I wanted once to touch this new instrument to see whether I could make any beautiful thing out of it. The play was written in Paris some six months ago, where I read it to some young poets, who admired it immensely. Of course there are modes of expression that a Frenchman of letters would not have used, but they give a certain relief or colour to the play.[8] A great deal of the curious effect that Maeterlinck produces comes from the fact that he, a Flamand by grace, writes in an

142   DECORATIVE ART IN AMERICA

alien language. The same thing is true of Rossetti, who, though he wrote in English, was essentially Latin in temperament."

During this part of our interview the correspondent of The Gaulois *was present. The conversation was consequently carried on in French, and my colleague remarked on the admirable way that Mr. Wilde spoke that language. This elicited from him a splendid tribute to Paris, "the center of art, the artistic capital of the world."*

" If the Censure refuses *Salomé,*" *said Mr. Wilde, for at the time of my first interview the decision of the Lord Chamberlain had not been announced,* " I shall leave England and settle in France, where I will take out letters of naturalization.[9] I will not consent to call myself a citizen of a country that shows such narrowness in its artistic judgment."

My colleague of The Gaulois *made a movement of surprise.*

" I am not English; I 'm Irish—which is quite another thing."

To continue with Salomé —"A few weeks ago," *said Mr. Wilde,* " I met Madame Sarah Bernhardt at Sir Henry Irving's. She had heard of my play and asked me to read it to her.[10] I did so, and she at once expressed a wish to play the title-rôle. Of course it has been a great disappointment to

THE CENSURE AND "SALOMÉ" 143

her and to her company not to have played this piece in London. We have been rehearsing for three weeks. The costumes, scenery, and everything has been prepared, and we are naturally disappointed; still all are looking forward now to producing it for the first time in Paris, where the actor is appreciated and the stage is regarded as an artistic medium. It is remarkable how little art there is in the work of dramatic critics in England. You find column after column of description, but the critics rarely know how to praise an artistic work. The fact is, it requires an artist to praise art; any one can pick it to pieces. For my own part, I don't know which I despise most, blame or praise. The latter, I think, for it generally happens that the qualities praised are those one regards with the least satisfaction oneself."

Just as I was taking leave of Mr. Oscar Wilde, the conversation went back to the question of prohibition.

"What makes the Lord Chamberlain's action to me most contemptible, and the only point in which I feel at all aggrieved in the matter, is that he allows the personality of an artist to be presented in a caricature on the stage,[11] and will not allow the work of that artist to be shown under very rare and very beautiful conditions." [12]

PARIS, THE ABODE OF ARTISTS

In France they limit the journalist, and allow the artist almost perfect freedom. Here we allow absolute freedom to the journalist, and entirely limit the artist. English public opinion, that is to say, tries to constrain and impede and warp the man who makes things that are beautiful in effect, and compels the journalist to retail things that are ugly or disgusting or revolting in fact.
— *The Soul of Man Under Socialism.*

Whenever a man does a thoroughly stupid thing, it is always from the noblest motive. — *The Picture of Dorian Gray.*

England has done one thing; it has invented and established Public Opinion, which is an attempt to organize the ignorance of the community and to elevate it to the dignity of physical force.
— *The Critic as Artist. Part II.*

The only thing that ever consoles man for the stupid things he does is the praise he always gives himself for doing them.
—*A Chinese Sage.*

PARIS, THE ABODE OF ARTISTS[1]

June, 1892.

To Monsieur X . . . . . of the Gaulois.

Sir:—My resolution is deliberately taken. Since it is impossible to have a work of art performed in England, I shall transfer myself to another father-land, of which I have long ago been enamoured. There is but one Paris, *voyez-vous*, and Paris is France.

It is the abode of artists; nay, it is *la ville artiste.* I adore Paris.[2] I also adore your language. To me there are only two languages in the world, French and Greek. Here [in London] people are essentially anti-artistic and narrow-minded. Now the ostracism of *Salomé* will give you a fair notion of what people here consider venal and indecorous.

To put on the stage any person or persons connected with the Bible is impossible. On these grounds the Censorship has prohibited Saint-Saëns' *Samson et Dalila*[3] and Massenet's *Hérodiade.*[4] Ra-

147

148   DECORATIVE ART IN AMERICA

cine's superb tragedy of *Athalie*[5] cannot be performed on an English stage. Really, one hardly knows whether the measure is the more hateful or ridiculous.

Of course, I do not deny that Englishmen possess certain practical qualities, but, as I am an artist, these qualities are not those which I can admire. Moreover, I am not at present an Englishman. I am an Irishman,[6] which is by no means the same thing.

No doubt, I have English friends, to whom I am deeply attached, but as to the English, I do not love them. There is a great deal of hypocrisy in England, which you in France, very justly find fault with.

The typical Briton is Tartuffe, seated in his shop behind the counter. There are numerous exceptions, but they only prove the rule.

OSCAR WILDE.

SARAH BERNHARDT AND "SALOMÉ"

TO SARAH BERNHARDT [1]

How vain and dull this common world must seem
  To such a One as thou, who should'st have talked
  At Florence with Mirandola, or walked
Through the cool olives of the Academe:
Thou should'st have gathered reeds from a green stream
  For Goat-foot Pan's shrill piping, and have played
  With the white girls in that Phæacian glade
Where grave Odysseus wakened from his dream.

Ah! surely once some urn of Attic clay
  Held thy wan dust, and thou hast come again
  Back to this common world so dull and vain,
For thou wert weary of the sunless day,
  The heavy fields of scentless asphodel,
The loveless lips with which men kiss in Hell.

SARAH BERNHARDT AND "SALOMÉ"[2]

March, 1893.

To the Editor of the Times.

Sir:—My attention has been drawn to a review[3] of *Salomé*[4] which was published in your columns last week. The opinions of English critics on a French work of mine have, of course, little, if any interest for me. I write simply to ask you to allow me to correct a misstatement that appears in the review in question.

The fact that the greatest tragic actress of any stage now living saw in my play such beauty that she was anxious to produce it, to take herself the part of the heroine, to lend to the entire poem the glamour of her personality, and to my prose the music of her flute-like voice—this was naturally and always will be a source of pride and pleasure to me, and I look forward with delight to seeing Mme Bernhardt present my play in Paris, that

152 DECORATIVE ART IN AMERICA

vivid centre of art, where religious dramas are often performed. But my play was in no sense of the word written *for* this great actress.[5] I have never written a play for any actor or actress, nor shall I ever do so. Such work is for the artisan in literature, not for the artist.

I remain, Sir,

Your obedient servant,

OSCAR WILDE.

THE ETHICS OF JOURNALISM

Gilbert. —As for modern journalism, it is not my business to defend it. It justifies its own existence by the great Darwinian principle of the survival of the vulgarest. I have merely to do with literature.

Ernest. —But what is the difference between literature and journalism?

Gilbert. —Oh! journalism is unreadable and literature is not read.

— *The Critic as Artist. Part I.*

The public have an insatiable curiosity to know everything except what is worth knowing. Journalism, conscious of this, and having tradesman-like habits, supplies their demands. In centuries before ours the public nailed the ears of journalists to the pump. That was quite hideous. In this century journalists have nailed their own ears to the keyhole. That is much worse.

— *The Soul of Man Under Socialism.*

All bad poetry springs from genuine feeling. To be natural is to be obvious, and to be obvious is to be inartistic.

— *The Critic as Artist. Part II.*

THE SHAMROCK

The spreading rose is fair to view,
And rich the modest violet's hue,
Or queenly tulip filled with dew,
And sweet the lily's fragrance;
But there's a flower more dear to me,
That grows not on a branch or tree,
But in the grass plays merrily
And of its leaves there are but three,
T 'is Ireland's native Shamrock.

My country's flower, I love it well,
For every leaf a tale can tell,
And teach the minstrel's heart to swell
In praise of Ireland's Shamrock:
The emblem of our faith divine,
Which blest St. Patrick made to shine,
To teach eternal truth sublime,
And which shall last as long as time,
And long as blooms the Shamrock.

Oh! twine a wreath of Shamrock leaves!
They decked the banner of our Chiefs
And calmed the Irish Exile's griefs.
Our country's cherished Shamrock;
The Muse inspired with words of praise
The poets of our early days,
To write in many a glowing phrase,
And sing in *powerful*, thrilling lays
The *virtues* of the Shamrock.

He who has left his island home
Beneath a foreign sky to roam,
And in a foreign clime unknown,
How dear he loves the Shamrock.
When on the feast of Patrick's Day
He kneels within the church to pray
For holy Ireland far away,
He feels again youth's genial ray,
While gazing on the Shamrock.

The brightest gem of the rarest flowers,
That ever bloomed in Eastern bowers
Possesses for him not half the powers
That dwell within the Shamrock;
Sweet memories, like refreshing dew,
The past with all its charm renew;
The church, the spot where wild flowers grew,
The faithful friends, the cherished few
He left to cull the Shamrock.

Land of the West, my native isle,
May heaven's love upon yon smile,
And banish foes that may beguile
The lovers of the Shamrock;
May God for ever cherish thee
In peace and love and harmony,
And rank thee proud mid nations free,
Thus pray thy children fervently
For Ireland and the Shamrock.

(Signed) OSCAR WILDE.

THE ETHICS OF JOURNALISM[1]

I

TO THE EDITOR OF THE PALL MALL GAZETTE.

*Sir :—*Will you allow me to draw your attention to a very interesting example of the ethics of modern journalism, a quality of which we have all heard so much and seen so little?

About a month ago Mr. T. P. O'Connor published in *The Sunday Sun* some doggerel verses entitled *The Shamrock*,[2] and had the amusing impertinence to append my name to them as their author. As for some years past all kinds of scurrilous personal attacks had been made on me in Mr. O'Connor's newspapers, I determined to take no notice at all of the incident.

Enraged, however, by my courteous silence, Mr. O'Connor returns to the charge this week. He now solemnly accuses me of plagiarizing[3] the poem he had the vulgarity to attribute to me.

158 DECORATIVE ART IN AMERICA

This seems to me to pass beyond even those bounds of coarse humour and coarser malice that are, by the contempt of all, conceded to the ordinary journalist, and it is really distressing to find so low a standard of ethics in a Sunday newspaper.

I remain, Sir,
Your obedient servant,
OSCAR WILDE.

II[4]

TO THE EDITOR OF THE PALL MALL GAZETTE.

Sir :—The assistant editor of *The Weekly Sun,* on whom seems to devolve the arduous duty of writing Mr. T. P. O'Connor's apologies for him,[5] does not, I observe with regret, place that gentleman's conduct in any more attractive or more honourable light by the attempted explanation that appears in the letter published in your issue of to-day. For the future it would be much better if Mr. O'Connor could always write his own apologies. That he can do so exceedingly well, no one is more ready to admit than myself. I happen to possess one from him.

The assistant editor's explanation, stripped of its unnecessary verbiage, amounts to this: it is now stated that some months ago, somebody, whose

THE ETHICS OF JOURNALISM 159

name, observe, is not given, forwarded to the office of *The Weekly Sun* a manuscript in his own handwriting, containing some fifth-rate verses with my name appended to them as their author. The assistant editor frankly admits that they had grave doubts about my being capable of such an astounding production. To me, I must candidly say, it seems more probable that they never for a single moment believed that the verses were from my pen. Literary instinct is, of course, a rare thing, and it would be too much to expect any true literary instinct to be found among the members of the staff of an ordinary newspaper; but had Mr. O'Connor really thought that the production, such as it is, was mine, he would naturally have asked my permission before publishing it. Great license of comment and attack of every kind is allowed nowadays to newspapers, but no respectable editor would dream of printing and publishing a man's work without first obtaining his consent.

Mr. O'Connor's conduct in accusing me of plagiarism when it was proved to him on unimpeachable authority that the verses he had vulgarly attributed to me were not by me at all, I have already commented on. It is perhaps left to the laughter of the gods and the sorrow of men. I would like, however, to point out that when Mr.

160   DECORATIVE ART IN AMERICA

O'Connor, with the kind help of his assistant editor, states, as a possible excuse for his original sin that he and the members of his staff "took refuge " in the belief that the verses in question might conceivably be some very early and youthful work of mine, he and the members of his staff showed a lamentable ignorance of the nature of the artistic temperament. Only mediocrities progress. An artist revolves in a cycle of masterpieces, the first of which is no less perfect than the last.[6]

In conclusion, allow me to thank you for your courtesy in opening to me the columns of your valuable paper, and also to express the hope that the painful exposé of Mr. O'Connor's conduct that I have been forced to make, will have the good result of improving the standard of journalistic ethics in England.   I am, Sir,

Your obedient servant,

OSCAR WILDE.

Sept. 22, 1894.

DRAMATIC CRITICS AND "AN IDEAL HUSBAND"

The work of art is to dominate the spectator; the spectator is not to dominate the work of art.
— *The Soul of Man Under Socialism.*

The tears that we shed at a play are a type of the exquisite sterile emotions that it is the function of Art to awaken. We weep, but we are not wounded. We grieve, but our grief is not bitter.
— *The Critic as Artist. Part II.*

The spectator is not the arbiter of the work of art. He is one who is admitted to contemplate the work of art, and, if the work be fine, to forget in its contemplation all the egotism that mars him —the egotism of his ignorance, or the egotism of his information.
— *The Soul of Man Under Socialism.*

The critic is he who can translate into another manner or a new material his impression of beautiful things.
— *The Preface to " The Picture of Dorian Gray."*

DRAMATIC CRITICS AND
"AN IDEAL HUSBAND"[1]

AN INTERVIEW WITH OSCAR WILDE

ON the morning following the production of An Ideal Husband,[2] *I met Oscar Wilde as he came down the steps of a club at the top of St. James' Street and I took advantage of the occasion to ask him what he thought of the attitude of the critics towards his play.*

"Well," *he replied, as he walked slowly down the street,* "for a man to be a dramatic critic is as foolish and as inartistic as it would be for a man to be a critic of epics or a pastoral critic, or a critic of lyrics. All modes of art are one, and the modes of the art that employs words as its medium are quite indivisible. The result of the vulgar specialization of criticism is an elaborate scientific knowledge of the stage—almost as elaborate as that of the stage-carpenter and quite on a par with that of

163

164 DECORATIVE ART IN AMERICA

the call-boy—combined with an entire incapacity to realize that a play is a work of art, or to receive any artistic impressions at all."

"*You are rather severe upon dramatic criticism, Mr. Wilde.*"

"English dramatic criticism of our own day has never had a single success, in spite of the fact that it goes to all the first nights."

"*But,*" *I suggested* "*it is influential.*"

"Certainly, that is why it is so bad."

"*I don't think I quite*"——

"The moment criticism exercises any influence, it ceases to be criticism. The aim of the true critic is to try and chronicle his own moods, not to try and correct the masterpieces of others."

"*Real critics would be charming in your eyes, then?*"

"Real critics? Ah! how perfectly charming they would be. I am always waiting for their arrival. An inaudible school would be nice. Why do you not found it?"

I was momentarily dazed at the broad vista that had been opened for me, but I retained my presence of mind, and asked:

"*Are there absolutely no real critics in London?*"

"There are just two."

"*Who are they?*" *I asked eagerly.*

CRITICS AND "AN IDEAL HUSBAND" 165

Mr. Wilde, with the elaborate courtesy for which he has always been famous, replied, "I think I had better not mention their names; it might make the others so jealous."

"*What do the literary cliques think of your plays?*"

"I don't write to please cliques; I write to please myself. Besides I have always had grave suspicions that the basis of all literary cliques is a morbid love of meat-teas. That makes them sadly uncivilized."

"*Still, if your critics offend you, why don't you reply to them?*"

"I have far too much time. But I think some day I will give a general answer in the form of a lecture in a public hall which I shall call *Straight Talks to Old Men.*"

"*What is your feeling towards your audiences— towards the public?*"

"Which public? There are as many publics as there are personalities."

"*Are you nervous on the night that you are producing a new play?*"

"Oh, no; I am exquisitely indifferent. My nervousness ends at the last dress rehearsal; I know then what effect my play, as presented upon the stage, has produced upon me. My interest in the play ends there, and I feel curiously envious of the

166 DECORATIVE ART IN AMERICA

public—they have such wonderfully fresh emotions in store for them."

I laughed, but Mr. Wilde rebuked me with a look of surprise.

"It is the public, not the play, that I desire to make a success."

"But, I' m afraid I don't quite understand"—

"The public makes a success when it realizes that a play is a work of art. On the three first nights [3] I have had in London, the public has been most successful, and, had the dimensions of the stage admitted of it, I would have called them before the curtain. Most managers, I believe, call them behind."

"I imagine then, that you don't hold with the opinion that the public is the patron of the dramatist?"

"The artist is always the munificent patron of the public. I am very fond of the public, and, personally, I always patronize the public very much."

"What are your views upon the much-vexed question of subject-matter in art?"

"Everything matters in art except the subject."

When I recovered, I said, "Several plays have been written lately that deal with the monstrous injustice of the social code of morality at the present time."

CRITICS AND "AN IDEAL HUSBAND" 167

" Oh," *answered Mr. Wilde, with an air of earnest conviction,* " it is indeed a burning shame that there should be one law for men and another law for women. I think "—*he hesitated, and a smile as swift as Sterne's " hectic of a moment " flitted across his face*—" I think that there should be no law for anybody."

" *In writing, do you think that real life or real people should ever give one inspiration ?* "

" The colour of a flower may suggest to one the plot of a tragedy; a passage in music may give one the sestet of a sonnet; but whatever actually occurs gives the artist no suggestion.

"Every romance that one has in one's life is a romance lost to one's art. To introduce real people into a novel or a play is a sign of an unimaginative mind,[4] a coarse, untutored observation and an entire absence of style."

" *I am afraid I can't agree with you, Mr. Wilde; I frequently see types and people who suggest ideas to me.*"

"Everything is of use to the artist except an idea."

After that I was silent, until Mr. Wilde pointed to the bottom of the street and drew my attention to the " apricot-coloured palace" which we were approaching. So I continued my questioning.

168   DECORATIVE ART IN AMERICA

"The enemy has said that your plays lack action."

"Yes, English critics always confuse the action of a play with the incidents of a melodrama. I wrote the first act of *A Woman of No Importance*,[5] in answer to the critics who said that *Lady Windermere's Fan*[6] lacked action. In the act in question, there was absolutely no action at all. It was a perfect act."

"What do you think is the chief point that critics have missed in your new play?"[7]

"Its entire psychology—the difference in the way in which a man loves a woman from that in which a woman loves a man; the passion that women have for making ideals (which is their weakness) and the weakness of a man who dares not show his imperfections to the thing he loves. The end of Act I, and the end of Act II, and the scene in the last act, when Lord Goring points out the higher importance of a man's life over a woman's—to take three prominent instances—seem to have been missed by most of the critics. They failed to see their meaning; they really thought it was a play about a bracelet. We must educate our critics—we must really educate them," *said Mr. Wilde half to himself.*

"The critics subordinate the psychological in-

CRITICS AND "AN IDEAL HUSBAND" 169

terest of a play to its mere technique. As soon as a dramatist invents an ingenious situation, they compare him with Sardou,[8] but Sardou is an artist not because of his marvellous instinct of stagecraft, but in spite of it. In the third act of *La Tosca*, the scene of torture, he moved us by a terrible human tragedy, not by his knowledge of stage methods. Sardou is not understood in England because he is only known through a rather ordinary travesty of his play *Dora*, which was brought out here under the title of *Diplomacy*. I have been considerably amused by so many of the critics suggesting that the incident of the diamond bracelet in Act III of my new play was suggested by Sardou. It does not occur in any of Sardou's plays, and it was not in my play until less than ten days before production. Nobody else's work gives me any suggestion. It is only by entire isolation from everything that one can do any work. Idleness gives one the mood in which to write, isolation the conditions. Concentration on one's self recalls the new and wonderful world that one presents in the colour and cadence of words in movement."

"*And yet we want something more than literature in a play*," said I.

" That is merely because the critics have always propounded the degrading dogma that the duty of

170   DECORATIVE ART IN AMERICA

the dramatist is to please the public. Rossetti did not weave words into sonnets to please the public, and Corot did not paint silver and grey twilights to please the public. The mere fact of telling an artist to adopt any particular form of art in order to please the public, makes him shun it. We shall never have a real drama in England until it is recognized that a play is as personal and individual a form of self-expression as a poem or a picture."

"I'm afraid you don't like journalists?" I remarked nervously.

"The journalist is always reminding the public of the existence of the artist. That is unnecessary of him. He is always reminding the artist of the existence of the public. That is indecent of him."

"But we must have journalists, Mr. Wilde."

"Why? They only record what happens. What does it matter what happens? It is only the abiding things that are interesting, not the horrid incidents of every-day life. Creation for the joy of creation, is the aim of the artist, and that is why the artist is a more divine type than the saint. The artist arrives at his moment with his own mood. He may come with terrible purple tragedies;[9] he may come with dainty rose-coloured comedies—

CRITICS AND "AN IDEAL HUSBAND"   171

what a charming title! " *added Mr. Wilde with
a smile*—" I must write a play and call it *A Rose-
Coloured Comedy.*"

" *What are the exact relations between literature
and the drama?*"

"Exquisitely accidental. That is why I think
them so necessary."

" *And the exact relations between the actor and the
dramatist?*"

*Mr. Wilde looked at me with a serious expression
which changed almost immediately into a smile, as
he replied,* " Usually a little strained."

" *But surely you regard the actor as a creative
artist?*"

" Yes," *replied Mr. Wilde with a touch of pathos
in his voice,* "terribly creative—terribly creative!"

" *Do you consider that the future outlook of the
English stage is hopeful?*"

" I think it must be. The critics have ceased to
prophesy. That is something. It is in silence that
the artist arrives. What is waited for never succeeds; what is heralded is hopeless."

*We were nearing the sentries at Marlborough
House, and I said:* " *Won't you tell me a little
more, please? Let us walk down Pall Mall—exercise is such a good thing.*"

"Exercise !" *he ejaculated with an emphasis*

172   DECORATIVE ART IN AMERICA

which almost warrants italics. "The only possible form of exercise is to talk, not walk."

And as he spoke, he motioned to a passing hansom. We shook hands, and Mr. Wilde, giving me a glance of approval, said : "I am sure that you must have a great future in literature before you."

"*What makes you think so ?*" *I asked, as I flushed with pleasure at the prediction.*

"Because you seem to be such a very bad interviewer. I feel sure that you must write poetry. I certainly like the colour of your necktie very much. Good-bye."

NOTES

Where there is no exaggeration there is no love, and where there is no love there is no understanding. It is only about things that do not interest one, that one can give a really unbiased opinion; and this is no doubt the reason why an unbiased opinion is always absolutely valueless. —*Mr. Pater's Last Volume.* *1890.*

NOTES

NOTES FOR THE INTRODUCTION

Page x

(¹) Cf. "I amused myself with being a *flâneur*, a dandy, a man of fashion."—*De Profundis.*

(²) Letter to James McNeill Whistler. *The World*, February 25, 1885; later in *The Gentle Art of Making Enemies.* 1890. (Page 163 of the 1904 edition) See *Mr. Whistler's " Ten O' Clock,"* Note 12, II, p. 199.

Page xi

(³) *The Truth of Masks* is the last essay of *Intentions*, though the first issued in its original separate form, under the title of *Shakespeare and Stage Costume. The Nineteenth Century*, No. XCIX, May, 1885, Vol. XVII.

(⁴) This theory is propounded at some length in a brilliant study entitled *An Artist in Attitudes : Oscar Wilde*, appearing in *Studies in Prose and Verse* by Arthur Symons : 1904. This study has also been translated into German by Franz Blei, and is included in his *In Memoriam. O. W.* Second Edition, 1905.

(⁵) Cf. "There are always new attitudes for the mind, and new points of view."—*The Critic as Artist. Part II.*

(⁶) *The Decay of Lying*, the first essay of *Intentions*, published first in *The Nineteenth Century*, No. CXLIII, January, 1889. Vol. XXV; later, in *The Eclectic Magazine*, February, 1889. It was considerably extended at the time of its later appearance.

Page xii

(⁷) *The Critic as Artist. Part II*, the fourth essay of *Intentions*, originally issued under the title of *The True Function and Value of Criticism. Concluded. The Nineteenth Century*, No. CLXIII,

176   DECORATIVE ART IN AMERICA

September, 1890, Vol. XXVIII; also, in *Mr. Pater's Last Volume.*
The Speaker, March 22, 1890, Vol. I.

(8) The Preface to *The Picture of Dorian Gray,* first published
in *The Fortnightly Review,* No. CCXCI, N. S., March, 1891, Vol.
LV, N. S.

Page xiii

(9) I. Richard Le Gallienne, in *The Academy,* July 4, 1891.

II. Agnes Repplier in *Essays in Miniature.* Charles L. Webster & Co., (1892); Houghton, Mifflin & Co. (Current Edition).

III. G. R. Carpenter in *Three Critics: Mr. Howells, Mr. Moore
and Mr. Wilde. The Andover Review,* December, 1891.

IV. Unsigned review in *The Speaker,* July 4, 1891, Vol. IV.

Page xiv

(10) The first conspicuous reference made in *Punch,* occurred on
February 14, 1880, Vol. 78. It is entitled *Nincompoopiana. The
Mutual Admiration Society.* About seven cartoons of this series
were printed, with the illustrations by George Du Maurier and the
captions of F. C. Burnand. They celebrated the " æsthetic " affectations of Maudle, Jellaby Postlethwaite and Mrs. Cimabue Brown.
Later on in 1881 and 1882, the references to Wilde became more
direct, as in *Oscar Interviewed,* January 14, 1882, Vol. 82, purporting to be an account of his arrival in the port of New York. In
addition to the pictorial satire, there were frequent parodies of his
poems—which poems were attacked with great bitterness.

Page xv

(11) Oscar Wilde arrived in New York harbour on the *Arizona* of
the Cunard Line on January 2, 1882. For a characteristic account
of this event, read *Ten Minutes with u Poet. The New York
Times,* Tuesday, January 3, 1882, page 5, cl. 6.

(12) Gilbert and Sullivan's *Patience; or, Bunthorne's Bride. An
Entirely New and Original Æsthetic Opera,* was first produced at
the Opera Comique, London, on Saturday, April 23, 1881. In
America, it was first presented under the management of R. D'Oyly
Carte at the Standard Theatre, New York, September 22, 1881.
Reginald Bunthorne, a Fleshly Poet, the " Ultra-poetical, super-
æsthetical " young man with his knee-breeches and sun-flowers, was

NOTES

generally accepted as a burlesque of Oscar Wilde. On the other hand, Mrs. Langtry, after attending a performance of *Patience* in New York, is said to have expressed her surprise at this interpretation of the character. "In England," she said, "Bunthorne is dressed after a countryman of yours—Mr. Whistler, a very distinguished artist. The tuft on the forehead and some other peculiarities of the make-up are characteristic of him." (*New York Herald*, Thursday, October 26, 1882, page 6.)

([13]) *The Colonel* by F. C. Burnand—an "æsthetic" comedy. was given its *première* at the Prince of Wales Theatre, London, Wednesday, February 2, 1881. The American production was at Abbey's New Park Theatre, Monday, January 16, 1882, with Lester Wallack in the title-rôle. It was a satire on all the forms of æstheticism, but Basil Giorgione, the Knight of the Lily, was made to bear the brunt of the ridicule; and because of the author's association with the *Punch* cartoons, this character was quite naturally assumed to be a travesty upon Oscar Wilde.

([14]) *Puck* began with occasional references such as that in *Fitz-noodle in America* for September 28, 1881, Vol. X. The more systematic bombardment commenced with No. 253, January 11, 1882, when the entire last page was devoted to "The Æsthete." In addition to this tribute, the larger part of that number and the succeeding one were generously allotted to his reception at the hands of "Fitznoodle" and "Hugo Dusenbury." This enthusiasm spent itself by the middle of March, but not until it had given Mr. R. K. Munkittrick the opportunity to unburden himself of a series of really delightful parodies of Wilde's *Impressions*, to which he applied such significant titles as "Impression Du Pork-Chop," "Impression Du Bull-Dog" and the like. These were pure fun, as was Helen Gray Cone's really brilliant *Narcissus in Camden. A Classical Dialogue*, between Whitman and Wilde (*The Century*, November, 1882); but not so were the parodies which appeared in *The World* under the general title of *The Æsthetic Boom*, and signed "OW!" However clever these were at times, they almost passed the bounds of decency by the undue emphasis which their author laid upon certain of the more amorous of Wilde's poems. It seems strange that *The World*, which of all American journals treated Wilde with the most courtesy, should have permitted the appear-

178 DECORATIVE ART IN AMERICA

ance of such verse on its editorial page. *Harper's Weekly* and *Harper's Bazar*, through the master hand of Thomas Nast, also exploited the foibles or peculiarities of the Apostle of Æstheticism and even *Life* entered the lists in a modest way. But the most flagrant example of so-called American Humour may be fonnd in *Ye Soul Agonies in Ye Life of Oscar Wilde*, a rare pamphlet of twenty-two pages purporting to be a comic history of the poet, with a pictorial cover, eight full-page illustrations and several sketches—all from the pen of Charles Kendrick, and representing Wilde at all ages from infancy. Although this pamphlet does not seem to have been issued with any malice, it was hardly an example of good taste, especially when it is recalled that copies were hawked by vendors on the streets outside the public halls in which Wilde lectured.

(15) There was none more ready than Wilde to recognize merit in the work of others. Even *The World* verses, mentioned above, are referred to in a personal letter (January, 1889), as "admirable parodies." On this subject he goes on to say: "Parody reqnires a light touch, a fanciful treatment, and, oddly enough, a love for the poet whom it caricatures. One's disciples can parody one—nobody else."

(16) See Note 2, page 181, for *Decorative Art in America*.

Page xvi

(17) *The Sun*, New York, Wednesday, January 18, 1882, page 2, cl. 2.

(18) *The Sun*, New York, Thursday, February 2, 1882, page 2, cl. 2.

(19) See Note 7, page 188, for *Joaquin Miller, The Good Samaritan*.

(20) *New-York Daily Tribune*, Sunday, November 5, 1882, page 3, cls. 3–4.

Page xvii

(21) See Note 3, page 182, for *Decorative Art in America*.

(22) See Note 1, page 181, for *Decorative Art in America*.

Page xviii

(23) The Preface to *The Picture of Dorian Gray*. See Note 8.

Page xix

(24) Cf. The second introductory keynote of *Decorative Art in America*, page 2.

(25) *The Decay of Lying*. See Note 6, page 175.

NOTES

179

Page xx

([26]) Cf. The third introductory keynote of *Decorative Art in America*, page 2.

([27]) *New York Herald*, Sunday, August 12, 1883, page 10, cl. 3.

([28]) *The Critic as Artist. Part II*; or, in its earlier form in *The Nineteenth Century*, September, 1890.

([29]) *The Soul of Man Under Socialism. The Fortnightly Review*, Febrnary, 1891, Vol. LV, O. S. ; or, in *The Eclectic Magazine*, April, 1891, Vol. LIII, N. S., and the several reprint editions in pamphlet and book-form.

Page xxi

([30]) The so-called *Envoi* is Wilde's Gallicism for the introduction which he contributed to *Rose Leaf and Apple Leaf,* by Rennell Rodd, a book of poems published through Wilde's agency in Philadelphia, 1882. Wilde was a friend of Rodd, an Englishman in the diplomatic service ; but the rather unusual character of the first issue of this book by J. M. Stoddart, made the author so conspicuous that its publication is said to have caused a breach in their friendship. The original edition was printed in brown ink on thin parchment, interleaved with green tissue. The book appeared again in 1882 in a more conventional form. The *Envoi* was reissued in 1904 as a " Privately Printed " book in London; and in a choice edition of 50 copies by Thomas B. Mosher, Maine, in 1905.

([31]) See Note 8, page 198, for *Mr. Whistler's "Ten O'Clock";* also Note 9, page 202, for *The Relation of Dress to Art.*

Page xxii

([32]) Wilde's theories are propounded in both his American lectnres on art (1882) ; in his two criticisms of Whistler's " *Ten O'Clock,*" included in this collection (1885); *The Soul of Man Under Socialism* (1891); as well as in a number of notes in *The Woman's World*, 1887–1889.

([33]) See Note 6, page 198, for *Mr. Whistler's "Ten O'Clock."*

([34]) See *James McNeill Whistler* by H. W. Singer. Charles Scribner's Sons, 1905, pages 74–5.

([35]) See Note 5, page 182, for *Decorative Art in America;* also matter referred to, page 6.

180   DECORATIVE ART IN AMERICA

Page xxiii

(36) See Note 6, page 198, for *Mr. Whistler's "Ten O'Clock."*

(37) See *The Relation of Dress to Art*, at the foot of page 53.

(38) *The Critic as Artist. Part II*, in *Intentions*; or its issue in magazine form, September, 1890.

(39) *The Soul of Man Under Socialism*, February, 1891.

Page xxiv

(40) Cf. The fourth introductory keynote of *Mrs. Langtry as Hester Grazebrook*, page 24.

Page xxvi

(41) This occurs in a personal letter, dated Paris, May 24, 1898.

Page xxvii

(42) *The Saturday Review*, December 8, 1900. Vol. XC.

(43) *The Critic as Artist. Part II.*

NOTES FOR "DECORATIVE ART IN AMERICA"

Page 3

(1) This discourse was delivered for the first time in New York City, May, 1882. It was heralded by circulars of yellowish Japan tissue, on which appeared a reproduction of the head from J. E. Kelly's etching of Wilde (See Frontispiece of *De Profundis*, G. P. Putnam's Sons), and the following announcement:—Art Decoration. The Practical Application of The Principles of The Æsthetic Theory to Exterior and Interior House Decoration, With Observations Upon Dress and Personal Ornaments. A Lecture By Oscar Wilde. To Be Given At Wallack's, Thursday Afternoon, May 11th, at Half-Past Two O'Clock.

Earlier in the spring, he had lectured on the same general subject. In Omaha, for example, he referred to many of the American houses as "illy designed, decorated shabbily and in bad taste, and filled with furniture that was not honestly made and was out of character." See also *The Freeman's Journal* (Dublin), Jan. 7, 1885.

(2) Oscar Wilde's first public appearance in America, under the management of R. D'Oyly Carte, was on the occasion of his lecture on *The English Renaissance* at Chickering Hall, Monday, January 9, 1882, at 8 o'clock. An interesting account of this even occurs in *The New York World*, Tuesday, January 10, 1882, page 2, columns 2-3, and in *The Nation*, January 12, Vol. XXXIV. The lecture was printed in *The New-York Daily Tribune* of January 10, page 2, and in *The Sun*, page 1. From these sources it has been reprinted more or less correctly in the following editions:

I. *Poems by Oscar Wilde; also his Lecture on the English Renaissance*. The Seaside Library, New York. January 19, 1882. (No. 1183 of Vol. 58.) Pp. 32.

182 DECORATIVE ART IN AMERICA

II. *Oscar Wilde's Poems and Lecture.* Ogilvie's Popular Reading. People's Library, New York, 1882. Pp. 30. III. *Poems by Oscar Wilde, together with his Lecture on the English Renaissance.* (*Now first published*) Paris, 1903. Pp. 216. IV. *Lecture on the English Renaissance. Rose Leaf and Apple Leaf: L'Envoi.* By Oscar Wilde. Portland, Maine. Thomas B. Mosher. 1905. Pp. 42.

Page 4

(3) Between January 16 and May 5, 1882, Wilde visited all the important centres of the North and West. In most cases, he lectured on *The English Renaissance*, varying his introduction and conclusion to suit the audience. The lecture tour embraced among other cities, Philadelphia, Washington, Baltimore, Boston, Hartford, New Haven, Rochester (in the order named); Cincinnati, Louisville,* St. Louis, Chicago, Racine, Milwaukee, St. Paul, San Francisco, Denver, Kansas City and Omaha. *See page 65 and Note.

Page 5

(4) See *Harper's Weekly*, Saturday, September 9, 1882. No. 1342, Vol. XXVI. " Oscar Wilde on Our Cast-Iron Stoves : Another American Institution sat down on."—Cartoon by Thomas Nast.

Page 6

(5) Cf. " The truths of art cannot be taught. They are revealed only—revealed to natures which have made themselves receptive of all beautiful impressions by the study and worship of all beautiful things."—*Lecture on the English Renaissance.*

Page 7

(6) For further expression of his beliefs as regards women's clothes and their making, cf. *Literary and Other Notes. The Woman's World*, February, 1888, or page 149 of *Essays, Criticisms and Reviews*; also, *Pall Mall Gazette*, or *Pall Mall Budget* for October-November, 1884.

Page 8

(7) See *Harper's Bazar*, Saturday, June 10, 1882. No. 23 of Vol. XV. "Wilde on *Us*. Something To ' Live Up To ' in Amer-

NOTES

183

ica."—Cartoon by Thomas Nast, representing Wilde with a miner's hat and boots in one hand, etc.

Page 9

(8) Wilde himself, however, had the courage of his convictions and caused a sensation by appearing at a Polo Game at Newport, with a white slouch hat.— *The New York World*, Sunday, July 16, 1882, page 6, cl. 3. He elaborated these ideas in his lectures on dress in England in 1884. In a letter printed in the *Pall Mall Budget* and *Pall Mall Gazette* for that year, he writes of head-gear: " In a hat made on right principles one should be able to turn the brim up or down according as the day is dark or fair, dry or wet, etc."; and of foot-gear: " A boot should be made of soft leather always, and if worn high at all, must be either laced up the front or carried well over the knee: in the latter case one combines perfect freedom for walking together with perfect protection against rain, neither of which a short stiff boot will ever give one; and when one is sitting in the house, the long soft boot can be turned down, as the boot of 1640 was."

Page 10

(9) This must refer to one of the many studies made for "The Symphony in White, No. 4" or "The Three Girls." The final design was a large panel painted some time in the early seventies and is now in the possession of Mr. Charles L. Freer of Detroit. It was originally intended to occupy the wall-panel opposite "La Princesse du Pays de la Porcelaine " in Mr. Leyland's dining-room. (See below.) Mr. Whistler began to paint the finished picture on more than one canvas with figures about life size, and although the painting "was never completed, Mr. Chapman owns a large canvas which Mr. Whistler left half-finished when he went to Venice."— *The Art of James McNeill Whistler* by T. R. Way and G. R. Dennis. Pages 26, 30 – 32 and 100. The three first and better known "Symphonies in White " were exhibited, 1863 – 7, as "The White Girl," "The Little White Girl " and "Symphony in White, No. 3."

(10) The celebrated dining-room known as the " Peacock Room " was in the residence of Frederick R. Leyland, 49 Prince's Gate London. Whistler's decorative scheme in blue and gold was carried out by him in 1876 – 77. Most interesting allusions to this work are

184 DECORATIVE ART IN AMERICA

made in *The History of Modern Painting* by Richard Muther, Vol. 3, page 662; *Recollections and Impressions of James A. McNeill Whistler* by Arthur Jerome Eddy, pages 128 – 130; *James McNeill Whistler* by H. W. Singer, pages 12, 36; *Whistler as I Knew Him* by Mortimer Menpes, pages 129 – 132; *The Art of J. McNeill Whistler* by T. R. Way and G. R. Dennis, pages 31, 99 – 101; *Pall Mall Budget*, June 16, 1892, Vol. 40; and *Whistler's Peacock Room*, *New York Herald*, Magazine Section, June 17, 1904. Of these, the last three contain illustrations of the panels. The *raison d'être* for the colour-scheme of this room was Whistler's painting "La Princesse du Pays de la Porcelaine" which hung over the mantel. This was first exhibited at the Paris Salon of 1865 and is reproduced in the volumes by H. W. Singer; T. R. Way and G. R. Dennis; *Pall Mall Budget*, June 2, 1892; and *Impressionist Painting* by Wynford Dewhurst. Both this picture and the peacock decorations (acquired in 1904) are now in the possession of Mr. C. L. Freer.

(11) This room is the Camera di San Paolo, Parma. At the bidding of the abbess of the convent, Donna Giovanna Piacenza, Correggio decorated her private room during the months of April – December, 1518. "From the cornice above the walls sixteen ribs rise to the centre of the vault, forming a like number of lunettes. Correggio covered the whole with frescoes, adapting his scheme of decoration to the structure of the vault. The design is a bower of foliage supported on a trellis of canes, with sixteen oval openings, through which a joyous band of naked Amorini, moving apparently along an outside gallery, are seen at play."—*Antonio Allegri da Correggio. His Life, His Friends, and His Time.* By Corrado Ricci, 1896. Following page 160 is a plate illustrating the cupola of this room.

Page 13

(12) "Wars there must be always; but I think that creating a common intellectual atmosphere might make men brothers."— *Lecture on the English Renaissance.*

Page 14

(13) See 'Oscar Wilde' in *People I Have Met. Short Sketches of Many Prominent Persons*, by Mary Watson, San Francisco, 1890.

NOTES 185

Cf. "In the Chinese restaurant, where these navvies meet to have supper in the evening, I found them drinking tea out of china cups as delicate as the petals of a rose-leaf, whereas at the gaudy hotels I was supplied with a delf cup, an inch and a half thick."— *Impressions of America*. Wandsworth, September, 1883.

Page 15

(14) Public Industrial Art School, a part of the public-school system of Philadelphia.

(15) Charles Godfrey Leland, author, editor and journalist, born in Philadelphia, August, 1824. His literary work extends over such dissimilar fields as are represented by *Hans Breitmann's Barty*, *The English Gypsies and Their Language*, *Abraham Lincoln*, and a series of *Art Manuals*.

(16) Mr. Wilde here turned to an adjoining table and held up to view the different articles which are mentioned.

(17) In a lecture on America and Art Schools, which Wilde delivered in London, April, 1884, he is reported to have expressed the hope that a time would come when boys would prefer to look at a bird or even draw one rather than throw "the customary stone."

In an earlier lecture, *Impressions of America*, September, 1883, he said: "Boys and girls should be taught to use their hands to make something, and they would be less apt to destroy and be mischievous."

NOTES FOR "JOAQUIN MILLER, THE GOOD SAMARITAN"

Page 19

(1) Cincinnatns Heine Miller, known by the pen-name of *Joaquin Miller*, which he assumed after he had written a paper in defence of the Mexican bandit, Joaquin Murietta. Born in Indiana, Nov., 1841, his father moved to Oregon when he was nine years of age. After an adventurous boyhood, which included an Indian campaign in 1857, he graduated from Columbia College, Oregon, in 1858. Admitted to the bar in 1860, he started for the Idaho gold mines in '61, but two years later he was back in Oregon as editor of *The Democratic Register* at Eugene. He resumed practice of law in '64, and for services against the Indians, was appointed Judge of Grant County in '66. From 1870 to 1887 his life was spent in Europe, and largely in New York and Washington, where he followed a literary career and published a number of poems (a collected edition in 1882), some prose and several plays. Since 1887 he has made his home in a cabin, which he calls "The Hights," from its position on the green hills overlooking Oakland and Alameda. It is here in the California which he loves, that he has dwelt in recent years, except for the time when he served as a newspaper correspondent in the Boxer Rebellion of 1900.

(2) Oscar Wilde delivered his *Lecture on the English Renaissance* at the Grand Opera House, Rochester, N. Y., on the evening of Tuesday, February 7th, 1882. By pre-arrangement among the students, his reception was most disorderly—so insulting in fact, that policemen were summoned to quiet the disturbance. For specific details, see *The New York Herald*, Wednesday, February 8, 1882, page 10; *The Boston Daily Globe*, Thursday, February 9, 1882, page 1; and *The Boston Evening Transcript*, same date, page 4.

Page 20

(3) Oscar Wilde and Joaquin Miller met for the first time at a

188   DECORATIVE ART IN AMERICA

reception given in New York by Mrs. Marion T. Fortescue on Friday, January 13, 1882. Mr. Miller immediately extended the hand of good-fellowship to the Irishman, although Wilde was already being persecuted by almost the entire American Press.

(4) His first visit to London was in 1870, for the purpose of securing a publisher for his poems. These were published by Longmans in 1871, under the title of *Songs of the Sierras.* He again visited London in 1873, in which year were issued *Songs of the Sunlands.* It is said that he made a sensation by appearing in the costume of a *vaquero*; he was much fêted and lionized, and called by some "The American Byron."

(5) Wilde delivered his lecture in St. Louis at the Mercantile Library Hall on Saturday, February 25, 1882.

Page 21

(6) Cf. "But you must not judge of æstheticism by the satire of Mr. Gilbert, any more than you judge of the strength and splendour of sun or sea by the dust that dances in the beam or the bubble that breaks on the wave."—*Lecture on the English Renaissance.*

(7) From the date of his first address up to that of the present letter, his audiences, if never enthusiastic, were at least attentive and courteous, except in Boston, Brooklyn and Rochester. The Rochester episode has already been recorded. Wilde lectured at Boston Music Hall on Tuesday, January 31, '82. The first rows of the orchestra had been reserved by sixty Harvard students, who came, dressed after the manner of Bunthorne in *Patience*, which at that time was being played at the Standard Theatre, New York City. Instead, however, of showing any embarrassment, he completely turned the tables by his witty sallies and good humour, thereby winning the esteem and good-will of the audience. For an account of the lecture, refer to any Boston newspaper for Feb. 1, 1882; *The Sun,* New York, Feb. 1st, or *The New York World,* Feb. 2nd. The most interesting allusions are the editorials in *The Boston Evening Transcript* of February 1st, and those of *The Sun* and *The World* of New York, on Boston's reception of Wilde, in their issues of Feb. 2nd. Under the latter date *The Transcript* had the fairness to supplement its first editorial with an acknowledgment of Wilde's fine bearing in the face of churlish provocation. To quote: "Mr. Wilde achieved a

NOTES

189

real triumph and it was by right of conquest, by force of being *a gentleman* in the truest sense of the word."

As regards the attitude of his Brooklyn audience at the Academy of Music, Friday, February 3rd, it was merely unsympathetic and ill-mannered in its interruptions of feigned applause. For details, refer to *The Sun, The New York World* and *The New York Herald* for February 4, 1882.

(8) At the date of this letter, these men and women included General and Mrs. McClellan, John Boyle O'Reilly, George W. Childs, Julia Ward Howe, Mrs. Robert H. Sherwood, Oliver Wendell Holmes, Clara Morris, Louisa Alcott, Kate Field, Henry Wadsworth Longfellow, all of whom extended to him some courtesy, if not their hospitality. Later he became acquainted with many of the most prominent people of this country and not least among them General Grant, and the Reverend Henry Ward Beecher, whose guest he became at his home in Peekskill, in the summer of 1882.

Page 22

(9) The "literary *gamin*," etc., to whom Wilde refers throughout this letter was the author of an editorial, signed T. W. H. which appeared in *The Woman's Journal*, Vol. XIII, No. 5, Saturday, Feb. 4, 1882. This was an attack on the personality and the theories of Wilde, terminating with the plea that he should be socially ostracized. Extracts from this article were reprinted in the *New-York Daily Tribune*, Sunday, February 5, 1882. To this, Mrs. Julia Ward Howe, who had received Wilde in Boston, replied in *The Boston Daily Globe*, February 15, page 4. This letter was copied in *The Boston Evening Transcript* of February 16, page 5: "As Colonel H . . . . n in *The Woman's Journal* takes exception to the entertainment of Mr. Oscar Wilde in private houses, . . . I as one of the entertainers alluded to . . . etc. Mr. Wilde is a young man in whom many excellent people have found much to like. . . . " Mrs. Howe further proved her friendship for Wilde by making him her guest at Lawton's Valley a part of the time that he was at Newport, where he lectured at the Casino, July 15th. The "T. W. H." episode was referred to later in an editorial entitled "A Stale Joke," *Harper's Weekly*, No. 1335, July 22, 1882, Vol. XXVI—an article in which Wilde was treated with customary

190 DECORATIVE ART IN AMERICA

severity. Though Wilde's allusions to his slanderer are lacking in restraint, it must be remembered that he was attacked without just provocation by a man whose high position in the community made this attack as injurious as it was undignified. It is interesting to note that this is the only display of feeling recorded of his visit in America. The one parallel expression of resentment occurs in the Whistler-Wilde controversy of 1890. See *Truth*, Jan. 9, 1890, and *The Gentle Art of Making Enemies*, page 236 – 42.

(10) So many were the "scribes," who ventured to express themselves upon Wilde's appearance and theories that it is difficult to fix upon the particular objects of his contempt. At the time of this letter, however, the two papers that had been the most virulent in their censure of him were *The Washington Post* and *The Saturday Evening Gazette*, Boston. The first, published on Sunday, January 22nd, 1882, a most insulting cartoon. When Colonel Morse, at that period manager for Mr. Carte, wrote to the editor expressing his indignation over such unjustifiable treatment, further insulting comments were made at the time of the publication of his letter, January 24th. As regards this very episode, the Chicago papers were especially hostile to Wilde. They went so far (he writes to Colonel Morse from Omaha) as to "accuse me of encouraging the attacks on me, and of having 'corrected the proofs of the Washington attack and approved of the caricature before it was published' — These are the words of *The Chicago Herald*." Such accusations were not unusual. *The Gazette*, in its issues of January 21st and January 28th, indulged in nothing short of abusive invective, part of which is quoted in *The Boston Daily Globe* for January 23rd and 30th. Under the first date, are quoted also extracts of a letter from one who is represented as being "one of the foremost literary men of New York." This is an anonymous and extremely priggish explanation that literary New York refused to receive in its ranks the soi-disant poet, who was trying to obtain admission to literary and social circles by means of letters of introduction secured through the agency of his manager. This was palpably false, and subsequent to the date of its original appearance in *The Boston Transcript* for January 13th, called forth some comment and ridicule from *The New York World* in an editorial under date of January 15th.

Apart from the two papers alluded to, the Press as a whole assumed

NOTES 191

an attitude which was mainly tolerant or flippant or, at the worst, satirical, though *The Springfield Republican* was occasionally insulting in tone and *The Boston Transcript* rather offensive in the personalities with which its editorials bristled until after the Boston lecture.

(11) Although Narcissus is one of the characters which Wilde uses most frequently in simile, this is probably a direct retort to the following passage in an editorial entitled *Oscar Wilde's Prototypes*, which appeared in *The Boston Evening Transcript*, January 14, 1882: "There has never been a lack of these creatures whose life is passed in posturing. Narcissus is perhaps the earliest recorded instance."

Note. The editor takes this occasion to acknowledge Mr. Joaquin Miller's courtesy in consenting to the publication of his letter to Oscar Wilde.

NOTES FOR "MRS. LANGTRY AS HESTER GRAZEBROOK"

Page 25

(1) This dramatic criticism was printed in *The New York World*, Tuesday, November 7, 1882, page 5, cl. 1.

(2) Mrs. Langtry made her American debut at Wallack's Theatre, New York, on Monday evening, November 6, 1882. She played the rôle of Hester Grazebrook in *An Unequal Match*, a comedy by Tom Taylor.

(3) Cf. "Art is the mathematical result of the emotional desire for beauty."—"*Vera*" and *the Drama*, page 36.

Page 26

(4) Helen of Troy, was, according to Euripides, the daughter of Lēda and Zeus. She is one of Wilde's favourite characters, alluded to frequently in his essays and poems. Apropos of both Helen and Mrs. Langtry, Wilde is reported to have made the following statement in an interview, chronicled in *The Halifax Morning Herald*, October 10, 1882: "I would rather have discovered Mrs. Langtry than have discovered America. Her beauty is in outline perfectly moulded. She will be a beauty at eighty-five. Yes, it was for such ladies that Troy was destroyed, and well might Troy be destroyed for such a woman."

Page 27

(5) Albert Moore, born in York, 1841; died in London, 1892. "From the Greeks he learnt the combination of noble lines, the charm of dignity and quietude, while the Japanese gave him the feeling for harmonies of colour, for soft, delicate, blended tones. By a capricious union of both these elements he formed his refined and exquisite style."—*The History of Modern Painting*, by Richard Muther, Vol. 3.

194 DECORATIVE ART IN AMERICA

([6]) Frederick, Lord Leighton, the classicist *par excellence*, born in Scarborough, 1830; died January, 1896. He was president of the Royal Academy from 1879 to the date of his death. — *The History of Modern Painting*, by Richard Muther, Vol. 3.

Page 28

([7]) Mrs. Langtry, who was under the management of Mr. Abbey, was to have made her debut at Abbey's New Park Theatre, 22nd Street and Broadway, on Monday evening, the 30th of October. This theatre, however, was destroyed by fire with all of the scenery, on that very afternoon. Through the courtesy and generosity of Mr. Wallack, Mr. Abbey was enabled to present Mrs. Langtry exactly one week later at the present Wallack's Theatre. There was consequently only a very brief interval for the preparation of new scenery.

Page 29

([8]) Cf. "As a rule, the hero is smothered in bric-à-brac and palm trees, lost in the gilded abyss of Louis Quatorze furniture, or reduced to a mere midge in the midst of *marqueterie;* whereas the background should always be kept as a background, and colour subordinated to effect." — *The Truth of Masks.*

([9]) The decorations of Madison Square Theatre in 1882, were by Louis C. Tiffany & Co. The curtain to which Mr. Wilde alludes was a very decorative scenic scheme in the Japanesque manner.

([10]) See : I. *Why either Claude or Titian?* a letter of protest in *The New York World*, November 8, 1882, page 5, cl. 4.

II. *Realism in Painting and in Drama*, a similar letter in *The New York World*, Nov. 9, 1882, page 2, cl. 4. The first cites the work of Salvator Rosa and Rubens as instances in which scenes and figures are given equal prominence; the second seeks to refute Wilde by recalling his expressed approval of the stage-setting at the London Lyceum and his plea for realistic dress. (*Note.* A careful study of Wilde's theories of costume, etc., as presented in *The Truth of Masks*, will show that he was not all inconsistent in his point of view.)

NOTES FOR "'VERA' AND THE DRAMA"

Page 33

(1) The play, *Vera, or the Nihilists,* a drama in a prologue and four acts, was, if we are to believe an interviewer, written as early as 1876.—*The New York World,* August 12, 1883. It was about to receive a hearing in London, December, 1881, under the management of Dion Boucicault, with Mrs. Bernard-Beere in the title-rôle, when for a reason still unexplained, it was suddenly withdrawn, and Wilde started for America. Current gossip had it that the socialistic sentiments of which it was the expression, were offensive to the Ambassador of the Czar, and that it was suppressed for political reasons. This, however, has never been authenticated. (*The New York Times,* December 26, 1881.)

We know that Wilde brought the manuscript of his play with him to America at the time of his first visit, 1882 (*New-York Daily Tribune,* Jan. 3, 1882), and that, among others, Lawrence Barrett expressed his admiration for it. Wilde endeavored to place the play through his manager, Mr. D'Oyly Carte, but whether it was eventually through him that Wilde was successful, is extremely doubtful; for he approached Mr. Wallack, Mr. Palmer and a number of other managers before Miss Prescott accepted it.

A very small acting edition was privately printed in 1882, but copies of this are now practically unobtainable. In an undated letter, which Wilde addressed to Colonel Morse from Boston (probably in the autumn of 1882), he thanks his manager for "sending the play to Washington." He adds: "I think to copyright under your name would be a very good plan." This he follows with directions for the distribution of a number of the copies. Mr. Morse accounts for some twelve copies disposed of in this way.

Wilde returned to America in 1883 for the purpose of attending his *première,* and reached New York on August 11th. On Monday,

196   DECORATIVE ART IN AMERICA

August 20th, the play was produced for the first time at the Union Square Theatre under the management of Marie Prescott's husband, W. Perzel. The latter claimed to have spent some $10,000 on the costumes, scenery, etc. ; but despite careful preparation and lavish expenditure, the play proved a total failure. It was withdrawn after one week's run, to the great loss of the manager who was said to have contracted with Wilde for a run of 100 nights at $50.00 a performance. Miss Prescott, in a letter published in *The New York Times* and *The New York Sun*, August 24, 1883, protested against the attitude of the dramatic critics, which, she insinuated, was one of pre-concerted condemnation. In *Vera*, Miss Prescott played the title-rôle, the only woman's part in the play; G. C. Boniface, the Czar ; Lewis Morrison, the Czarevitch ; and Edward Lamb, Prince Paul.

In 1902, a version of *Vera* was published in England purporting to be printed from "the author's own copy, showing his corrections of and additions to the original text." In this it is stated that "This play was written in 1881." The edition, which is represented as a limited one of 200 numbered copies, privately printed, was issued at 12s. 6d.

(2) It is nevertheless a fact that Mr. Wilde tried to secure Miss Clara Morris for the part. In an unpublished letter to R. D'Oyly Carte, he writes from St. Paul, Minnesota, March 16, 1882: "I have received your letter about the Play: I agree to place it entirely in your hands for production on the terms of my receiving half the profits, and a guarantee of £200 paid down to me on occasion of its production. As regards the cast, I am sure you see yourself how well the part will suit Clara Morris. I am, however, quite aware how *difficile* she is. . . ." He also thought of Miss Rose Coghlan for the part, and in this connection it is interesting to recall that it was she who secured, for America, his fifth play, *A Woman of No Importance*. But it was on Miss Morris he had set his heart. He writes again to Mr. Carte in 1882: "I feel it will succeed, if she (Clara Morris) act and you manage." And in the same letter regarding the other rôles : "Could you get Kyrle Bellew or Johnson Forbes Robertson for the Czarevitch? Flockton would be an able Prince Paul."

NOTES FOR "MR. WHISTLER'S 'TEN O'CLOCK'"

Page 41

(1) This review appeared first in *The Pall Mall Gazette*, Saturday, February 21, 1885, and was later included in the weekly issue of *The Pall Mall Budget*, Friday, February 27, 1885, Vol. 33. An extract also appears in *The Gentle Art of Making Enemies*.

(2) Mr. Whistler's lecture on art, which he whimsically termed *Ten O'Clock*, because that was the hour of his address, was delivered in London, February 20, 1885; at Cambridge, March 24th; at Oxford, April 30th. It was published in pamphlet form by Chatto & Windus, 1888; also by Houghton, Mifflin & Co. in America; and is included in *The Gentle Art of Making Enemies*, page 135.

Page 42

(3) Cf. "There was something almost sublime in his inhuman devotion to the purely visible aspect of people, as of a great surgeon who will not allow human pity to obstruct the operation of his craft." *Mr. Whistler. The Athenæum*, No. 3952, July 25, 1903.

Page 43

(4) It must be remembered that not long before this, in October, 1884, Wilde had delivered his lectures on Dress, in which he suggested certain radical reforms in the costumes of men and women, thereby giving rise to an interesting controversy in the pages of *The Pall Mall Gazette*, which lasted till the middle of November.

(5) Cf. "Velasquez, whose Infantas clad in inæsthetic hoops, are, as works of Art, of the same quality as the Elgin Marbles."— *Whistler's "Ten O'Clock."*

Page 44

(6) Of Whistler's attitude towards the development of public taste, Swinburne expressed himself as follows, in his article entitled

198 DECORATIVE ART IN AMERICA

Mr. Whistler's Lecture on Art: "But it does not follow that all efforts to widen the sphere of appreciation, to enlarge the circle of intelligence must needs be puny and unprofitable. Good intentions will not secure results; but neither—strange as it may seem—will the absence of good intentions." *The Fortnightly Review,* June, 1888, Vol. 49, pages 745–53; or *The Eclectic Magazine,* August, 1888, Vol. 48, N. S., pages 154–158. To this Whistler replied in *The World* (London), June 3, 1888. See *The Gentle Art of Making Enemies: Freeing a Last Friend;* also *"Et tu, Brute!"*

(7) "We have then but to wait—until, with the mark of the Gods upon him, there come among us again the chosen—who shall continue what has gone before. Satisfied that, even were he never to appear, the story of the beautiful is already complete—hewn in the marbles of the Parthenon—and broidered, with the birds, upon the fan of Hokusai, at the foot of Fusi-yama."—*Whistler's "Ten O'Clock."* (The Conclusion.)

(8) Cf. "The master stands in no relation to the moment at which he occurs—a monument of isolation—hinting at sadness—having no part in the progress of his fellow-men."—*Whistler's "Ten O'Clock."*

Page 45

(9) Cf. "Indeed, so far from its being true that the artist is the best judge of art, a really great artist can never judge of other people's work at all, and can hardly in fact, judge of his own. . . . It is exactly because a man cannot do a thing that he is the proper judge of it." *The Critic as Artist. Part II.* (*N. B.* In this passage the term "artist" is used to denote the painter or poet—the creator.)

(10) Cf. "Art does not address herself to the specialist. Her claim is that she is universal, and that in all her manifestations she is one." —*The Critic as Artist. Part II.* (*Intentions,* 1891.) "I believe, myself, in the correlation of the arts—that painting, poetry, and sculpture are only different forms of the same truth."—*An Interview with Oscar Wilde. New-York Daily Tribune,* Jan. 8, 1882.

(11) Whistler's marginal note to the extract from this lecture in *The Gentle Art of Making Enemies,* reads: "*Reflection.*—It is not enough that our simple Sunflower thrive on his 'thistle'—he has now grafted Edgar Poe on the 'rose' tree of the early American Market in 'a certain milieu' of dry goods and sympathy; and 'a

NOTES 199

certain entourage' of worship and wooden nutmegs. Born of a Nation, not absolutely 'devoid of any sense of beauty'—Their idol—cherished—listened to—and understood! Foolish Beaudelaire!—Mistaken Mallarmé!"

(¹²) As a result of this criticism from Wilde, occurred the following interesting exchange of letters :

I. *Tenderness in Tite Street.* (Signed with the "Butterfly device.")—*The World*, February 25, 1885. (Whistler's *Gentle Art of Making Enemies*, page 162.)

To the Poet:

Oscar,—I have read your exquisite article in the *Pall Mall*. Nothing is more delicate, in the flattery of "the Poet" to "the Painter," than the *naïveté* of "the Poet" in the choice of his Painters—Benjamin West and Paul Delaroche!

You have pointed out that "the Painter's" mission is to find "*le beau dans l'horrible,*" and have left to "the Poet" the discovery of "*l'horrible*" dans "*le beau*"!

Chelsea.

II. *To the Painter.—The World*, Feb. 25, 1885. (Whistler's *Gentle Art of Making Enemies*, page 163.)

To the Painter :

Dear Butterfly,—By the aid of a biographical dictionary, I made the discovery that there were once two painters, called Benjamin West and Paul Delaroche, who rashly lectured upon Art. As of their works nothing at all remains, I conclude that they explained themselves away.

Be warned in time, James ; and remain, as I do, incomprehensible. To be great is to be misunderstood.*—*Tout à vous,*

OSCAR WILDE.

*From *Essay II, Self-Reliance,* by Ralph Waldo Emerson.

(*N. B.* Whistler's customary reflection reads: "I do know a bird, who, like Oscar, with his head in the sand, still believes in the undiscovered. If to be misunderstood is to be great, it was rash in Oscar to reveal the source of his inspirations: the '*Biographical Dictionary!*'")

NOTES FOR "THE RELATION OF DRESS TO ART"

Page 49

(1) This essay appeared first in *The Pall Mall Gazette*, Saturday, February 28, 1885, and was later included in the weekly issue of *The Pall Mall Budget*, Friday, March 6, 1885, Vol. 33.

Page 50

(2) Cf. "Subordination in art does not mean disregard of truth; it means conversion of fact into effect."—*The Truth of Masks*. "The quarrel between the school of facts and the school of effects touches them not."—*London Models*. See page 91. "English public opinion tries to constrain . . . the man who makes things that are beautiful in effect, and compels the journalist to retail things that are ugly . . . in fact."—*The Soul of Man Under Socialism*. See the first keynote, page 146. (*N. B.* A great number of examples might be given to illustrate Wilde's habitual use of certain pairs of words, as in the above instance. See *Phrases* in Index.)

(3) Cf. "Nobody of any real culture ever talks nowadays about the beauty of a sunset. Sunsets are quite old-fashioned. They belong to the time when Turner was the last note in art."—*The Decay of Lying*.

Page 51

(4) This probably refers to "Japanese Girls on the Terrace"; but Wilde could have found a number of equally good examples such as "La Princesse du Pays de la Porcelaine," "The Golden Screen," "Die Lange Leizen—of the Six Marks," or "Irving as Philip II of Spain," which was first exhibited eight years before this article.

(5) Cf. "Mr. Whistler made many beautiful studies of nude figures, mostly with transparent draperies of brilliant colour, quite classical in character."—Chapter on Pastels, etc., *The Art of James McNeill Whistler*, by T. R. Way and G. R. Dennis.

202　DECORATIVE ART IN AMERICA

(6) Cf. "It is the secret of much of the artificiality of modern art, this constant posing of pretty people, and when art becomes artificial, it becomes monotonous."—*London Models.* See page 99.

Page 52

(7) Cf. "'All right, sir,' said the professor of posing."—*London Models.* See page 91.

(8) Cf. *London Models,* page 100.

(9) This was one of Wilde's most cherished theories. In the letter entitled *More Radical Ideas Upon Dress Reform,* 1884, he writes: "The over-tunic should be made full and moderately loose; it may, if desired, be shaped more or less to the figure, but in no case should it be confined to the waist by any straight band or belt; on the contrary, it should fall from the shoulder to the knee or below it, in fine curves and vertical lines, giving more freedom and consequently more grace." Cf. *The Freeman's Journal* (Dublin), Jan. 6, 1885.

(10) Wilde's position is even more strongly defined in a *Letter on Woman's Dress,* 1884, in which he defends himself against a correspondent in *The Pall Mall Gazette,* who signs herself "Girl Graduate": "All the most ungainly and uncomfortable articles of dress that fashion has ever in her folly prescribed, not the tight corset merely, but the farthingale, the vertugadin, the hoop, the crinoline, and that monstrosity, the so-called 'dress-improver' also—all of them have owed their origin to the same error, the error of not seeing that it is from the shoulders only that garments should be hung."

Page 53

(11) Whistler's point of view, on the other hand, was: "We are told that the Greeks were, as a people, worshippers of the beautiful, and that in the fifteenth century Art was engrained in the multitude . . . Listen! there was never an artistic period. There never was an Art-loving nation."—*Whistler's "Ten O'Clock."*

(12) Whistler's point of view was: "Why, after centuries of freedom from Art, and indifference to it, should it now be thrust upon them (the people) by the blind—until wearied and puzzled, they know no longer how they shall eat or drink—how they shall sit or stand—or wherewithal they shall clothe themselves—without af-

NOTES 203

flicting Art."—*Whistler's* "*Ten O'Clock.*" Cf. *Introduction*, page xxiii; *Decorative Art in America*, page 13; and note to same, page 184.

Page 54

(13) Cf. "My business as an artist was with Ariel. I set myself to wrestle with Cailban."—*De Profundis.* (*N. B.* This is another instance of Wilde's repeated use of certain pairs of words.)

NOTES FOR "THE TOMB OF KEATS"

Page 56

(1) This sonnet was first published in *The Dramatic Review*, January 23, 1886, page 249. It was included by Mr. Alfred H. Miles in *The Poets and the Poetry of the Century*, Vol. VIII (1891–4), page 519, and will in all probability be contained in the revised edition of this series, bearing the imprint of George Routledge & Sons and E. P. Dutton & Co., of which several volumes have already been issued. Mr. Thomas B. Mosher of Maine has printed it in a collected edition, *The Poems of Oscar Wilde*, 1905; and quite recently (1906) it has reappeared in what practically constitutes a transcription of the Mosher edition, published by F. M. Buckles & Co., New York, in two volumes.

Wilde, himself, never added any one of his later poems to his original book of *Poems* (1881); and no edition revised by Wilde was issued after 1882. The limited Edition de Luxe, which was sold with the imprint of Elkin Mathews & John Lane in 1892, was no more than the remnant of David Bogue's last 1882 edition, with a special title-page by Charles Ricketts and a new cover, designed by him.

(2) These were the love letters which Keats wrote to his fiancée, Fanny Brawne, from July 1, 1819, to some time early in August, 1820. Thirty-seven of them were published as *Letters of John Keats to Fanny Brawne*, with Notes by Harry Buxton Forman. London, 1878. Mr. Forman included them with two letters acquired later (Letters III and XXXVI), in his four volume edition of *The Poetical Works and Other Writings of John Keats*, 1883, Vol. IV, page 125–189; and more recently in *The Letters of John Keats*, 1895. Mr. Forman seems to think it necessary to justify his publication of these letters, for in his Preface to the last mentioned edition, page xvi, he writes: "I still think Keats' letters without those to Fanny Brawne very much like *Hamlet* without the Prince of Denmark. When I

206 DECORATIVE ART IN AMERICA

made up my mind, after weighing the whole matter carefully, to publish those letters in 1878, I was fully alive to the risk of vituperation, and not particularly solicitous on that branch of the subject. [!] . . . The press turned out to be about equally divided on it. . . . Above all, the letters are irrevocably with us." Perhaps Mr. Forman made the above statement to fortify himself in the face of the implied criticism, contained in Sidney Colvin's Preface to *Keats* in the "English Men of Letters" Series, 1887: "A biographer cannot ignore these letters now that they are published; but their publication must be regretted by all who hold that human respect and delicacy are due to the dead no less than to the living, and to genius no less than obscurity."—Remark on *Letters of J. K. to F. B.* in Preface, page vi.

Mr. Colvin omitted the letters from his own edition of the *Letters of John Keats,* published in 1891. Fanny Brawne died in 1865 as Mrs. Lindon.

(³) The letters were sold under the hammer at the rooms of Messrs. Sotheby on Monday, March 2, 1885. The following is a sample of England's commentary on the sale: "The love letters of Keats are naturally somewhat monotonous in their sweet song of gushing affection to the young lady. . . . The sale was but thinly attended, but the prices obtained for the collection of Keats' letters were high throughout, not one selling for less than £8 15s., the average being above £15, several bringing £20, and the last two of the collection £34 and £39. In this last of three closely written 8vo. pages, he says: 'The last two years taste like brass upon my palate. . . . Hamlet's heart was full of such misery as mine is, when he said to Ophelia, "Go to a nunnery, go, go !"' [Letter XXXIX, the last, which Forman dates Kentish Town, August, 1820, beginning page 501 of the 1895 edition of *The Letters.*] The total realized on these love letters of Keats amounted to £544."—*London Times,* March 4, 1885. See also *New York Times,* Sunday, March 22, 1885, page 4, cl. 4.

(⁴) "And they crucified him, and parted his garments, casting lots."—*St. Matthew,* xxvii, 35. "Then the soldiers, when they had crucified Jesus, took his garments, and made four parts, to every soldier a part; and also *his* coat: now the coat was withou seam, woven from the top throughout. They said therefore among

NOTES 207

themselves, Let us not rend it, but cast lots for it, whose it shall be."—*St. John*, xix, 23–4.

Wildes selection of the word *dice* in the place of *lots* illustrates the poet's fine word sense. Cf. Note 9.

Page 57

(5) This essay was printed in *The Irish Monthly ; A Magazine of General Literature*, Dublin, Fifth Yearly Volume, July, 1877, page 476. It was written, it would seem, early in the spring of 1877, as we know Wilde to have been in Italy in March of that year (see *London Models*, Note 2, page 241). Wilde sent a number of poems to *The Irish Monthly*, this being, however, his only contribution in prose. In fact, with the exception of *The Grosvenor Gallery*, a critique which appeared in *The Dublin University Magazine* for the same month, no other prose of his appeared in book or periodical until *L'Envoi to Rose Leaf and Apple Leaf* (see Note 30, page 179). *The Lecture on the English Renaissance*, it should be remembered, was an unauthorized version (see Note 2, page 181 fol.). One bit of art criticism appeared in *Saunders' Irish Daily News*, May 5, 1879.

Remark. This essay has been taken out of the chronological order adhered to for the balance of the essays, letters, etc., comprising this volume, for the purpose of placing in juxtaposition Wilde's two references to Keats, and more especially to contrast his style and point of view at two different periods of his career: that of the lyric poet, which covered his earlier years up to 1881, and that of the art critic from 1885 to 1891. The years 1881-1885 formed a transition period, devoted largely to proposed reform in dress and handicraft, and an active campaign for the establishment of industrial art schools and the cultivation of taste in house-furnishing, coincident with the Morris movement.

(6) Via Ostiensis is the old Roman road to Ostia, which at the time of the Republic and early Empire was a flourishing city and the harbour of Rome. Porta San Paolo, the ancient Porta Ostiensis, was one of the fifteen Gates in the Aurelian Walls, and is immediately east of the Pyramid of Cestius.

(7) The Pyramid of Cestius, originally on the Via Ostiensis, but enclosed by Aurelian within the city walls, is the tomb of Caius

208   DECORATIVE ART IN AMERICA

Cestius Epulo, who is known to have died before B.C. 12. The pyramid is 116 feet high and composed of concrete, overlaid with slabs of marble.

(8) Modern Rome has nine obelisks of varying size at the following locations: (1) Piazza del Popolo; (2) The Pincio; (3) Piazza della Trinità; (4) Piazza del Quirinale; (5) Piazza dell' Esquilino; (6) Piazza Colonna—84 ft. high; (7) Piazza della Minerva—very small; (8) Piazza di San Giovanni in Laterano—105 ft. high; (9) Piazza di San Pietro.

(9) "And the Lord went before them by day in a pillar of a cloud, to lead them the way; and by night in a pillar of fire, to give them light."—*Exodus*, xii, 21. Wilde frequently reverts to this metaphor, as in *English Poetesses*, page 74: " Sappho, who, to the antique world, was a pillar of flame." Quite characteristic is his substitution of *flame* for *fire*, as being more enphonious and hence, according to his theory, not only justifiable but correct. Cf. Note 4.

Page 58

(10) This is the old burying-ground, no longer in use. From the outer edge of the moat may be seen the grave of Keats. In what is now the New Protestant cemetery, was placed the heart [!] of Shelley (see Note 22, page 212 fol.); and John Addington Symonds was buried there in 1893. The old cemetery is sadly in need of repairs; walls have been torn down, and its general condition is deplorable (see Note 16, page 210). Next to the grave of Keats is that of his ever faithful friend Joseph Severn, in whose arms he expired. It was through Severn that the present tombstone with the lyre was placed over Keats, and in 1882 Severn's own body was reinterred in the present plot of ground, over which was set a mate to the stone over the poet's grave. Some idea of the general appearance of the cemetery and graves may be obtained by referring to the illustrations in *The Graves of Keats and Severn*. *The Century Magazine*, No. 4, February, 1884, Vol. XXVII, page 603, and *Keats in Hampstead, ibid.*, No. 6, October, 1895, Vol. L, page 898. See also " The Burial-place of Keats," etched by Arthur Evershed from a drawing by Samuel Palmer, a rather crude etching which appears

NOTES

209

at page 106, Vol. I, of H. Buxton Forman's edition of *The Poetical Works and Other Writings of John Keats*, 1883.

([11]) "February 14, [1821]: Among the many things he has requested of me to-night, this is the principal, that on his grave shall be this:

'Here lies one whose name was writ in water.' "

—*Joseph Severn's Account of the Last Days of Keats.*

See H. Buxton Forman's 1883 edition of Keats' Works, Vol. IV, page 212.

([12]) Cf.

"Men's evil manners live in brass; their virtues
We write in water."

—*King Henry VIII*, Act IV, Scene 2.

"All your better deeds
Shall be in water writ, but this in marble."

—*Philaster*, Act V, Scene 3.
Beaumont and Fletcher.

On these lines Shelley began the following lovely sonnet:

Fragment On Keats,
Who Desired That On His Tomb Should Be Inscribed:—

"'Here lieth One whose name was writ on water.'
But ere the breath that could erase it blew,
Death, in remorse for that fell slaughter,
Death, the immortalizing winter, flew
Athwart the stream,—and time's printless torrent grew
A scroll of crystal, blazoning the name
Of Adonais.''—

In *The Century Magazine*, February, 1906, page 611, are some more exquisite verses on this theme, *The Name Writ in Water (Piazza di Spagna, Rome)*, by Robert Underwood Johnson. It is the "Spirit of the Fountain" which speaks, and the Spirit's last words are:

"Little he knew 'twixt his dreaming and sleeping,
The while his sick fancy despaired of his fame,
What glory I held in my loverly keeping:
Listen! my waters still whisper his name."

([13]) "Keats was buried in the Protestant cemetery at Rome, one of the most beautiful spots, etc. (as quoted by Wilde). In one of those mental voyages into the past, which often precede death, Keats

210   DECORATIVE ART IN AMERICA

told Severn that 'he thought the intensest pleasure, etc.' (as quoted by Wilde) : . . . and another time, after lying a while, still and peaceful, he said, ' I feel the flowers growing over me.' And there they do grow, even all the winter long—violets and daisies mingling with the fresh herbage, and, in the words of Shelley ' making one in love with death, to think that one should be buried in so sweet a place.' "—*Life and Letters of John Keats*, by Lord Houghton, 1848. Wilde seems to have borrowed a little too freely, if anything, from Lord Houghton's account. Wilde's paragraph is to all intents and purposes a paraphrase of the above extract. See the two following notes.

Page 59

(14) The following is what Shelley actually did write in his Preface to *Adonais*: "It might make one in love with death, to think that one should be buried in so sweet a place."

(15) In a letter which Keats wrote to his friend, James Rice, on February 16, 1820, he expresses this same love for flowers, which he dwelt on so often during his last days: " How astonishingly does the chance of leaving the world impress a sense of its natural beauties on me! . . . I muse with the greatest affection on every flower I have known from my infancy—their shapes and colours are as new to me as if I had just created them with a superhuman fancy. It is because they are connected with the most thoughtless and the happiest moments of our lives."

(16) It is welcome news to every lover of poetry as well as to every admirer of Keats, that a movement long on foot to establish a Keats-Shelley Memorial in Rome promises to have a successful issue. Though it does not have in view a monument of the type conceived by Wilde, it has an object which is much finer and more praiseworthy, in that it concerns the purchase of the house in which Keats breathed his last, in order that it may become the welcome Mecca of all students of the Poet. Now that the greathearted of America and England are joining in this Memorial, which has the approval and support of the Kings of England and of Italy, President Roosevelt and Sir Rennell Rodd, there is every reason to believe that not only will the house on Piazza di Spagna be saved to us for all time, but that the lovely cemetery which holds

NOTES

211

the grave of Adonais, will be spared further indignities and restored to a state of beauty worthy of the several great men who have made its name immortal.

([17]) In 1875, a committee of Englishmen and Americans, headed by Sir Vincent Eyre, provided for the repair of the tombstone, and placed on an adjacent wall a medallion portrait of the poet, presented by its sculptor, Mr. Warrington Wood. The lines of poetry are an acrostic written by the head of the committee.

([18]) The lady in question was Mrs. Procter, to whose description Wilde refers in *Keats' Sonnet on Blue*, page 69. Lord Houghton quotes her in his *Life, Letters and Literary Remains of John Keats*. See Note 18, page 225.

Page 60

([19]) The Sphinx seems to have cast a spell over Wilde, perhaps a baleful one; for there is the ring of truth in his cry in *The Sphinx*, his one curiously repulsive poem:

"Get hence, you loathsome mystery! Hideous animal, get hence!
You wake in me each bestial sense, you make me what I would not be."

At any rate, he continually used the word in simile and in description, both to lend colour to his language and suggestiveness to his subject. We have his long poem, just alluded to, written in Paris as early as 1883, and finally published in 1894, with strange Egyptic illustrations from the hand of Ricketts. Here, in the sixth verse, we have apparently the key of his theme:

"Come forth you exquisite grotesque! half woman and half animal!"

In *The Happy Prince* (1888), page 18, the word is used for its suggestion of Eastern mystery: "He told him of the Sphinx, who is as old as the world itself, and lives in the desert, and knows everything."

In *The Grave of Shelley* (1877 and 1881), in connection with the pyramid (of Cestius), the allusion has the same object:

"Surely some Old-World Sphinx lurks darkly hid
Grim warder of this pleasaunce of the dead."

In *A Woman of No Importance* (1894), as a figure of speech: "Women as a sex are Sphinxes without secrets."

212   DECORATIVE ART IN AMERICA

Practically the same epigram had seen service in his story, *Lady Alroy*. *The World* (London), May 25th, 1887, and so great was its fascination for him, that he elevated it to the dignity of title for the same story, since it was included as *The Sphinx Without a Secret*, in *Lord Arthur Savile's Crime and Other Stories* (1891). The titles of the other three tales were not altered.

Again in *The Decay of Lying* (1889), the word appears as: "The solid, stolid British intellect lies in the desert sands like the Sphinx in Flaubert's marvelous tale."

In 1896, from Reading Gaol in a letter to Robert Ross: "The 'gilded sphinx' is, I suppose, as wonderful as ever."

And three years later, in 1899, he inscribed the following sentiment in a presentation copy of *The Importance of Being Earnest:* "To the wonderful Sphinx: to whose presence on the first night the success of this comedy was entirely due," etc.

Furthermore, improbable as it may seem, Wilde appears not only to allude to the Sphinx when he mentions Egypt, but to mention Egypt only that he may allude to the Sphinx.

(20) Monte Testaccio is an isolated mound some one hundred and fifteen feet high and about a thousand paces in circumference, which rises above the Tiber. It was formed of broken pottery, large earthen jars (testæ), brought principally from Spain and Africa.

(21) This simile seems to have lingered in his mind, as it occurs again in a sonnet written at about the same period:

> "Like burnt-out torches by a sick man's bed
> Gaunt cypress-trees stand around the sun-bleached stone."
> — *The Grave of Shelley.*

And a number of years later it recurs in the following: "The cypress-trees were like burnt-out torches."—*The Fisherman and His Soul.* 1891.

Certain similar catch-phrases, couplets, etc., were thus employed by Wilde a number of times, in the same manner that Shelley made use at least three times of the "phenomenon" which he notes at the end of the third stanza of his *Ode to the West Wind*. See also Notes 24 and 29, pages 214 and 217; and *Phrases* in Index.

(22) Shelley was drowned in the Gulf of Spezia, in July, 1822.

NOTES

213

Several days after the recovery of his body, it was cremated in the presence of Byron, Leigh Hunt and Trelawny. "What surprised us all was that the heart remained entire. In snatching this relic away from the fiery furnace, my hand was severely burnt."— Trelawny's *Recollections of Sheelly*.

"Shelley's heart was given to Hunt, who subsequently, not without reluctance and unseemly dispute, resigned it to Mrs. Shelley. It is now at Boscombe. His ashes were carried by Trelawny to Rome and buried in the Protestant cemetery."—*Shelley* by John Addington Symonds in "English Men of Letters," page 181.

Trelawny's inscription on the tombstone reads as follows:

> "Percy Bysshe Shelley
> Cor cordium
> Natus, etc. . . . "

An illustration of Shelley's grave may be found in the etching by W. B. Scott, which appears as frontispiece to Vol. II of *Poetical Works of Percy Bysshe Shelley*, etc., edited by H. Buxton Forman, 1886. The apparently general belief that it is Shelley's actual heart which is buried in Rome, and the statement made by J. A. Symonds and other authorities that the heart is in England and the ashes in Rome, are difficult to reconcile.

It is unfortunate that the great cannot write their own death notices. Their friends always disagree. For instance, the several accounts, which have been written of the last hours, the funeral, etc., of Oscar Wilde, differ in almost every important detail.

(23) The "St. Sebastian" of Guido Reni is in Room VI of Palazzo Brignole Sale, also called Palazzo Rosso, No. 18, Strada Nuova.

It should be recalled that St. Sebastian was one of Wilde's favorite characters, and that he, himself, borrowed the name of Sebastian as the first part of the *nom de plume* which he adopted after his release from Reading Gaol. He not only appears to have delighted in the sound of the name, and the martyrdom which it connotes, but shows by the following lines that he found in the convict's dress certain features suggestive of this saint:

> "Like ape or clown, in monstrous garb
> With crooked arrows starred."

— The Ballad of Reading Gaol, Canto IV, Verse 7.

214   DECORATIVE ART IN AMERICA

From the arrow-starred victim of Individualism rampant to the martyred saint was but a short step for the lover of curious paradox. The Rev. Charles Robert Maturin (1782 – 1824), that eccentric novelist, dramatist and display-loving *poseur* whom Wilde calls his grand-uncle, and whom he resembled in more ways than one, wrote in 1820 his masterpiece, *Melmoth the Wanderer*. This book greatly interested Wilde—in fact it has been suggested that the anonymous introduction to the edition of 1892 might be traced to his pen. The book was certainly recalled to him during his imprisonment, as in a letter to Ross at that period he mentions his interest 'in seeing how his grand-uncle's *Melmoth* and his mother's *Sidonia* had been two of the books that fascinated Rossetti's youth!'

Sebastian Melmoth: the martyr and the wanderer! Here perhaps is found Wilde's honest opinion of himself!

Remark. M. Henry-D. Davray, the translator into French of *De Profundis*, has recently stated as a fact the conclusions that are deduced from the theory given above. Whether M. Davray received his information direct from Wilde or from some friend of Wilde, or has been led to this belief through a similar process of deduction, remains for him to state.

(24) This group of words or the idea which it conveys, was used again in several different combinations. It is found in his sonnet, *Wasted Days (From a Picture Painted by Miss V. T.)*. Kottabos, Vol. III, Michaelmas Term, 1877, beginning:

> " A fair slim boy not made for this world's pain,
> With hair of gold thick clustering round his ears,"

and in a later version of the same, greatly altered as *Madonna Mia* (in all editions of *Poems*):

> " A Lily-Girl, not made for this world's pain,
> With brown, soft hair close braided by her ears,"

and again in *London Models*, 1889: " He is often quite charming with his large melancholy eyes, his crisp hair, and his slim brown figure." (See page 95.)

(25) A recent number of *The Century Magazine* (No. 4, February, 1906, Vol. LXXI, page 535), contains a very interesting illustrated article by the late William Sharp, entitled *The Portraits of*

NOTES

215

Keats, With Special Reference to Those by Severn. In this article are included the original miniature by Joseph Severn, the George Keats replica, the Haydon sketch and life-mask, the Hilton oil painting, the Girometti medallion, several of the better known sketches and paintings by Severn, together with interesting allusions to the many replicas genuine and unauthentic. Refer also to *Keats in Hampstead. The Century*, No. 6, October, 1895, Vol. L, page 898, which illustrates a bust of Keats by Anne Whitney, placed in the Parish Church of St. John's, Hampstead, in 1894. See *Note on the Portraits of Keats*, Vol. I, page xxxiii, of H. Buxton Forman's 1883 edition of Keats' works. In this note and throughout the four volumes, are given illustrations of the more famous portraits. A chalk drawing by William Hilton, R.A., not included in *The Century*, is of interest. A beautiful reproduction of a portrait by Severn, done from all appearances in chalk, serves as frontispiece to *Odes, Sonnets & Lyrics of John Keats*, published in a very limited edition by the Daniel Press, Oxford. The publisher remarks that the drawing is in the possession of Mrs. Furneaux, and "has never until now been copied." This portrait does not seem to be generally known and deserves attention as a very lovely picture, even if it may not be the "trustworthy likeness" which Mr. Daniel claims. It is certainly as close a resemblance as the painful caricature which disfigures the Cambridge Edition of the poet's works. See Note 21, page 226, for a special reference to Joseph Severn.

(26) The Haydon pen and ink sketch is the one which B. R. Haydon made in his MS. Journal for November, 1816, shortly after his meeting with Keats. This is generally conceded to be the first portrait of Keats which has been left to us. "This fine profile head was a sketch for the portrait of Keats introduced by Haydon into his large picture of 'Christ's Entry into Jerusalem,' now in St. Peter's Cathedral at Cincinnati."—*The Portraits of Keats*, by William Sharp. See preceding Note, 25.

(27) This is a bust by the American, Fuller, forming part of a monument erected in memory of the Rajah of Koolapoor (Kolapoor, Kohlapore), who died in Florence in 1870. The monument is in the Cascine, the park of Florence, some two miles from its entrance.

216 DECORATIVE ART IN AMERICA

Page 61

(28) After considerable revision in the sestet, this sonnet was republished as *The Grave of Keats* in *The Burlington*, No. 1, January, 1881, page 35. It was included in *Poems*, 1881 (July) and all later editions; and was reprinted in *The Best of Oscar Wilde*, collected by Oscar Herrmann (New York); *Every Day in the Year*, edited by Jas. L. and Mary K. Ford (New York); *Golden Gleams of Thought*, edited by Rev. S. P. Linn (Chicago); with an extract in *The Poets' Praise*, collected by Estelle D. Adams (London). Wilde was the most painstaking of poets despite his affected carelessness and indifference. His scholarship is clearly proven by the neatly annotated copies of *Herodotus, Sallust, Cicero*, etc., used by him at Oxford. Hardly one of his poems which appeared in *The Irish Monthly, Kottabos, The World, Time*, etc., was republished in the collected edition, without some change. The fifth edition of *Poems* shows differences of text, which seem hardly important enough to have warranted alteration, in some twenty separate instances. This habit of careful revision never left him; for all the plays were revised for publication; the second edition of *The Ballad of Reading Gaol* shows by collation some ten new readings; and later editions show three further variants of the second. As an illustration of this point, may be told an anecdote recounted by Mr. Sherard in *Oscar Wilde. The Story of an Unhappy Friendship:* During Wilde's trip in America, he had occasion to tell his "host one evening that he had spent the day in hard literary work, and when asked what he had done, he had said: 'I was working on the proof of one of my poems all the morning, and took out a comma.' 'And in the afternoon?' 'In the afternoon—well, I put it back again.'"

To show the development of this sonnet to its final form it is now given in full as

THE GRAVE OF KEATS.

Rid of the world's injustice, and *his* pain,
He rests at last beneath God's veil of blue:
Taken from life *when* life and love were new
The youngest of the martyrs here is lain,
Fair as Sebastian, and as *early* slain.

NOTES

217

> No cypress shades his grave, *no* funeral yew,
> But *gentle* violets *weeping* with *the* dew
> *Weave on his bones an ever-blossoming chain.*
> O proudest heart that broke for misery!
> O *sweetest lips since those of Mitylene!*
> O *poet-painter of our* English Land!
> Thy name was writ in water—*it shall stand:*
> *And* tears *like mine will* keep thy memory green,
> *As Isabella did her* Basil-tree.

The changes in the text are indicated in italics.

([29]) The larger part of this line and the whole of the third line were used afterwards in *Ravenna*, III, ll. 7 – 8:

> " Taken from life while life and love were new,
> He lies beneath God's seamless veil of blue."

Ravenna was the Newdigate Prize Poem in heroic couplets, which Wilde recited in the Theatre at Oxford, June 26, 1878. It was published subsequently by Thomas Shrimpton and Son, Broad Street, Oxford, 1878. See *Notes for "London Models,"* Note 2, page 241.

([30]) The allusion is obviously to Keats' *Isabella; or, The Pot of Basil. A Story from Boccaccio.* Stanza LII, ll. 7 – 8:

> " and o'er it set
> Sweet Basil, which her tears kept ever wet."

This incident in the words of John Payne's translation from Boccaccio's *Story of Isabella* (Il Decamerone, Giornata IV, Novella 5) runs as follows: " She had not dug long before she came upon her unhappy lover's body . . . ; she would fain, an she but might, have borne away the whole body, to give it fitter burial; but seeing that this might not be, she with a knife cut off the head, as best she could. . . . Then, taking a great and goodly pot, of those wherein they plant marjoram or sweet basil, she laid therein the head, folded in a fair linen cloth, and covered it up with earth, in which she planted sundry heads of right fair basil of Salerno; nor did she ever water these with other water than that of her tears. . . . She would bend over it and fall to weeping so sore and so long, that her tears bathed the basil, which, by dint of such long and assiduous tending, . . . grew passing fair and sweet of savour."

NOTES FOR "KEATS' SONNET ON BLUE"

Page 65

(1) This article was contributed to *The Century Guild Hobby Horse*, No. 3, July, 1886, Volume I, page (81) 83. This quarterly was a magazine *de luxe* (12½" x 9½"), which was published at the Chiswick Press from January, 1886, through October, 1892 — twenty-eight beautiful numbers in all. In April, 1884, a single number (11" x 9"), with the same title and woodcut for the cover, was published under the imprint of G. Allen. This first issue, however, was quickly withdrawn by the publisher, so that few copies of it are in circulation.

(2) Wilde's Western tour brought him to Louisville some time in February, 1882, probably at a date between the 15th and the 23rd.

(3) Mrs. Philip Speed (Emma Keats) died in the month of September, 1883. "It may be added that the mask [Haydon's life-mask] of Keats bears a striking resemblance to one of Keats' relatives now living in America, and that it especially recalls the features of his niece, Mrs. Emma Keats Speed, of Louisville, Kentucky."—Statement by the Editor. *The Century*, No. 4, February, Volume XXVII, 1884, page 603.

(4) George Keats (1797–1842), the brother of the poet, immigrated to America in the spring of 1818, shortly after his marriage to Georgiana Augusta Wylie. He went ostensibly to better his fortunes, with the hope of assisting his brother financially. He has had many detractors, however, who censured him for his money dealings with the poet. Charles Brown was especially bitter in his denunciations of him and was prevented by him from carrying out his proposed biography of Keats. George visited his brother in England during the winter of 1819–20.

After having tried his hand at several trades, he went into the lumber business and died a wealthy man and one of the best known citizens of Louisville. "George Keats not only loved his brother

220 DECORATIVE ART IN AMERICA

John but reverenced his genius and enjoyed his poetry, believing him to belong to the front rank of English bards."—*Memoir of George Keats*, by J. F. C. (The Rev. James Freeman Clark), *The Dial*, April, 1843.

(5) Mr. John Gilmer Speed, son of the lady whom Wilde met, edited *The Letters and Poems of John Keats*, in 3 vols., New York, 1883.

(6) Wilde seems to have made some error here, unless it be possible that such an annotated edition of Dante has escaped the notice of the many editors of Keats' work. Wilde probably had in mind the copy of *Milton* in which Keats wrote his comments on *Paradise Lost*. Part of these appeared in *The Dial*, April, 1843. See also *The Athenæum*, October 26, 1872, and *Notes on Milton's "Paradise Lost,"* page 256, Vol. III of H. Buxton Forman's Glasgow edition of Keats' works, 1901. Keats was, however, an ardent admirer of Dante, to whom he was introduced in Cary's translation. In a copy of this he wrote his sonnet *On a Dream*.

Page 66

(7) A facsimile of the manuscript preceded Wilde's essay, page 81. It does not appear to be a very good reproduction, though it is conceivable that the ink of the original had faded (Wilde speaks of "faded scraps of paper," etc.), making it difficult of reproduction. Mr. H. Buxton Forman, the authority on Keats, refers to it in the following terms in *Poetry and Prose by John Keats. A Book of Fresh Verses and New Readings, etc.*, London, 1890, page 25:

"A manuscript of the Sonnet on blue, written in answer to one of Reynolds' on dark eyes, found its way to America; and a so-called facsimile of it, now shorn of its first line, appeared in *The Century Guild Hobby Horse* for July, 1886. Line 6 and those following seem to have exercised the poet a good deal. Mr. Horwood's variation is not shown by this copy; but, as far as *The Hobby Horse* reproduction is legible, the intentions seem to have been as follows:"

Since Mr. Forman's transcription does not appear to embrace all the variants which occur in this version, and a single capital be-

NOTES

comes of interest, when collation extends to such minutiæ, a more detailed transcript of the thirteen lines in the facsimile is given below:

Ll. 1 . . . . [Torn from MS.] . . . .
2. Of Cynthia, the Wide Palace of the sun
3. The tent of Hesperus and all his train
4. The Bosomer of Clouds gold, grey and dun
5. Blue 't is the Life of Waters — Ocean

                         Waterfalls   ⎫
      his   Pools numberless   ⎬
6. And all vassal Streams ; *Lakes, Pools and Seas* ⎭
        Λ

⎰ 7. *And Waterfalls and Fountains never ran*
⎱   *well'd*
     8. *Or flow'd or slep't but still*

7. May rage and foam and fret but never can
8. Subside but to a dark blue Nativeness
9. Blue! gentle Cousin to the forest green
10. Married to green in all the sweetest flowers
     th Forget me not
11. *The Violet* the Bluebell and that Queen
         Λ

     Secrecy
12. Of *Hiddenness* the Violet. What strange powers
                 But how great ⎱
13. Hast thou as a mere Shadow? *then how high* ⎰
   When   an
14. *Trembling* in eye thou art alive with fate —
       Λ

Note. The carets occur where shown; the italicized words are crossed in the MS., but appear in the same relative position.

(8) Lord Houghton (1809–85), Richard Monckton Milnes, traveller, philanthropist, unrivalled after-dinner speaker, poet and Mæcenas of poets. He obtained the laureateship for Tennyson and was among the first to recognize Mr. Swinburne. Among his works are *Poems, Legendary and Historical* (1844); *Palm Leaves* (1844); and most important of all *The Life, Letters and Literary Remains of John Keats* (1848), 2 vols.

(9) Charles Armitage Brown (1786–*c.*1842), a retired merchant, when he met Keats at Hampstead. He accompanied the poet on his "tour to the Hebrides," July–August, 1818, and took him into his home after the death of Keats' brother in December, 1818. He was the poet's warm friend and adviser, and after his

222 DECORATIVE ART IN AMERICA

death went to Italy, where he became acquainted with Trelawny and Landor. At the villa of the latter, he met Lord Houghton and when finally he decided to give up his idea of a biography of Keats and to emigrate to New Zealand, he placed in Lord Houghton's hands all the material he had collected for this purpose. The so-called Houghton MSS. from which was compiled *The Life, Letters*, etc., consist of Brown's manuscript memoir, transcripts made by him of a few of Keats' poems, reminiscences by Charles Cowden Clarke, Henry Stephens, Joseph Severn and other intimates of Keats, as well as letters from the above.

Page 67

(10) This sonnet appears, Vol. II, page 295 of *The Life, Letters and Literary Remains of John Keats*, by Lord Houghton (1848).

(11) The sestet of Reynolds' sonnet reads as follows:

> "The golden clusters of enamouring hair
> Glow 'd in poetic pictures sweetly well;—
> Why should not tresses dusk, that are so fair
> On the live brow, have an eternal spell
> In poesy?—dark eyes are dearer far
> Than orbs that mock the hyacinthine-bell."

(12) John Hamilton Reynolds (1796–1852), poet and friend of Keats. Author of *Safie, an Eastern Tale* (1814); *The Eden of Imagination* (1814); *The Naiad* (1816). In the first and last of these he shows the influence of Byron; in the second that of Leigh Hunt, through whom it is probable that he met Keats. Before the completion of *Endymion*, Keats projected a series of metrical versions of Boccaccio's tales with Reynolds, his own contribution to be *Isabella*, and Reynolds', *The Garden of Florence*. The last was eventually published together with *The Ladye of Provence* in 1821, over the pseudonym "John Hamilton." In the meantime Reynolds had produced in 1819 a farce entitled *One, Two, Three, Four, Five*, and parodies of Wordsworth, entitled *Peter Bell*. Keats' letters to Reynolds are noteworthy as being among his most unreserved and interesting. (See also Note 14.)

(13) "Woodhouse's transcript of the sonnet corresponds verbally with the text of this edition [the residuum of Wilde's facsimile]:

NOTES 223

he gives the date as the 8th of Febrnary, 1818."—*Poetry and Prose by John Keats.* Edited by H. Buxton Forman, 1890, page 26.

"The Woodhouse MSS. consist of a commonplace book in which Richard Woodhouse, the friend of Keats, transcribed about mid-summer, 1819, the chief part of Keats' poems at that date unpublished. The transcripts are in many cases made from early drafts of the poems."—Preface to *Keats* by Sidney Colvin, page vii.

(14) See *A Sonnet by Keats,* in *The Athenæum,* No. 2536, June 3, 1876, page 764. Mr. Horwood's article is sufficiently interesting to warrant a full quotation, and though the verbal changes in the sonnet are all pointed out by Wilde, it is given in full, to illus-trate the curious variations in punctuation and capitalization, which characterize the several versions of many of Keats' poems.

"In 1821, John Hamilton Reynolds, the friend of Keats, pub-lished a volume of poems with the title, *'The Garden of Florence and other Poems,* by John Hamilton.' At pages 124 and 126 are two sonnets on Sherwood Forest; and a manuscript note in my copy says, that 'It was in answer to these two sonnets that Keats sent the anthor the lines on Robin Hood, which are published with his *Lamia,* etc.' At page 128 is a sonnet ending with an expression of preference of dark eyes to blue eyes. Appended to this is a manu-script addition (made evidently not long after the volume was printed), of which the following is a copy: 'Keats, npon reading the above sonnet, immediately expressed his own preference for blue eyes in the following lines:

'[Ll.] 1. Blue! 't is the hue of heaven—the domain
2. Of Cynthia,—'the bright palace of the sun,
3. The tent of Hesperus and all his train,
4. The bosomer of clouds, gold, grey, and dun.

5. Blue! 't is the life of waters:—Ocean,
6. With all his tributary streams, pools numherless,
7. May rage and foam and fret; but never can
8. Subside, if not to dark blue nativeness.

9. Blue! gentle cousin to the forest green;
10. Married to green in all the sweetest flowers,—
11. Forget-me-not; the Blue-bell; and that Queen
12. Of secrecy, the Violet.—What strange powers

13. Hast thou, as a mere shadow:—but how great
14. When in an eye thou art, alive with fate!'

224   DECORATIVE ART IN AMERICA

I do not find this sonnet in any of several editions of Keats' poems which I have, nor is it mentioned in Lord Houghton's *Life of Keats*.

A. J. Horwood."

Mr. Horwood no doubt had the revised edition of Lord Houghton's *Life of Keats* published in 1867.

Page 68

(15) "These strike me as decidedly genuine variations, but indicative of an earlier state of the poem than that adopted in the text." — *The Poetical Works*, etc., *of John Keats*. Edited by H. Buxton Forman, 1883. Vol. II, pages 257-8.

(16) Mr. Forman makes further comment (see Note 7, page 220) on this subject in *The Complete Works of John Keats*, Glasgow, 1901, Vol. II, pages 198-9, and offers the following objection: "The scholiast of the *Hobby Horse* 'fac-simile' demurred to my acceptance of *The Athenæum* variant of line 6 as genuine, on the ground that we 'have before us Keats' [*sic*] first draft of the sonnet,' and that, 'having got his line right in his first draft, Keats probably did not spoil it in his second.' This reasoning assumes the *Hobby Horse* draft to be the first and ignores the probability that, as in other cases, there were scrappy pencillings, any of which might have passed into another version written out at a different time."

(17) "The punctuation of *The Athenæum* version is characteristic of Keats, and I have adopted it in part." — *The Poetical Works*, etc., 1883. Edited by H. Buxton Forman, Vol. II, page 258. On the preceding page is the sonnet, the title reading:

SONNET.

Written in answer to a Sonnet ending thus:—

Dark eyes are dearer far
Than those that mock the hyacinthine bell.
By J. H. Reynolds.

In collating Mr. Forman's version with those of Lord Houghton (1) and *The Athenæum* (2), the following variations are disclosed:

NOTES

225

Ll. 1-4 follow the text and punctuation of (1), adding a comma after "Hesperus," l. 3.

L. 5 follows the text and punctuation of (2), but begins "'t is" with a capital.

" 6 follows the text of (1) and punctuation of (2).

" 7 " ' " and punctuation of (1).

" 8 " " " " " " " (2).

" 9 reads: "Blue! Gentle cousin of the forest-green."

" 10 follows the text and punctuation of (2).

" 11 " " ·· of (2) and punctuation of (1), but omits hyphen in Blue-bell.

" 12 follows the text and punctuation of (1), but begins "violet" with a capital.

" 13 follows the text and punctuation of (1).

" 14 follows the text of (1) and punctuation of (2).

The current Cambridge Edition of Keats, edited by Horace E. Skidder and published by Houghton, Mifflin & Co., has this sonnet on page 43, and seems to borrow its punctuation and capitalization from both the Houghton and Forman texts, thereby forming another variant—*et sic ad inf.*

Page 69

(18) "At page 100, Vol. I, of his first *Life of Keats*, Lord Houghton has quoted a literary portrait which he received from a lady [Mrs. Procter. See Note 18, page 211] who used to see him at Hazlitt's lectures at the Surrey Institution [probably during 1817-1818] . . . 'His eyes were large and *blue*, and his hair *auburn*.' . . . Reader, alter in your copy of the *Life of Keats*, Vol. I, page 103, 'eyes' light hazel, 'hair' lightish brown and wavy."—*Recollections of Charles Cowden Clarke.*

Yet only a few pages before, Clarke writes: "John was the only one resembling him (his father) in person and feature, with brown hair and dark hazel eyes."

"The eyes mellow and glowing; large, dark and sensitive."—*Lord Byron and Some of his Contemporaries*, etc., by Leigh Hunt, 1828.

"At one of our visits, Mr. Severn maintained that Keats' eyes were

226 DECORATIVE ART IN AMERICA

hazel." *The Graves of Keats and Severn.* Editor of *The Century*, No. 4, February, 1884, Vol. XXVII, page 603.

In this connection, curiously enough a similar confusion exists concerning the colour of Wilde's eyes:

"His eyes are blue, or light grey, and instead of being 'dreamy' are bright and quick."—*Oscar Wilde's Arrival. New-York Daily Tribune,* Jan. 3, 1882, page 5, cl. 4.

"His eyes were of a deep blue, but without that far-away expression which is popularly attributed to them."—*Oscar Wilde's Arrival. The New York World,* Jan. 3, 1882, page 1, cl. 4.

"The eyes were large, dark and ever-changing in expression."—*The Lady's Pictorial.* 1882.

"La pure lumière bleue, un peu enfantine, de son regard."—*Oscar Wilde et son œuvre,* by J.-Joseph Renaud. *La Grande Revue,* 15 Février, 1905, page 401 ; also in his preface to *Intentions.* Paris : P.-V. Stock, 1905.

Lord Alfred Douglas, on the other hand, affirms that Wilde's eyes were green. Therefore, according to his friends and interviewers, his eyes were deep blue, light grey, dark, or green.

(19) Charles Cowden Clarke (1787–1877), warm friend of Keats, co-author of *Recollections* (see following note): also of *Note on the School-House of Keats at Enfield. The St. James's Holiday Annual, 1875.*

> "You first taught me all the sweets of song."
> Keats' *Epistle to Charles Cowden Clarke,* l. 53.

(20) *Recollections of Writers by Charles and Mary Cowden Clarke,* 1878, as reprinted, with slight changes, from *The Gentleman's Magazine,* February, 1874.

(21) Joseph Severn (1793–1879), the ardent and faithful friend of Keats until his death, and faithful to Keats' memory through the remainder of his own long life. It is to Severn that we owe our knowledge of Keats' last days at the house on the Piazza di Spagna —those bitter hours made so real by the painter's sketch of Keats during his last illness (see *Century Magazine,* February, 1906, page 545). If not a great painter, he was a great friend, whose name can no more be disassociated from that of the poet than the tombstone with the palette be removed from the stone with the lyre;

NOTES 227

for in 1882 Severn's body was placed by the side of Keats' in the Protestantcemetery at Rome. See Note 10, page 208 ; Note 11, page 209 ; Note 13, page 210 ; or for special reference to Severn's portraits of Keats, Note 25, page 214.

(22) This is line 5 of the Sonnet, *To My Brother George*, originally published as the first poem under the general title of *Sonnets* in *Poems by John Keats*, London : Printed for C. & J. Ollier, etc., 1817.

NOTES FOR "ENGLISH POETESSES"

Page 73

[1] This essay originally appeared in *Queen, The Lady's Newspaper*, No. 2189, December 8, 1888, Vol. LXXXIV.

[2] Cf. "Mrs. Browning, the first really great poetess of our literature."—*Literary and Other Notes. The Woman's World*, November, 1887, or *Essays, Criticisms and Reviews*, page 115. See also Note 13, page 230.

[3] The New Year hymn no doubt refers to *Old and New Year Ditties*, published in *Goblin Market and Other Poems* (1864). In a letter which Dante Gabriel Rossetti wrote to Hall Caine, he mentioned, however, that "Swinburne thinks *The Advent* perhaps the noblest of all her poems."

[4] Swinburne was an ardent admirer of Christina Rossetti's poetry. To her he addressed *A Ballad of Appeal.* "*To Christina G. Rossetti,*" in *A Midsummer Holiday, and Other Poems* (1884); to her, he dedicated *A Century of Roundels* (1883); and at her death, wrote an elegy entitled, *A New Year's Eve*, printed in the *Nineteenth Century*, February, 1895.

Page 74

[5] Σαπφώ, or, in her own dialect Ψάπφα, was one of the two great leaders of the Æolian school of poetry, of which Alcæus was the other.

[6] Her lyric poems formed nine books, but of these only fragments have come down to us. The longest is a splendid ode to Aphrodite. The fragments are edited by Neue, Berlin (1827), and in Bergk's *Poetæ Lyrici* (1867).

[7] Athos (Haghion Oros, Monte Santo, i. e. Holy Mountain), the mountainous peninsula, also called Acte, which projects from Chal-

230 DECORATIVE ART IN AMERICA

dice in Macedonia. This peninsula has, for a thousand years, been studded with numerous monasteries, cloisters and chapels whence it derives its modern name. In these monasteries some valuable MSS. of ancient authors have been discovered.

Page 75

(8) Sappho was a native of Mitylene or, as some said, of Eresos in Lesbos. See line 10 of *The Grave of Keats*, Note 28, page 217.

(9) *The Cry of the Children* (1843).

(10) *Sonnets from the Portuguese*, first printed as: *Sonnets by E. B. B., Reading. (Not for publication.)* 1847.

Page 76

(11) *Vision of Poets* in *Poems* (1844); *Casa Guidi Windows* (1851); and *Aurora Leigh* (1857).

(12) Casa Guidi was the celebrated home of the Brownings in Florence—the house now marked with a commemorative tablet.

(13) Cf. "Mrs. Browning, the first great English poetess, was also an admirable scholar, though she may not have put the accents on her Greek, and even in those poems that seem most remote from classical life, such as *Aurora Leigh*, for instance, it is not difficult to trace the fine literary influence of classical training."—*Literary and Other Notes. The Woman's World*, January, 1888.

(14) Elizabeth Barrett married Robert Browning in 1846 and shortly afterwards travelled south to Italy by way of Paris, crossing the Alps in the same year.

Page 77

(15) Richard Hengist Horne, the author of *The Death of Marlowe*, to whom she wrote continuously before her marriage. These letters were published under the title of *Letters of E. B. Browning to R. H. Horne.*

Page 78

(16) Cf. "I have worked at poetry; it has not been with me reverie, but art."—*Letters of E. B. Browning to R. H. Horne.*

Page 79

(17) Delphi in Phocis, the seat of the world-renowned temple of Apollo, in the center of which was a chasm, and over this a tripod,

NOTES

231

whereon was seated the priestess Pythia whenever the oracle was to be consulted.

Page 80

(18) I.   Emily Jane Pfeiffer (1827–1890):—*Glan Arlach* (1877); *Sonnets and Songs* (1880); and *Under the Aspens* (1882); etc.

II.   Harriet Eleanor Hamilton-King (1840–   ):—*The Disciples* (1878); *A Book of Dreams* (1882); and *Ballads of the North* (1889).

III.   Augusta Webster (Julia A. J. Davies), (1837–1894):— Psendonym "Cecil Home"; *Dramatic Studies* (1866); *Portraits* (1870), including *The Castaway; The Book of Rhyme* (1881); also dramatic pieces and translations such as *Medea* (1866).

IV.   (Mrs.) Graham R. Tomson (1860–   ):—*The Bird-Bride* (1889); and *Summer Night and Other Poems* (1891). A sympathetic review of the first book with selections from it was included by Wilde in *Some Literary Notes. The Woman's World*, June, 1889.

V.   A. Mary F. Robinson-Darmesteter (1857–   ):—*A Handful of Honeysuckle* (1878); *The Crowned Hippolytus* (1881); *The New Arcadia* (1884); *An Italian Garden* (1886); and *Poems, Ballads and a Garden Play* (1888). "Miss Robinson's poems have always the charm of delicate music and graceful expression," Wilde writes of the last volume, in *A Note on Some Modern Poets. The Woman's World*, December, 1888.

VI.   Jean Ingelow (1820–1897):—*A Rhyming Chronicle of Incidents and Feelings* (1850); *Poems* (1871); (1876); (1885)— three series. "Jean Ingelow, whose sonnet on "A Chess King" is like an exquisitely carved gem," Wilde writes of her in *Literary and Other Notes. The Woman's World*, November, 1887.

VII.   May Kendall (1861–   ):—*Dreams to Sell* (1887) and *Songs from Dreamland* (1894)—all in a humorous vein.

VIII.   Edith Nesbit (Bland), (1858):—*Lays and Legends* (1886); *Leaves of Life* (1888). "There are some wonderfully pretty poems in it, poems full of quick touches of fancy, and of pleasant ripples of rhyme; and here and there a poignant note of passion flashes across the song, as a scarlet thread flashes through the shuttlerace of a loom, giving a new value to the delicate tints, and bringing the scheme of colour to a higher and more perfect key." Such was Wilde's

232 DECORATIVE ART IN AMERICA

criticism of the last volume, reviewed in *Some Literary Notes*. *The Woman's World*, March, 1889.

IX. May Probyn:—*Poems* (1881):—*A Ballad of the Road and Other Poems* (1883); and *Pansies, A Book of Poems* (1895). "A poetess with the true lyrical impulse of song, whose work is as delicate as it is delightful," Wilde writes of her in *Literary and Other Notes*. *The Woman's World*, November, 1887.

X. Mrs. George Lillie Craik (Dinah Maria Mulock), (1826–1887):—*Poems of Thirty Years, New and Old* (1881).

Wilde wrote more specifically of these poems in an article entitled *A Note on Some Modern Poets*, which he contributed to *The Woman's World* (of which he was the editor) for December, 1888. See also the reprint of this in *Essays, Criticisms and Reviews* (1901), pages 32–34.

XI. Mrs. Wilfred Meynell (Alice C. Thompson):—*Preludes* 1875) and *Later Poems* (1901).

XII. Elizabeth Rachel Chapman:—*The New Purgatory and Other Poems* (1887). This book was reviewed by Wilde in *Literary and Other Notes. The Woman's World*, January, 1888: "All of Miss Chapman's poems are worth reading, if not for their absolute beauty at least for their intellectual intention."

Page 81

[19] Cf. "Carlyle's stormy rhetoric."—*Mr. Pater's Last Volume*.

[20] Cf. "Those long sentences of Mr. Pater's come to have the charm of an elaborate piece of music, and the unity of such music also." And later in the same review, "If imaginative prose be really the special art of this century, Mr. Pater must rank amongst our century's most characteristic artists."—*Mr. Pater's Last Volume*. "Even the work of Mr. Pater, who is, on the whole, the most perfect master of English prose now creating amongst us, is often far more like a piece of mosaic than a passage in music."—*The Critic as Artist. Part I.*

[21] Cf. "His style is chaos illumined by flashes of lightning. As a writer he has mastered everything except language," etc.—*The Decay of Lying* and *Literary and Other Notes. The Woman's World*, January, 1888. "One incomparable novelist we have now in England, Mr. George Meredith. There are better artists in France,

NOTES

233

but France has no one whose view of life is so large, so varied, so imaginatively true, etc."— *The Soul of Man Under Socialism.* " Meredith is a prose Browning, and so is Browning."— *The Critic as Artist. Part I.*

(22) Cf. "Mr. Robert Louis Stevenson, that delightful master of delicate and fanciful prose."— *The Decay of Lying.*

(23) Cf. "Ruskin's winged and passionate eloquence."—*Mr. Pater's Last Volume.*

(24) Cf. "Women seem to me to possess just what our literature wants—a light touch, a delicate hand, a graceful mode of treatment and an unstudied felicity of phrase. We want some one who will do for our prose what Mme. de Sévigné did for the prose of France." —*Some Literary Notes. The Woman's World,* January, 1889.

Page 82

(25) Juliana Berners, Bernes, or Barnes (*c.* 1388 – ?):—Is believed to have lived in the beginning of the fifteenth century and to have been Prioress of Sopwell Nunnery, Hertfordshire. Published a work on field sports and heraldry, *The Boke of St. Albans* (1486). This book contains treatises on hawking, hunting and kindred sports. Cf. *Literary and Other Notes. The Woman's World,* November, 1887.

N. B. From this point throughout the essay, all names marked with an asterisk (*) have been referred to by Wilde in almost identical terms in his review of *Women's Voices* (1887): "An anthology of the most characteristic poems by English, Scotch and Irish women, selected and arranged by Mrs. William Sharp." This review occurs under *Literary and Other Notes. The Woman's World,* November, 1887, from which quotations have already been made.

(26) Anne Askew * (1521-1546):—Protestant martyr; was twice arraigned for heresy and on the second instance, refusing to recant, was burned at Smithfield.

(27) Queen Elizabeth,* the pupil of Ascham, could speak Latin and Greek fluently, and French and Italian as well as she did English. She was the author of a number of poems as well as translations of *Boëthius* and *Sallust.* George Puttenham includes in his *Arte of*

---

* Cf. *Literary and Other Notes. The Woman's World,* November, 1887.

234   DECORATIVE ART IN AMERICA

English Poesie (1589), the fourteen line poem referred to and terms it "A Ditty of her Majesties owne making, passing sweet and harmonical." Lines 11–12 read as follows:

"The daughter of debate, that eke discord doth sowe,
Shal reap no gaine, where former rule hath taught stil peace to growe."

Elizabeth wrote a number of letters to James VI of Scotland, which were published by the Camden Society in 1849.

(28) Mary Herbert,* Countess of Pembroke (*c.* 1555–1621):—Sister of Sir Philip Sidney. To her, the latter dedicated his *Arcadia;* Spenser, his *Ruines of Time;* Daniel, his *Delia.* For her, Nicholas Breton wrote *The Pilgrimage of Paradise.* She was one of the most distinguished *littérateurs* of her time, herself author of *The Doleful Lay of Clorinda*, published with *Astrophel and Stella;* the translator in blank verse from the French of *Antonie*, a tragedy by Robert Garnier; collaborator with Sidney in a metrical version of the Psalms (unpublished); and editor of her brother's posthumous works.

Page 83

(29) Lady Elizabeth Carey* (or Carew). There were two ladies of the same name: the mother (*fl.* 1590), a patroness of poets, to whom Spenser and Nash dedicated works; and the daughter, to whom Nash dedicated *Terrors of the Night*, referring in that dedication to translations of poems from Petrarch. It is generally conceded that the daughter was the author of this tedious tragedy, published 1613.

(30) Lady Mary Wroth* (*fl.* 1621), daughter of Sir Robert Sidney and niece of Sir Philip, whose *Arcadia* she imitated in *The Countesse of Mountgomerie's Urania.* Ben Jonson's dedication reads as follows:—'To the Lady Most Deserving Her Name and Blood, Lady Mary Wroth. Madam,—In the age of sacrifices, the truth of religion,' etc.—*The Alchemist* (1612).

(31) Elizabeth,* Queen of Bohemia (Stuart), (1596–1662):— Daughter of James I of England. She became the wife of the Elector Palatine, Frederick V, who was chosen King of Bohemia in 1619 and deposed in 1620, his reign of one winter gaining him the name of "The Winter King." She, however, is remembered as "The Queen

*Cf. *Literary and Other Notes. The Woman's World*, November, 1887.

NOTES 235

of Hearts " and is immortalized in the poem of Sir Henry Wotton written *c.* 1620, and printed first in *Reliquiæ Wottoniæ* (1651). See Palgrave's *Golden Treasury*, CX:

> "You meaner beauties of the night . "

(32) Margaret Cavendish,* Duchess of Newcastle (Lucas), *c.* 1624–1674:—Wrote and published a great multitude of verses, essays and plays (1653–1668). Pope glorified her thus:

> "There, stamped with arms, Newcastle shines complete."—*The Dunciad.*

Wilde quotes in *Literary and Other Notes* three verses from a book of her *Poems*, published 1693.

(33) Afra, Aphra or Ayfara Behn* (Johnson), (1640–1689):— Dramatist. In 1671 she brought out *Forc'd Marriage*. Her plays are published in three or four volumes. Author of many verses, a long allegorical poem entitled *Voyage to the Isle of Love*, and the story *Oroonoko*. Referring to this, Mr. Swinburne writes:—"This improper woman of genius was the first literary abolitionist—the first champion of the slave on record in the history of fiction."

(34) Katherine Philips* (Fowler), (1631–1664):—Wrote verse under the pseudonym of "Orinda," to which an admiring public added the epithet "Matchless." Cowley has written an elegy, *On the Death of Mrs. Katherine Philips* and an *Ode on Orinda's Poems*. She was a very prolific writer. Her collected verses were printed in 1667. Her translation of Corneille's *Pompée* was acted with great success in Dublin.

(35) Annie Finch,* Countess of Winchilsea (*d.* 1720):—Poetess friend of Pope and Rowe. *The Spleen, a Pindarique Ode*, appeared in 1701 in *Giddon's Miscellany* and her *Miscellany Poems, Written by a Lady* in 1713. From the former, Pope borrowed for *An Essay on Man*, "We faint beneath the aromatic pain." Wordsworth made the statement, which Wilde quotes, in a prefatory essay to his volume of 1815, having already sent a commendatory sonnet of his own to Lady Mary Lowther. Wilde, in *Literary and Other Notes*, does not consider Wordsworth's statement accurate, "as it leaves Gay entirely out of account." A new edition of *The Poems of Anne, Countess of Winchilsea*, has been published in Chicago, 1902.

*Cf. *Literary and Other Notes*. *The Woman's World*, November, 1887.

236 DECORATIVE ART IN AMERICA

Page 84

(36) Lady Russell* (Rachel Wriothesley), (1636–1723) :—Daughter of the 4th Earl of Southampton ; celebrated as the amanuensis of her husband in his famous trial, and author of letters since transcribed from the MS. in Woburn(e) Abbey, first published in 1773.

(37) Eliza Haywood * (Fowler), (c. 1693–1756) :—Wrote a great number of dramas, etc. *Secret Histories, Novels and Poems* (1725), dedicated to Richard Steele. Of her, Pope wrote :

> " Two babes of love close clinging to her waist;
> Fair as before her works † she stands confessed,
> In flowers and pearls by bounteous Kirkall dressed."
>
> —*The Dunciad.*

† The "two babes " were her scandalous books, *The Court of Carimania* and *The New Utopia.*

(38) Anne Wharton,* Marchioness of Wharton (Lee), (c. 1632–1685) :—The author of a metrical paraphrase of *The Lamentations of Jeremiah* and other verse. Edmund Waller wrote of her in *On an Elegy on the Earl of Rochester,*

> " Her wit as graceful, great and good ;
> Allied in genius, as in blood."

(39) Lady Mary Wortley Montagu * (Pierrepont), (1689–1762):—Famous as one of the greatest letter-writers of any age. Has also written verses, town eclogues, and epigrams, and some charming translations of Turkish poems submitted to her when she was in Constantinople.

(40) Mrs. Susannah Centlivre (1667–1723) :—Dramatist. *The Perjured Husband* (1700) was her first production. *Plays* (19 in all), with her life, was issued in 3 vols., 1761. Pope's comment reads :

> "At last Centlivre felt her voice to fail."—*The Dunciad.*

(41) Lady Anne Barnard * (Lindsay), (1750–1825) :—Her poem of *Auld Robin Gray*, was published anonymously when she was but 22 (1772).

(42) "Vanessa," Esther (Hester) Vanhomrigh (c. 1689–1723), was the daughter of a Dutch merchant who had settled in England. Swift became acquainted with Mrs. Vanhomrigh and her two daugh-

*Cf. *Literary and Other Notes. The Woman's World*, November, 1887.

NOTES 237

ters during a visit to London in 1708, when Esther was not more than 19 years old. She became enamoured of him and her infatuation lasted until the day of her death, which was the indirect result of their estrangement. Swift celebrated their love in *Cadenus and Vanessa*, a long poem written in 1713, revised in 1719 and published after her death by the terms of her testament.

(43) Dean Swift's "Stella" was Hester (Esther) Johnson (1681–1728), whom he first met as an inmate of Sir William Temple's family. To her he addressed his famous *Journal*. One of the great puzzles of literary history remains, whether or not Swift married Miss Johnson.

(44) Hester L. (Salisbury), (Thrale) Piozzi * (1741–1821):— Author of *Anecdotes of Dr. Johnson* (1786); *Letters to and from Dr. Johnson* (1788). Her poem, *The Three Warnings*, appeared in a volume of *Miscellanies* issued in 1776 by Mrs. Williams. Mrs. Piozzi was arch-priestess of the Della Cruscan mutual admiration society, and her contributions to the *Florence Miscellanies* (1785) afforded a subject for Gifford's satire in his *Baviad*:

> "See Thrale's gay widow with a satchel roam,
> And bring in pomp her laboured nothings home!"

Page 85

(45) Mrs. Anna Letitia Barbauld * (Aiken), (1743–1825):— Author of *Poems* (1773), *Hymns in Prose for Children* (1775). Some of her lighter verse is quite readable.

(46) Hannah More * (1745–1833):—Author of a pastoral drama, *The Search after Happiness* (1773); *The Inflexible Captive* (1774); *Legendary Poems; Percy, a Tragedy* (1776); *The Fatal Falsehood, a Tragedy* (1779); *Sacred Dramas* (1782), including *Sensibility; Florio*, a volume of verse (1786); and later a great amount of didactic prose. Her collected works were issued in 11 vols. (1833).

Wilde mentions her at greater length in a review of Mrs. Walford's *Four Biographies from Blackwood* in *Some Literary Notes. The Woman's World*, March, 1889.

(47) Joanna Baillie* (1762–1851):—Called by Scott "The Immortal Joanna," author of *Fugitive Verses* (1790); *Plays on the Passions* (1798–1836); and *The Family Legend* (1810).

*Cf. *Literary and Other Notes. The Woman's World*, November, 1887.

238   DECORATIVE ART IN AMERICA

(48) Mrs. Hester Chapone * (Mulso), (1727-1801) :—Contributed to Johnson's *Rambler*. Was especially a writer of essays. *Letters on the Improvement of the Mind* (1772); and *Miscellanies* (1775).

(49) Anna Seward * (1747-1809) :—At an early age was the author of elegiac verses on Garrick and Major André. Wrote a poetical novel, *Louise* (1782); and *Poems*, 3 vols., bequeathed to and issued with a memoir by Sir Walter Scott (1810).

(50) L. E. L.* (Pseudonym for Letitia Elizabeth Landon), (1802-1838), afterwards Mrs. Maclean:—First a contributor to *The Literary Gazette*. Published the following verse: *The Fate of Adelaide* (1821); *The Improvisatrice* (1824); *The Troubadour* (1825); *The Golden Violet* (1827); etc. Was also a dramatist and novelist. She has been described, despite Disraeli's comment, as a very fascinating woman. Her life was a sad one and her death very tragic. See Christina G. Rossetti's lovely poem, "L. E. L." :

"Whose heart was breaking for a little love."

(51) (Mrs.) Ann Radcliffe * (Ward), (1764-1823) :—Once called the "Salvator Rosa of English novelists." Her first novel was *The Castle of Athlin and Dunbayne* (1789), which was followed by *The Mysteries of Udolpho* (1794) and *The Italian* (1797).

(52) Georgiana Cavendish,* Duchess of Devonshire (Spenser), (1757-1806) :—The author of verses, many of which exhibit much elegance of expression. Her *Ode to Hope* was commented on by Walpole, who wrote of her, "She effaces all without being a beauty." Her best known poem is *The Passage of the Mountain of St. Gothard*, first published in France with a French translation (1802), and printed in several foreign languages before its appearance in England in 1816.

(53) I.—Lady Helen Selina Dufferin* (Sheridan), (1807-1867) :— granddaughter of Richard Brinsley Sheridan. Famed especially for her lyrics, e. g., *Terence's Farewell* and *The Irish Emigrant.*

II.—The Hon. Caroline Elizabeth Norton * (1808-1876) :—*The Sorrows of Rosalie* (1829); *The Undying One* (1831). Married a second time to Lord Gifford. The third sister Georgina, became Duchess of Somerset, the trio being known as "The Three Graces."

*Cf. *Literary and Other Notes. The Woman's World*, November, 1887.

NOTES 239

(54) (Mrs.) Mary Tighe* (Blackford), (1772–1810):—Of her poems, the most famous was a version in melodious Spenserian stanzas of the tale of Cupid and Psyche from the *Golden Ass of Apuleius*. In 1853 there had already been six editions of *Psyche* published. Keats mentions her also in his verses, *To Some Ladies*.

(55) Constantia Grierson* (*c.* 1706–1733):—This lady is said to have been proficient in Hebrew, Latin, Greek and French, and was well-known in her time as a writer of elegant verse, of which an example was included by Mrs. Barber in her volume *Poems on Several Occasions* (1734). She edited *Terence* (1727) and *Tacitus* (1730) for her husband, George Grierson, George III's printer in Ireland. Was on terms of intimacy with Swift and Thomas Sheridan.

(56) Felicia Dorothea Hemans (Browne), (1793–1835):—*Lays of Many Lands* (1826); *Records of Women* (1828).

(57) (Mrs.) Mary Robinson,* known as "Perdita" (1758–1800):—Actress and author; mistress of George, Prince of Wales (George IV). A complete edition of her verses appeared under the title of *The Poetical Works of the Late Mrs. Mary Robinson. Including Many Pieces Never Before Published.* 3 vols. 1806.

The Ode to the Snowdrop is her best known poem.

(58) Emily Brontë* (1818–1848):—Besides being the author of *Wuthering Heights*, she wrote a number of beautiful poems, such as *The Night Wind, A Death Scene, Last Lines* and *Old Stoic*.

*Cf. *Literary and Other Notes*. *The Woman's World*, November, 1887

NOTES FOR "LONDON MODELS"

Page 89

(1) This essay was published in *The English Illustrated Magazine*, No. 64, January, 1889, page 313, with an ornamental head-piece by James West and fifteen illustrations from drawings by Harper Pennington, engraved by Walker and Boutall, except for the full page which was the work of H. Fitzner Davey.

J.-Joseph Renaud in *Oscar Wilde et son œuvre* (*La Grande Revue*, 15 Février, 1905), says that in Wilde's house there hung a portrait of "le maître de la demeure avec une canne, par Arthur Pennington."

(2) John Pentland Mahaffy (1839 –   ), C. V. O. (1904), Senior Fellow of Trinity College, Dublin; Professor of Ancient History, etc. He is the author of translations and works on Philosophy; *Greek Social Life from Homer to Menander* (1874); *Rambles and Studies in Greece* (1878); etc., etc. It was with Professor Mahaffy that Wilde made a tour of Greece, via Italy, during the summer of 1877. At this period and at the time of his first visit to Italy in 1876, were written or conceived many of his early poems, e. g., *Sonnet on Approaching Italy* (Turin); *San Miniato; Ave Maria Plena Grata* (Florence); *Italia* (Venice); *Sonnet Written in Holy Week at Genoa; Rome Unvisited; Urbs Sacra Æterna; Easter Day* (Rome); *The Grave of Shelley* (Rome); *Impression de Voyage; Ravenna* (March, 1877), (see Note 29, page 217); *Heu Miserande Puer*, page 61; etc., etc. For a commentary on this trip and the early career of the poet, see *An Irish Winner of the Newdigate. The Irish Monthly*, No. 65, November, Sixth Yearly Volume, 1878, page 630; also the charming sonnet *To Oscar Wilde, Author of "Ravenna,"* by Augustus M. Moore, page 610 of the same number.

(3) Pheidias or Phidias (Φειδίας), (B.C. *c*. 490–432), the pride of Greece, sculptor of Athene Promachos on the Acropolis at Athens, the Athene of the Parthenon (See Wilde's *Charmides*, verses 18–23), and the chryselephantine statue of Zeus at Olympus,

242 DECORATIVE ART IN AMERICA

which was considered by the Ancient World as the masterpiece of the whole range of Grecian art.

(⁴) Polygnotus (Πολύγνωτος), one of the most celebrated of Greek painters, who settled in Athens at about B.C. 463. By some he was called the inventor of painting, the art, as distinguished from the handicraft. His most famous paintings in the Lesche, or Hall of the Cnidians at Delphi, represented the Fall of Troy and scenes from the underworld (Pausanias, x, 25–31). He was commissioned by Cimon to decorate the public buildings of Athens, such as the Temple of Theseus, the Anacēum and the Poēcile. He also executed a series of paintings in the Propylæa of the Acropolis. His pictures were without background, as tinted outlines on the white wall.

(⁵) Elpinike ('Ελπινίκη), daughter of Miltiades, the wife of Callias, a wealthy Athenian, who, as a condition of marriage, paid in behalf of her brother, Cimon, the fine of fifty talents, which had been imposed on Miltiades.—*Herodotus*, VI, 132–36; *Miltiades*, Nepos.

(⁶) This was Cimon (Κίμων), (B.C. 504–*c*. 449), son of the great Miltiades and Hegesipyle. He first distinguished himself at the time of the invasion of Xerxes (480), and won great victories in 466, on both land and sea. From about 471 to 461, he was the greatest power in Athenian politics

Page 90

(⁷) Niagara seems to have been Wilde's *bête noire*. His first visit to the Falls was on the Western tour of 1882. He stopped there on February 9th, at the Prospect House, Ontario, and wrote in the Private Album of the Hotel: "The roar of these waters is like the roar when the mighty wave of democracy breaks against the shores where kings lie couched at ease."—*New York Herald*, February 10, 1882, page 7. Subsequently, however, he seems to have greatly enjoyed baiting the American Press, by questioning the grandeur of the Falls. See *Mrs. Langtry on the Hudson. New York Herald*, October 30, 1882, page 4, in which Wilde's rather whimsical comments on Niagara are given at some length and taken with apparent seriousness by the interviewer. Here are a few of his later *mots* on the same subject:

NOTES 243

"Niagara will survive any criticism of mine. I must say, however, that it is the first great disappointment in the married life of many Americans, who spend their honeymoons there."—*Oscar Wilde Returns. New York World*, August 12, 1883, page 5.

"Niagara is a melancholy place filled with melancholy people, who wander about trying to get up that feeling of sublimity, which the guide-books assure them they can do without extra charge."—*London Topics of To-day. New York Times*, Nov. 25, 1883, page 5.

"I was disappointed with Niagara. Most people must be disappointed with Niagara. Every American bride is taken there, and the sight of the stupendous waterfall must be one of the earliest, if not the keenest, disappointments in American married life."—*Impressions of America*. September, 1883.

His remark, "I am not exactly pleased with the Atlantic. It is not so majestic as I expected," is in the same category, and called forth almost enough humorous verse to reach from Liverpool to New York.

Page 91

(8) Cf. "Popular is he, this poor peripatetic professor of posing."—*The Relation of Dress to Art*, page 52.

(9) Cf. "The Attorney-General said, 'There are some people who would do away with critics altogether.'
I agree with him, and am of the irrationals he points at.
. . . .
No! let there be no critics! they are not 'a necessary evil,' but an evil quite unnecessary, though an evil certainly."—*Whistler v. Ruskin: Art and Art Critics*. Chelsea, Dec., 1878; also *The Gentle Art of Making Enemies*, pages 29-30.

(10) Cf. "It is only an auctioneer who can equally and impartially admire all schools of Art."—*The Critic as Artist. Part II.*

(11) Cf. "That . . . what is ugly in fact may, in its effect, become beautiful, is true."—*The Relation of Dress to Art*, page 50; also Note for same, page 201.

Page 94

(12) Heinrich Fuessli (Henry Fuseli), R.A., was born at Zurich in 1741, and died in London, 1825. He settled in England about 1767, and adopted painting as a profession. "A fan-

244 DECORATIVE ART IN AMERICA

tastic and prolific designer rather than a painter, he had neither the judgment to control, nor the technical knowledge to adequately represent, the fancies of his powerful, but ill-regulated imagination."—*Cyclopædia of Painters and Painting.* Edited by John Denison Champlin, Jr., Vol. II., page 100.

Cf. "He (Thomas Griffiths Wainewright) tells us frankly that his great admiration for Fuseli was largely due to the fact that the little Swiss did not consider it necessary that an artist should only paint what he sees."—*Pen, Pencil, and Poison.*

Page 95

(13) Cf. "A lovely brown boy, with crisp clustering hair."—*The Tomb of Keats,* page 60; also Note to same, page 214.

(14) The word "crouch" makes better sense. "Couch" is probably a printer's error overlooked by Wilde or the proof-reader.

Page 98

(15) Cf. The first keynote of *The Relation of Dress to Art,* page 48.

(16) *Manette Salomon,* by Edmond and Jules de Goncourt (1830–1870), 2 vols., 1868.

(17) *Les Frères Zemganno,* by Edmond de Goncourt (1822–1896), published in 1879.

Page 99

(18) Cf. "The professional model is ruining painting, and reducing it to a condition of mere pose and *pastiche.*"—*The Relation of Dress to Art,* page 51.

Page 100

(19) Cf. "All costumes are caricatures. The basis of Art is not the Fancy Ball."—*Ibid.,* page 52.

NOTES FOR "'DORIAN GRAY' AND ITS CRITICS"

Page 103

[1] This letter appeared in *The St. James' Gazette*, Thursday, June 26, 1890, nnder the heading, *Mr. Oscar Wilde's Bad Case.*
For other replies by Wilde to the criticism of *The Picture of Dorian Gray*, see *The Daily Chronicle*, July 2, 1890 and *The Scots Observer*, July 12, August 2 and 16, 1890.

[2] This very virulent attack on the book and the author was printed on Tuesday, June 24, 1890.

[3] *The Picture of Dorian Gray*, issued simultaneously in England and America, as the "long story" of *Lippincott's Monthly Magazine*, pages 3–100, July, 1890—No. 271, Vol. XLVI, of the American edition. The text of this first issue was in thirteen chapters in all. Since then twelve distinctive editions have been published in English, of which three bear the imprint of London; seven, that of New York; and two, that of Paris. Of the first three mentioned, one is the *soi-disant* "Privately Printed" issue, dated 1890, which follows the Lippincott text; the other two were published by Messrs. Ward, Lock & Co., 1891 and 1894, and were the only editions authorized and sanctioned by Wilde. With the former of these two, was issned a supplementary Edition de Lnxe of 250 signed copies, nsed largely for presentation purposes. In the two authorized editions the text has been materially altered and extended, by additions and changes in the sub-divisions, to twenty chapters. They contain, also, a Preface (first published in *The Fortnightly Review*, March, 1891), composed of epigrams which represent his attitndes toward literatnre, as the verbal manifestation of Art. These epigrams are sometimes referred to as *The Credo* or *The Dogmas.* Of the remaining editions in English, all follow the Ward & Lock text, except five of the American editions, which were pirated from the first magazine issne. Of the remaining two American editions, the sixth

246 DECORATIVE ART IN AMERICA

was published by the Charterhouse Press, 1904, and transferred to Brentano's in 1905. The seventh or current edition is Brentano's reissue of the last, with corrections and revisions as regards certain biographical and bibliographical addenda. A translation in French in twenty chapters, was published in 1895 (1900), followed by two editions in cheaper form. The German translations are two in number: one, the work of Johannes Gaulke, published in 1901; another, the work of Felix Paul Greve, published in 1903, and now in its third edition. The first is in thirteen chapters; the second, in twenty. There are also translations in Italian and Swedish.

(4) Cf. "The first condition of criticism is that the critic should be able to recognize that the sphere of Art and the sphere of Ethics are absolutely distinct and separate."—*The Critic as Artist. Part II.* "Art is out of the reach of morals, for her eyes are fixed upon things beautiful and immortal and ever changing. To morals belong the lower and less intellectual spheres. However, let these mouthing Puritans pass; they have their comic side."— *Ibid.* Cf. *The Rise of Historical Criticism*, foot of page 26.

Page 104

(5) An extract from this letter with especial reference to this part, is quoted in *The Critic*, under heading of *The Lounger*, August 23, 1890, No. 347, Vol. XIV, N. S.—*The Critic* takes sides with Wilde upon the point in question.

(6) Cf. "The plays are not great; . . . As a matter of fact most of them are the outcome of wagers. So was *Dorian Gray*. I wrote it in a few days, merely because a friend of mine insisted that I could never write a novel."—Translated from *Oscar Wilde* in *Prétextes* by André Gide. This study appeared originally in *L'Ermitage*, June, 1902. It was translated into German by Berta Franzos for the *Rheinisch-Westfälischen Zeitung*, Nr. 547, 560, 568 (1903). Franz Blei made another translation, which he included in *In Memoriam. Oscar Wilde*, Leipzig, 1904 (1905). The latter was re-translated into English, and issued under Blei's title by Percival Pollard, Greenwich, Conn., 1905. Stuart Mason has translated it from the original French and published it as *Oscar Wilde. A Study.* Oxford, 1905.

NOTES 247

Page 105

(7) This second letter appeared Friday, June 27, 1890.

Page 106

(8) Wilde is more than probably referring to the novels of Mrs. Humphry Ward. Cf. "*Robert Elsmere* is of course a masterpiece—a masterpiece of the '*genre ennuyeux,*' the one form of literature that the English people seem to thoroughly enjoy. A thoughtful young friend of ours once told us that it reminded him of the sort of conversation that goes on at a meat tea in the house of a Nonconformist family, and we can quite believe it. . . . It is simply Arnold's *Literature and Dogma* with the literature left out."

—*The Decay of Lying.*

(9) It is interesting to note that this is the same point made by Elizabeth Barrett in one of her letters to R. H. Horne, when he takes her to task for apparent disregard of rhyme.

Page 107

(10) Wilde has had attributed to him a translation of *The Satyricon of Petronius*—indeed, a translation with a long introduction, bibliography, and most scholarly notes, was issued in Paris, 1902, with the following note printed on a transparent slip pasted over the publisher's imprint: "The present translation was done direct from the original Latin by 'Sebastian Melmoth' (Oscar Wilde)." The authenticity of this work, however, is questioned, if not altogether denied by Mr. Robert Ross, his literary executor, on the ground that no one can show any part of the MS. in the author's handwriting.

(11) Wilde himself was an Honour man. The following is noted in *Oxford Honours.* 1220—1894. Clarendon Press. 1894:

Wilde (Oscar O'F. Magd.)

1 Cl. Mod. 1876 [First Class Honour in Classics, awarded by Moderator of Magdalen.]

English Verse. 1878. [Newdigate Prize: *Ravenna.*]

1 Cl. 1878. [First Class Honour in Classics.]

Page 108

(12) "The only real people are the people who never existed, and

248 DECORATIVE ART IN AMERICA

if a novelist is base enough to go to life for his personages he should at least pretend that they are creations, and not boast of them as copies."—*The Decay of Lying.*

(13) Cf. "As a method, Realism is a complete failure."—*The Decay of Lying.*

Page 109

(14) This third letter appeared Saturday, June 28, 1890, under the heading: *Mr. Oscar Wilde's Defence.*

Page 110

(15) Cf. *The Censure and "Salomé,"* pages 139-40.

Page 113

(16) This fourth letter appeared Monday, June 30, 1890, under the same heading as the last: *Mr. Wilde's Defence.*

(17) The following letter, to which he has reference, appeared Saturday, June 28.

"To the Editor of the St. James Gazette:

Sir: — If Mr. Oscar Wilde is the last man in England (according to his own account), who requires advertisement, his friends and publishers do not seem to be of the same opinion. Otherwise it is difficult to account for the following audacious puff-positive which has been sent through the half-penny post to newspaper editors and others :—

'Mr. Oscar Wilde will contribute to the July number of *Lippincott's Magazine* a complete novel, entitled *The Picture of Dorian Gray,* which, as the first venture in fiction of one of the most prominent personalities and artistic influences of the day, will be everywhere read with wide interest and curiosity. But the story is in itself so strong and strange, and so picturesque and powerful in style, that it must inevitably have created a sensation in the literary world, even if published without Mr. Wilde's name on the title page. Viewed merely as a romance, it is—from the opening paragraph down to the tragic and ghastly climax—full of strong and sustained interest; as a study in psychology it is phenomenal; and judged even as a piece of literary workmanship, it is one of the most brilliant and remarkable productions of the year.' Such, Sir,

NOTES 249

is the estimate of Mr. Wilde's publisher or paragraph-writer. Note the adjectival exuberance of the puffer—complete, strong, strange, picturesque, powerful, tragic, ghastly, sustained, phenomenal, brilliant and remarkable ! For a man who does not want advertisement this is not bad. I am, Sir, Your obedient servant,

A London Editor."

June 27.

Page 114

(18) Mr. R. H. Sherard mentions in *Oscar Wilde. The Story of an Unhappy Friendship*, that Wilde had a great aversion for all neologisms, especially those terminating in "ette."

Page 115

(19) Cf. "There is the despot who tyrannizes over the body. There is the despot who tyrannizes over the soul. . . . The first is called The Prince. The second is called The Pope."—*The Soul of Man Under Socialism.*

NOTES FOR "MR. KIPLING AND THE ANGLO-INDIANS"

Page 119

([1]) This letter was printed under the heading *An Anglo-Indian's Complaint* in *The Times* (London), Saturday, September 26, 1891.

([2]) Under the title *An Anglo-Indian's Complaint* there appeared in *The Times*, September 25, '91, a long letter signed "An Indian Civilian," in which among other grievances was one against Wilde for attributing vulgarity to the Anglo-Indian.

([3]) Wilde's allusion to the Anglo-Indians and vulgarity occurred first in *The True Function and Value of Criticism. Concluded. The Nineteenth Century*, September, 1890, No. 163, Vol. XXVIII. This essay, in a somewhat modified form, appeared later as *The Critic as Artist. Part II* in *Intentions*. Why Wilde should refer to the magazine issue and not to *Intentions*, is difficult to understand, for *Intentions* was published as early as May, 1891. An extract from the passage in question, is quoted here as the first part of the introductory keynotes.

NOTES FOR " A HOUSE OF POMEGRANATES "

Page 123

(¹) This letter was printed in *The Speaker* (London), December 5, 1891. Vol. IV.

Page 124

(²) The paragraph in question occurred under "The Week," page 648, of the preceding number of *The Speaker*, November 28, 1891.

(³) *A House of Pomegranates* by Oscar Wilde.
The Design & Decorations of This Book by C. Ricketts & C. H. Shannon.

James R. Osgood, McIlvaine & Co. London, MDCCCXCI.

The Chiswick Press makes the following observation regarding this book of fairy tales in the advertising column of *The Century Guild Hobby Horse*, October, 1892, No. 28, Vol. VII:

" *A House of Pomegranates, The Young King, The Birthday of the Infanta, and other Beautiful Tales,* by Oscar Wilde. With four full-page illustrations by C. H. Shannon, and numerous decorations in the text by C. Ricketts. With end papers executed in pale olive, and the cover in moss green, pale coral and ivory-white. 8vo. cloth, uncut edges and large margins, 21 s. — "

(⁴) Charles Shannon designed also the title-pages and bindings for *Lady Windermere's Fan* (1893), *A Woman of No Importance* (1894), and *The Duchess of Padua,* unpublished, but announced as "in preparation," in the Publisher's List of 1894. The covers of *The Importance of Being Earnest* (1899) and *An Ideal Husband* (1899) also suggest his handiwork. Wilde evidently thought highly of his talent as he presented him with a large paper copy of the last play, with the following inscription: "To Charles Shannon: in sincere admiration: in affection: etc."

254　DECORATIVE ART IN AMERICA

(5) Charles Ricketts, of the London firm of Hacon and Ricketts, publishers of the Vale Press Books, to which he contributed a larger part of the illustrations, initial letters, etc. In addition to his work in *A House of Pomegranates*, Mr. Ricketts designed the cover for the 1892 limited edition of Wilde's *Poems*, issued by Elkin Mathews and John Lane; drew the cover and illustrations, etc., for *The Sphinx*, published by the same firm in 1894; and was commissioned to supply initial letters and a cover design for *The Incomparable and Ingenious History of Mr. W. H.*, announced in Lane's Publisher's List for 1894, but never issued.

Page 125

(6) As an exposition of his views regarding the illustration of books, cf. "At present there is a discord between our pictorial illustrations and our unpictorial type. The former are too essentially imitative in character and often disturb a page instead of decorating it."—*Some Literary Notes*. *The Woman's World*, January, 1889.

(7) In fairness to the author of the paragraph to which Wilde objects, the latter should have acknowledged the critic's favorable comment on the illustrations, if not on the cover design.

NOTES FOR "THE RELATION OF THE ACTOR TO THE PLAY"

Page 129

(1) This letter was printed under the title of *Puppets and Actors* in *The Daily Telegraph*, London, February 20, 1892.

Page 130

(2) This is quoted in a most interesting article on Wilde, entitled *Poets and Puppets—and Censors*. *The Saturday Review*, London, July 2, 1892, No. 1914, Vol. LXXIV.

Also, see the analysis of this letter in an article entitled *Puppet and Playwright*. *The Saturday Review*, February 27, 1892, No. 1896, Vol. LXXIII.

Page 131

(3) Cf. "When a great actor plays Shakespeare, we have the same experience. His own personality becomes a vital part of the interpretation." *The Critic as Artist. Part II.*

(4) Cf. " His dancing was funny," cried the Infanta; "but his acting is funnier still. Indeed he is almost as good as the puppets, only of course not so natural." — *The Birthday of the Infanta.*

Page 132

(5) John Gray, author of *Silverpoints* (1893). This book is especially remarkable for its cover which was one of the early successes of modern artistic binding.

255

NOTES FOR "THE CENSURE AND 'SALOMÉ'"

Page 137

(¹) This interview was published first in *The Pall Mall Gazette*, London, Wednesday, June 29, 1892, and on the following day in *The Pall Mall Budget*, June 30, 1892, Vol. 40, page 947. It was accompanied by a caricature of Wilde as a French *religieux*, entitled "Monsienr Vilde."

(²) *Salomé* has indeed been the subject of strange vicissitudes. Written in French by Wilde with slight revisions by his friend, the late Marcel Schwob, so exquisite was the music of its prose and so dramatic its plot that Mme. Bernhardt undertook to produce it, although it was by no means a one-rôle piece. In *The Story of an Unhappy Friendship*, Robert Sherard tells how its *première* was delayed and how for obvious reasons Mme. Bernhardt neglected to present it, as had been her intention, in 1895. The play was produced in Paris by Luigne Poë in 1896, and is mentioned by Wilde in his letter of March 10, 1896, written to Robert Ross from prison: *De Profundis. Aufzeichnungen und Briefe*, translated by Max Meyerfeld, page 102; or *De Profundis. Précédé de Lettres Écrites de la Prison*, translated by Henry-D. Davray, page 17. Reference is likewise made to this in the introduction to J.-Joseph Renaud's translation into French of *Intentions;* or see *Oscar Wilde et son œuvre. La Grande Revue*, Feb. 15, 1905, pages 400–414. In Germany, it has created a furore from the time of its production at the Neue Theater, Berlin, September 29, 1903. It has also appeared on the boards in Italy (see *Il processo e l'estetica di Oscar Wilde*. L. Gamberale. *Revista d'Italia*, June, 1904). On the other hand, in English, there seem to have been no more than two productions thus far. The first was of a quasi-private nature by the New Stage Clnb, at the Bijon Theatre, Archer

258   DECORATIVE ART IN AMERICA

Street, W., London, May 10th and 13th, 1905. The second was a series of public performances in New York, given at The Berkeley Lyceum, 19 West 44th Street, by the Progressive Stage Society, from Monday, November 13th to Thursday, November 16th, *incl.*, 1905. The first performance was for members of the society only. See also Note 4, page 263 fol.

Page 139

(3) See *Poets and Puppets—and Censors. The Saturday Review*, London, July 2, 1892, No. 1914, Vol. LXXIV. This extract is quoted to show what is considered an inconsistency in Wilde's attitude towards the actor, if compared with the views expressed in *Puppets and Actors.* This paragraph, beginning with "Every rehearsal," and ending with "and not to me" is quoted in *The Sun*, New York, April 6, 1895.

Page 141

(4) *Hérodiade*, 5 acts, Brussels, Théâtre de la Monnaie, 1881.

(5) *La Reine de Saba*, Paris, Opéra, February 29, 1862.

(6) *Die Makkabäer*, German Opera in 3 acts, Berlin, April 17, 1875.

(7) *Divorçons*, a comedy by Victorien Sardou, produced in 1880.

(8) It is stated, however, on the authority of Mr. Sherard that Wilde received some assistance, though slight, from Marcel Schwob. It was to him that Wilde dedicated *The Sphinx*, "in Friendship and in Admiration." In the same year (1894), *Mimes* was published. Wilde was given one of the Japan vellum copies with the inscription: "à mon cher Oscar Wilde, son admirateur, son ami, Marcel Schwob."

Mayer-André-*Marcel* Schwob was born 1867. In addition to *Mimes*, he wrote among other books *Étude sur l'argot français* (1889); *Cœur double* (1891); *le Roi au masque d'or* (1892); *Croisade des enfants* (1895); *Vies imaginaires* (1896); and *La lampe de Psyche* (1903). He also adapted *Hamlet* with E. Morand for Sarah Bernhardt, who produced it in 1899.

Page 142

(9) This announcement called forth much satirical comment, notably, *Lines to our New Censor*, a satirical poem in five quatrains

NOTES

259

by W. W. (William Watson) in *The Spectator*, Saturday, July 9, 1892, No. 3341, Vol. 69, which was afterwards reprinted in *The Poems of William Watson*, edition of 1893. A rather amusing cartoon of Wilde as a French conscript was printed above the caption "A Wilde Idea. Or, More Injustice to Ireland! " in *Punch*, July 9, 1892, Vol. CIII.

Compare this announcement with the first paragraph of *Paris, the Abode of Artists*.

([10]) Compare this statement, that on page 139, and the tenor of Wilde's letter to *The Times*, pages 151–2, with E. Gómez Carrillo's Preface to the Spanish translation of *Salomé*. This rather salacious fantasy is entitled *El Origen de la " Salomé,, de Wilde* and states as a fact that Wilde wrote the play for Sarah Bernhardt or rather that it was largely her personality that suggested the form of the play. The following are characteristic extracts :

"Los labios del poeta crispábanse, sonriendo á la visión de Salomé desnuda. En su entusiasmo de artista sensual, creía ver á Sarah Bernhardt adolescente, bailando, desnuda, ante el mundo." —Page 16.

"La idea de ver á Sarah Bernhardt, rejuvenecida, bailando desnuda ante el Tetrarca volvió á obsesionarle. Y abandonando su lengua natal, principió en francés su *Salomé*."—Page 19.

Wilde's reason for writing *Salomé* has also been touched upon by Meltzer under the heading *Footlights*, in *The World*, December 17, 1893, page 20. The Sarah Bernhardt theory is probably founded on rumour, if not made out of the whole cloth.

Page 143

([11]) This is a reference to *The Poet and the Puppets*, a travesty by Mr. Charles Brookfield with music by J. M. Glover. This skit began at The Comedy Theatre in May, 1892, and had a run of several months. It was an exceedingly clever burlesque of *Lady Windermere's Fan*, or rather of the eccentricities of its author. Of it, it is said: "Mr. Charles Hawtrey transformed himself for the nonce into the 'Poet' and so well, that it was not even necessary for him to sing 'Neighbor O'Flaherty's Child' to disclose the identity. Later he sang most amusingly, 'A Poet Lived in a

260   DECORATIVE ART IN AMERICA

Handsome Style.'" See *The Theatre*, London, June 1, 1892, Vol. 29 of Complete Series; *The Spectator*, Nov. 26, 1892, No. 3361, Vol. 69; *The Times* (London), Friday, May 20, 1892, page 10, cl. 6; *The Saturday Review*, May 28 and July 2, 1892, and *The Athenæum* May 28, 1892.

[12] Compare with Wilde's attitude towards the stage, as expressed in this interview, *The Relation of the Actor to the Play*, etc., Mr. Richard Mansfield's recent defence, *Man and the Actor*. This illuminating and brilliant essay may be found in *The Atlantic Monthly*, May, 1906, page 577. "The art of acting," writes Mr. Mansfield, "is the crystallization of all arts. It is a diamond in the facets of which is mirrored every art."

NOTES FOR "PARIS, THE ABODE OF ARTISTS"

Page 147

(1) This letter was written or, what is more probable, this statement was made on the occasion of the interview recorded in the preceding article. It is quoted under date of June 30, 1892, by the Paris correspondent of a London newspaper.

(2) Wilde's great love of Paris is evident from the fact that after his release from prison, it was this city which seemed always to draw him to itself, from the more secluded localities where he was urged to remain by his well-wishers. Paris was the home of his early successes, and he numbered among its *littérateurs* and artists more friends and admirers than he could command in England. It was in Paris that he died. See Robert Sherard's *Story of an Unhappy Friendship;* the essays of Ernest La Jeunesse or André Gide in *In Memoriam. O. W.*; and the articles of J.–Joseph Renaud in *La Grande Revue*, February 15, 1905; and Henry–D. Davray in *Mercure de France*, June 15, 1905.

(3) *Samson et Dalila,* in 3 acts (*Op.* 47), Weimar, December, 1877.

(4) See Note 4, page 258.

Page 148

(5) Athalie or Athaliah, the daughter of Omri, King of Israel, mother of Ahaziah and grandmother of Joash (II Kings, viii, 26 and xi, 1-2). *Athalie* was presented first in 1691 before Louis XIV at Saint-Cyr.

(6) Cf. *The Censure and "Salomé,"* page 142 and Note 9, page 258 fol.

NOTES FOR "SARAH BERNHARDT AND 'SALOMÉ'"

Page 150

(1) This sonnet was first published in *The World*, London, June 11, 1879. Later it was included in Wilde's *Poems* under the title of *Phèdre*, one of Mme. Bernhardt's most famous rôles. Of this rôle Wilde wrote: " For my own part, I must confess that it was not until I heard Sarah Bernhardt in *Phèdre* that I absolutely realized the sweetness of the music of Racine."—*Literary and Other Notes. The Woman's World*, January, 1888.

Page 151

(2) This letter was printed in *The Times* (London), Thursday, March 3, 1893.

(3) The review in question appeared under *Books of the Week*, Thursday, February 23, 1893, page 8, cl. 3: " This is the play written for Mme. Sarah Bernhardt. It is an arrangement in blood and ferocity, morbid, bizarre, repulsive, etc." It is interesting to compare this criticism with the sympathetic review of Henry Norman, in *The Illustrated London News*, Saturday, March 4, 1893, No. 2811, page 278; also with *Salomé: a Critical Review*, by Alfred Douglas, in *The Spirit Lamp, an Oxford Magazine*, edited by Lord Alfred Douglas, No. 1, May, 1893, Vol. IV.

(4) *Salomé. Drame en un acte*. Paris, Librairie de l'Art Indépendant. Londres, Elkin Mathews et John Lane. 1893. A 12mo. with purple wrappers lettered in silver. Pp. 84. The edition was limited to 600 copies (500 for sale) with a small supplementary edition on hand-made paper, numbered and signed by the author (at least 10 such copies were issued).

The English version is Lord Alfred Douglas' translation, with illustrations by Aubrey Beardsley, first published in 1894 in an edition of 500 copies, small 4to, and 100 copies on large paper. A small 16mo. reprint of this (4½" x 5¾") was issued by the Paper

264   DECORATIVE ART IN AMERICA

Covered Book Store, San Francisco, 1896. A full-size reprint with a few extra plates, was published by Melmoth & Co., London, 1904, in an edition of 250 numbered copies on hand-made paper and 50 numbered copies on Japanese vellum. (See also Note, below.) The German versions are three in number: Hedwig Lachmann's translation, with illustrations by Marcus Behmer, 1903 (in its second edition); Isidore L. Pavia and Hermann Freiherr von Teschenberg's translation, 1903 (in its fifth edition); and Dr. Kiefer's translation, which was the stage version used at the Neue Theater, Berlin, September 29, 1903. Frau Lachmann's version was used as the libretto for a score of an opera by Richard Stranss, produced in Dresden, December 5, 1905.

The Swedish translation is by Edv. Alkman, 1905, in an edition of 500 copies, with a supplementary edition of 50 nnmbered copies on large paper.

The Polish translation is by Hew. Gonsowska (Gasowskiej), 1904, with fonr pictorial head-pieces and tail-pieces.

The Spanish translation is by J. Pérez Jorba and B. Rodríguez, with numerous illustrations by L. Valera and an introduction by E. Gómez Carrillo. See Note 10, page 259.

The Russian translations are two in number: one by B. and L. Andruson, 1904, edited by K. D. Balmont; another, by the Baroness Rodoshevski, 1905.

The play has also been presented on the Italian stage: "*Salomé* che Mario Fumagalli ed Edwige Reinach portarono trionfalmente in giro per l'Italia."—Preface to *De Profundis*, translated by Olga Bicchierai, Venice, 1905, page 6.

Note. It is announced that John Lane Company will issue in July a new English edition of *Salome*, 16mo., unillustrated, but with a cover design by Aubrey Beardsley. Following this will come an illustrated edition (6½" x 8") with an introduction by Robert Ross, the pictures of Beardsley on Japan vellum and an ornamental cover. There will also be a portfolio of *Salome* drawings, in full-size reproductions (9" x 6⅜"), which will appear in the autnmn.

NOTES FOR "THE ETHICS OF JOURNALISM"

Page 157

(1) This letter appeared first in *The Pall Mall Gazette*, Thursday, September 20, 1894; was printed later in *The Pall Mall Budget*, Thursday, September 27, 1894, New Series, No. 1357, 26th Year; and in *The Sun*, New York, April 6, 1895, page 4, cl. 1.

(2) *The Shamrock* was printed in *The Weekly Sun*, Sunday, August 5, 1894. From this paper it was copied in *The Sun*, New York, Sunday, August 19, 1894. Its appearance in the latter was noticed by the Reverend William J. McClure of Mt. Kisco, N. Y., who wrote a letter published in *The Sun*, New York, Thursday, August 23, 1894, calling attention to a scrap album in his possession which contained the original of this poem clipped from *The Cork Weekly Herald*. Mr. McClure showed several variations in the lines and asked to know how Wilde's name came to be associated with the verses. In an editorial, August 31, 1894, *The Sun*, New York, commented upon the above letter and requested its colleague, *The Weekly Sun*, to explain matters. In the meantim so long was the silence on the subject, that Mr. McClure addressed a second letter to *The Sun*, Monday, October 8, 1894. In this he referred to a letter received from Robert H. Sullivan, who had discovered in a volume, entitled *Gathered Leaflets*, this same poem above the signature of Helena Calanan (spelled with a single "l"). As a matter of fact the mystery had already been cleared away in England. In brief, a poem entitled *The Shamrock*, signed "Oscar Wilde," was claimed to have been discovered by a correspondent of *The Weekly Sun* (see the Assistant Editor's letter) in a Cork newspaper for 1888. It then appeared, however, that the author was Helena Callanan, a blind girl. A letter from her, dated The Asylum for the Blind, Infirmary Road, Cork, was published in *The Weekly*

266   DECORATIVE ART IN AMERICA

Sun, Sunday, September 23, 1894, together with the poem as originally written. It came to light that this was first printed in *The Cork Weekly Herald*, 1881. From there, it had been copied by the *Boston Pilot*, *The Sidney Freeman*, and *The New Orleans Morning Star*, appearing later as a " Cork Blind Asylum Poem " in a collection entitled *Gathered Leaflets* (*Scattered Leaflets*), 1885. Such is the history of *The Shamrock*. Strangely enough the version given in *The New York Sun* varies from that of *The Weekly Sun*, from which it purports to be copied, and quite materially from the original of Miss Callanan. It is here reprinted from the first mentioned version as the least unreadable of the three, but even in this version, it is such doggerel as to make it difficult to understand how its publication could have been prompted by anything but malice. However noble the sentiment, it hardly comes within the category of rhyme, not to mention poetry.

(3) This accusation, based on the implication of *The New York Sun*, was made in *The Weekly Sun*, September 16, 1894.

Page 158

(4) This letter was printed first in *The Pall Mall Gazette*, Monday, September 24, 1894; was reprinted in *The Pall Mall Budget*, Thursday, September 27, 1894, New Series 1357 (as before). The first paragraph was reprinted in *The Sun*, New York, April 6, 1895.

(5) The letter referred to, bears so directly upon the answer that it is here reprinted in full:

" To the Editor of the Pall Mall Gazette:

Sir:— Mr. Oscar Wilde's letter in your issue of yesterday calls for a few words of explanation from me. Let me in the first place say that we regret exceedingly the suggestion of plagiarism. ╮

The story of the association of Mr. Wilde's name with the poem is a curious and perplexing one. Our own part in the matter is, however, easily explained. Some three months ago one of our correspondents sent to us in MS. a poem entitled *The Shamrock*. The name of Oscar Wilde was appended to it. Accompanying the poem was a letter in which our correspondent said, 'I have copied this

NOTES 267

poem on the "Shamrock" from an old Irish newspaper which I happened on by accident. It is so beautiful and its sentiment is so fine and tender, that it came to me as a revelation. Oscar Wilde may be a *flâneur* and a cynic, but it is quite evident from this poem that deep down in his heart he has kept the fire of patriotism burning with something of a white purity. I think the poem is one which *The Weekly Sun* might well rescue from oblivion.'

This then, Sir, was the way in which we came to give the poem publicity in *The Weekly Sun*, and this the spirit in which the name of the elegant ornament of polite society came to be connected with it in our pages. Mr. Oscar Wilde places our ascription of the poem to himself, on the level of certain 'scurrilous attacks' which haunt his imagination. The suggestion is characteristic. I am not concerned here to defend the poem. It may be and doubtless is assailable, but even the most fastidious critic cannot deny that it is full of melodic charm and breathes a spirit of pure and exalted patriotism. So conspicuous, indeed, was its elevation of tone that we were reluctant to believe that it could have been the product of a mind like Mr. Oscar Wilde's, and were driven to take refuge in the charitable belief that it belonged to the period of a forgotten and generous youth.

Faithfully yours,
The Assistant Editor."

Weekly Sun Office,
 Tudor St., E. C., Sept. 21st.

N. B. The above letter appeared in the same issues of *The Pall Mall Gazette* and *Budget* as Wilde's reply, and in *The Weekly Sun,* Sunday, September 23, 1894.

Page 160

(6) The gist of this controversy and this particular part of the letter is quoted (or rather misquoted) in *The Critic,* October 13, 1894, No. 660, Vol. 25 of the Complete Series (London Letter). Apropos of his dogma that "the artist moves in a cycle of masterpieces," he is said to have been asked why it was, he had never collaborated. His reply was: "The cycle is not a cycle made for two."—*The Theatre,* London, March 1, 1895, page 185.

NOTES FOR "DRAMATIC CRITICS AND AN 'IDEAL HUSBAND'"

Page 163

([1]) This interview appeared in *Sketch*, London, January, 1895, and is from the pen of Gilbert Burgess. It was reprinted under the title of *A Highly Artistic Interview* in *The New-York Daily Tribune*, Sunday, January 27, 1895.

([2]) The *première* of *An Ideal Husband* occurred at the Haymarket, Thursday, January 3, 1895. It was not issued in book form until 1899, at which date it was published by Leonard Smithers in an edition of 1000 copies, with a supplementary edition of 100 signed copies on large paper and 12 signed copies on Japan vellum. The text was subjected to considerable revision prior to its appearance in the library edition. It is included in *The Plays of Oscar Wilde*. Boston, John W. Luce and Co., 1905, Vol. II.

Page 166

([3]) *Lady Windermere's Fan*, at the St. James Theatre, Saturday, February 20, 1892; *A Woman of No Importance*, at the Haymarket Theatre, Wednesday, April 19, 1893; and *An Ideal Husband*, already referred to.

Page 167

([4]) Cf. Notes 12 and 13, pages 247-8, and page 108.

Page 168

([5]) *A Woman of No Importance* has been issued in the following editions:

I. *A Woman of No Importance*. London, John Lane, 1894, in an edition of 500 copies, with 50 additional on large paper.

II. *A Woman of No Importance*. Paris, Privately Printed, 1903, in an edition of 250 numbered copies.

III. *The Plays of Oscar Wilde*. Boston, John W. Luce and Co., 1905, Vol. I. There are translations in German and Italian.

270 DECORATIVE ART IN AMERICA

(6) *Lady Windermere's Fan* has been issued in the following editions:

I. *Lady Windermere's Fan. A Play about a Good Woman.* London, Elkin Mathews and John Lane, 1893, in an edition of 500 copies, with 50 additional on large paper.

II. *Lady Windermere's Fan, etc.* Paris, Privately Printed, 1903. in an edition of 250 numbered copies.

III. *Lady Windermere's Fan, etc.* New York, Samnel French, n. d. (1904). The text is that of the library edition followed by I and II.

IV. *Lady Windermere's Fan, etc.* London, Samuel French, Ltd., n. d. This is the acting edition in its unrevised form.

V. *The Plays of Oscar Wilde.* Boston, John W. Luce and Co., 1905, Vol. I. There is also a translation in German.

(7) It is interesting to compare the actual opinions of the leading critics of England and America, few of whom have treated this play with favour. For comments of the Press and leading reviews, see the following:

The Athenæum, Jan. 12, 1895; *The Saturday Review,* the same date; *The Academy,* Jan. 19th; *The Illustrated London News,* Jan. 12th; *The Times* (London), Jan. 4th; *The Theatre,* Feb. 1, 1895; *Punch,* Feb. 2, 1895; *The Critic* (New York), Jan. 26 and March 16; *Life,* March 28th, 1895; any of the New York daily papers for Wednesday, March 13th, 1895. The play was produced the night before the last mentioned date at the Old Lyceum Theatre, New York City.

Page 169

(8) Victorien Sardou (1831 –   ) : Member of l'Académie Française June 7, 1877; author of *Dora* (1877); *Divorçons* (1880); *Fédora* (1882); *Théodora* (1886); *La Tosca* (1887), etc., etc.

Page 170

(9) Purple was one of Wilde's favourite words and he used it often with tragedy, as "the purple dignity of tragedy."—*The Critic as Artist. Part II.* "I thought I could bear a real tragedy if it came to me with purple pall."—*De Profundis.*

INDEX

Nothing that actually occurs is of the smallest importance.
—*Phrases and Philosophies for the use of the Young.*

INDEX

Abbreviations: 2 (K. 1, 3)=page 2, first and third introductory Keynotes; *N.,* indicates that all following references are to the notes; 175(3, 6–9)=page 175, notes 3 and 6 to 9 inclusive; Q.=quoted; Q.i.f.=quoted in full; bibl.=bibliography; W.=Oscar Wilde; a change from comma to semicolon after a series of pages following Q., denotes that all subsequent pages contain allusions only: for example, in Q., 255(3), 272(9); 175(7), the first two notes contain quotations, the last an allusion only.

Abbey, Mr., the theatre manager, *N.,* 194(7).
Abbruzi, a brigand from the, 52.
Academe, the, 150.
Academy, The, N., 176(9), 270(7).
Acrobats, the grace of, 97–8.
Actor, the, as interpreter, 32 (K. 3, 4), 128 (K. 1–3), 130–2, 136 (K. 1), 171: *N.,* 255(3).
Adonais (Keats), *N.,* 209(12), 211 (16).
Adonais, Shelley's, Preface to, *N.,* Q., 58 fol.: *N.,* Q., 210(13–4).
Advertisement, its value, 35; should not be used to forestall the critic's or public's opinion, 113–4: *N.,* "London Editor's" comment, 248(17) fol.
Æsthetic Boom, "OW!" 's parodies of W.'s poems, *N.,* 177(14) fol.
Æsthetics, The New, xiv: W.'s theories and dogmas, xix, xxi–xxiii, 2 (K. 1–4), 40 (K. 3, 4), 48 (K. 4, 5), 64 (K. 4), 88 (K. 1, 2), 102 (K. 4–6), 108, 118 (K. 2), 120, 122 (K. 1, 2), 126, 128 (K. 2, 3), 132–3, 136 (K. 2), 154 (K. 3), 167, 170: *N.,* 182(5), 244(12), 246(4), 247(12) fol., 248(13).
Ajax, 90.
Alchemist, Ben Jonson's, 83: *N.,* 234(30).
Alcott, Louisa, *N.,* 189(8).
Alkman, Edv., *N.,* 264(4).
Alroy, Lady. See *Lady Alroy.*
America, Lecture on, Q., 18.

Amsterdam, the Jews' quarter of, 49.
Andover Review, The, N., 176(9).
Andruson, B. and L., translators of *Salomé, N.,* 264(4).
Anecdotes, of W., *N.,* 193(4), 216(28), 243(7), 267(6).
Anglo-Indian's Complaint, An, N., 251(1).
Anglo-Indians, 119–20: *N.,* 251 (1–3).
Anstey (Thomas Anstey Guthrie), 115.
Apollo's shrine, 79: *N.,* 230(17) fol.
Ariel, 54, 132: *N.,* 203(13).
Arizona, the steamer, *N.,* 176 (10–1).
Arnold, Matthew, 81: *N.,* 247(8).
Art (general), xi, xiv, xvii–xxi, xxvii, xxix (K. 2), 2 (K. 1, 4), 3, 11, 13, 26, 36, 45, 48 (K. 3–5), 49, 52–3, 56 (K. 3), 64 (K. 4), 88 (K. 2–4), 102 (K. 4–6), 103–15 *passim,* 118 (K. 2), 120, 122 (K. 1, 4), 125–6, 136 (K. 2), 139–41, 143, 147, 152, 162 (K. 1–3), 163, 166–7, 170–1: *N.,* 182(5), 193(3), 197(5), 198(6–10), 199(12, 11), 201(2), 202(11–2) fol., 243(10), 244(19), 246(4).
Art, American, xx, 2 (K. 4), 3–5, 9, 11–5: *N.,* 181(1), 185(13).
Art, conditions of, 50, 88 (K. 4), 102 (K. 4), 118 (K. 2), 122 (K. 1, 2), 167, 169: *N.,* 182(5), 198(8).

273

274 INDEX

Art, Decorative xvii–xx, 2 (K.
2, 3), 4–6, 9–12, 14–5, 29, 122
(K. 1, 2): N., 183(9, 10), 184
(11), 194(9), 207(5).
Art, Dramatic. See *Dramatic Art.*
Art, Illustrative, 122 (K. 3): N.,
254(6).
Art, Pictorial, xxi, 10, 26–30, 40
(K. 1–5), 43–46, 48 (K. 5), 49–
52, 54, 88 (K. 1, 6), 89–100
passim, 139: N., 183(9, 10) fol.,
184(11), 193(5), 194(6, 10),
197(3, 5), 198(9), 199(12, I, II),
201(2–5), 202(6), 214(25) fol.,
215(26), 226(21), 241(1), 242
(4), 243(12) fol., 244(18).
Art Schools, for children, xvii,
14–5: N., 185(14–5, 17), 207(5).
Arte of English Poesie, Putten-
ham's, Q., 82: N., 233(27) fol.
Artist, The, Q., 56.
Artist in Attitudes, An, by Arthur
Symons, Q., xi: N., 175(4).
Artists' Models. See *Models.*
Askew, Anne, 82: N., her mar-
tyrdom, 233(26).
Atalanta in Calydon, Swinburne's,
129.
Athalie, Racine's, 148: N., 261(5).
Athenæum, The, 67–8: N., 197(3),
220(6), 223(14) fol., 224(16–7)
fol., 260(11), 270(7).
Athens, 89, 100: N., 241(3) fol.,
242(4–6).
Athos, 74: N., 229(7) fol.
Atlantic Ocean, W.'s disappoint-
ment in the, N., 243(7).
Atlantic Monthly, The, N., 260(12).
Auld Robin Gray, Lady Anne
Barnard's, admired by Scott,
84: N., 236(41).
Aurelian Walls, 60: N., 207(6, 7).
Aurora Leigh, E. B. Browning's,
76: N., 230(11, 13).
Ave Maria Plena Grata, N., 241(2).

Baillie, Joanna, 85: N., her
verses; Scott's epithet, 237(47).
Ballad of Reading Gaol, The, N.,
Q., 213(23); 216(28).
Balmont, K. D., editor of the
Russian translation of *Salomé*,
N., 264(4).
Baltimore, Maryland. N., 182(3).
Barbauld, Anna Letitia, 85: N.,
237(45).
Barnard, Lady Anne, Scott's re-
mark, 84: N., 236(41).
Barrett, Lawrence, his admira-
tion for *Vera*, N., 195(1).
Basil-tree, the, 61: N., 217(28, 30).
Baviad, William Gifford's, N., Q.,
237(44).

Beardsley, Aubrey, N., 263(4)
fol., 264 (Note).
Beaudelaire, Charles, 45; Q., 49:
N., 199(11).
Beaumont and Fletcher, N., Q.,
209(12).
Becky Sharp, 85.
Beecher, Rev. Henry Ward, N.,
entertains Wilde, 189(8).
Beerbohm, Max, Q., xxvii: N.,
180(42).
Behn, Aphra, 83: N., her plays,
verses, etc.; Swinburne's statement, 235(33).
Bellew, Kyrle, for the part of
Czarevitch in *Vera*, N., 196(2).
Bernard-Beere, Mrs., N., 195(1).
Berners, the Abbess Juliana, 82:
N., her life and works, 233(25).
Bernhardt, Sarah, the interpreter
of *Salomé*, 137; the greatest
artist on any stage, 138; for
whom it is the fashion to write
single-rôle pieces, 139; prevented by engagements from
giving an invitation performance of *Salomé*, 140; met
W. at Henry Irving's; asked
to have *Salomé* read to her;
at once wished to play title-
rôle, 142; to produce play
in Paris, 143; W.'s sonnet
to her, 150; her desire to take
part of *Salomé* a source of
pleasure to W., 151; the play
not written for her, 152: N.,
her failure to produce play, as
anticipated, 257(2); for whom
Marcel Schwob adapted *Hamlet*,
258(8); who inspired *Salomé*,
according to E. Gómez Carrillo,
259(10); her acting in *Phèdre*,
263(1); for whom *Salomé* was
written, according to *The Times*,
263(3).
Bernhardt, Sarah, Sonnet to,
Q.i.f., 150: N., 263(1).
Best of Oscar Wilde, The (1904),
collected by Oscar Herrmann;
edited by W. W. Massee, N.,
216(28).
Bicchierai, Olga, N., 264(4).
Birthday of the Infanta, The, N.,
Q., 255(4).
Blei, Franz, N., 175(4), 246(6).
Boccaccio, N., Q., 217(30), 222
(12).
Bogue, David, publisher of W.'s
Poems, N., 205(1).
Boke of St. Albans, Juliana Ber-
ners', 82: N., 233(25).
Boniface, G. C., as the Czar in
Vera, N., 196(1).
Boston, Mass, xvi, 90: N., 182(3),

INDEX

188(7), 189(8, 9) fol., 190(10) fol., 191(11), 195(1), 266(2).
Boston Music Hall, *N.*, 188(7).
Boucher, Maurice, 132.
Boucicault, Dion, *N.*, 195(1).
Brawne, Fanny, W.'s sonnet on Keats' love letters to, Q.i.f., 56: *N.*, Keats' love letters to: their publication; Mr. H. B. Forman's comment on publication, 205(2) fol.; Mr. Sidney Colvin's attitude, 206(2); sale by auction; quotation from letter XXXIX, 206(3).
Brignole Sale, Palazzo,*N.*,213(23).
Briton, the typical, Tartuffe seated in his shop behind the counter, 148.
Brompton, 85, 100.
Brontë, Emily, 85: *N.*, her poems, 239(58).
Brookfield, Charles, *N.*, 259(11) fol.
Brooklyn, N. Y., *N.*, 188(7) fol.
Brown, Charles Armitage, 66: *N.*, 219(4); his life, 221(9) fol.
Browning, Elizabeth Barrett, 58; the one great poetess whom England has given the world: by whose side Swinburne would put Christina Rossetti, 73; approachable only by Sappho, 74; the latter only a memory, the former an imperishable glory to our literature; *The Cry of the Children, Sonnets from the Portuguese*, 75; *Vision of the Poets*, etc.; her debt to Greek literature and Italy, 76; the strength and sincerity of her poetry; the deliberate ruggedness of her rhyme; its pleasurable element of surprise, 77; her ideal of the poet's mission, with quotations, 78; as the wisest of the Sibyls; her influence on the awakening of woman's song, 79; 80–1, 84, 86: *N.*, the first really great poetess of our literature, 229(2); chronology of the poems mentioned, 230(9–11); home in Florence, 230(12); first great English poetess; an admirable scholar, 230(13); her marriage and journey to Italy, 230(14); letters to R. H. Horne, 230(15); her life's work "not reverie, but art," 230(16); 247(9).
Browning, E. B., Letters of, to R. H. Horne, 77: *N.*, *Q.*, 230(16); 230(15), 247(9).
Browning, Robert, 130: *N.*, 230 (12, 14), 233(21).

Bunthorne, Reginald—in *Patience, N.*, 176(12) fol., 188(7).
Burgess, Gilbert, xxv; Q., 163–72: *N.*, 269(1).
Burlington, The. A Monthly Magazine, edited by Helen B. Mathers, *N.*, 216(28).
Burlington House, 51, 96.
Burnand, Sir Francis Cowley, xv: *N.*, 176(10), 177(13).
Byron, 58, 77: *N.*, 213(22), 222(12), 225(18).

Caine, Hall, *N.*, 229(3).
Caliban, 54: *N.*, 203(13).
California, 14, 66: *N.*, 182(3), 184(13) fol., 187(1), 188(4).
Callanan, Helena, author of *The Shamrock*, Q., 155–6: *N.*, 265 (2) fol.
Cambridge, England, *N.*, 197(2).
Camelot, 72 (K. 1).
Canaan, a patriarch of, 52.
Carew, Elizabeth, 83: *N.*, patroness of poets, 234(29).
Caricatures, of W., xiv, xv: *N.*, 176(10), 177(14) fol., 182(4, 7) fol., 190(10), 257(1).
Carlyle, 81: *N.*, his rhetoric, 232(19).
Carpenter, G. R., *N.*, 176(9).
Carrillo, E. Gómez, *N.*, *Q.*, 259(10), 264(4).
Carte, R. D'Oyly, W.'s manager in America, 32: *N.*, 176(12), 181(2), 190(10), 195(1), 196(2). See *Letters, unpublished.*
Casa Guidi, 76: *N.*, 230(12).
Casa Guidi Windows, E. B. Browning's, 76: *N.*, 230(11).
Catch phrases, used by W. See *Phrases.*
Cenci, Shelley's, 129.
Censor, Lines to our New, William Watson's, *N.*, 258(9) fol.
Censorship, Government, over imaginative literature; the arts, 110; the drama (according to W.'s interviewer), 137–8; apparently regards the stage as the lowest of all arts, 139; allows the low and shameful in life to be portrayed, but suppresses ennobling subjects from the Bible; its injury to actors, 140; bars the great religious operas (examples cited), 141; yet allows the private individual to be caricatured on the stage, 143; 147–8.
Censure and "Salomé," The, xxiv, 135, 137–43: *N.*, 248(15); Notes for, 257–60; 261(4, 6), 264(5).

INDEX

276

Centlivre, Susannah, 84: *N.*, her plays; Pope's comment, 236(40).
Century Guild Hobby Horse, The, N., its history, 219(1); 220(7), 224(16), 253(3).
Century Magazine, The, N., 177 (14), 208(10), 209(12), 214(25) fol., 216(26), 219(3), 225(18) fol., 226(21).
Cestius, Caius, 58: *N.*, 207(6, 7) fol., 211(19).
Chain of Pearl, A, by Diana Primrose, 83.
Chapman, Elizabeth R., 80: *N.*, her poems; W.'s comment, 232(18, XII).
Chapone, Hester, 85: *N.*, her essays, 238(48).
Charles I, of England: dress at the time of, 7; 83.
Charmides, N., 241(3).
Chelsea, 51: *N.*, 199(12), 243(9).
Chéret, 123.
Chicago, Illinois, *N.*, 182(3), 190(10).
Chickering Hall, N. Y., *N.*, 181(2).
Childs, George W., *N.*, 189(8).
Chinese Quarter, the, at San Francisco, 14; *N.*, 185(13).
Chinese Sage, A, *Q.*, 146.
Christ, on the cross, 139; 140.
Chronicle, The Daily (London), *N.*, 245(1).
Cicero (*Select Letters*), the copy of, which W. used and annotated with copious marginal notes during his course at Oxford, *N.*, 216(28).
Cimon, 89: *N.*, 242(5, 6).
Cincinnati, Ohio, *N.*, 182(3), 215(26).
Clarke, Charles Cowden, 69: *N.*, *Q.*, 225(18); 22(9), 226(19, 20).
Claude Lorraine, 29: *N.*, 194(10).
Cleopatra, 84.
Coghlan, Miss Rose, for the part of Vera; in *A Woman of No Importance, N.*, 196(2).
Colonel, Burnand's, xv: *N.*, 177 (13).
Colvin, Sidney, *N.*, *Q.*, 206(2), 223(13).
Commination Service, 54.
Common sense, the enemy of romance, 102 (K. 7).
Cork Weekly Herald, The, N., 265(2) fol.
Corneille, Pierre, *N.*, 235(34).
Corot, Jean B. C., 170.
Correggio, 10: *N.*, 184(11).
Correggio, Antonio Allegri da. His Life, etc., by Corrado Ricci, *N.*, *Q.*, 184(11).

Cowley, Abraham, 83: *N.*, 235(34).
Craik, Mrs. George Lillie. See *Mulock*.
Critic, The (New York), *N.*, 246(5), 267(6), 270(7).
Critic as Artist, The. Part I, Q., 18, 24, 40, 64, 72, 88, 154: *N.*, *Q.*, 232(20), 233(21).
Critic as Artist, The. Part II, Q., xi, xii, xx, xxiii, xxvii, xxix, 2, 18, 32, 40, 88, 102, 118, 122, 128, 146, 154, 162: *N.*, *Q.*, 175 (5), 198(9, 10), 243(10), 246 (4), 255(3), 270(9); 175(7), 179(28), 180(38, 43), 251(3).
Criticism, dramatic, lack of prejudice necessary for, 136 (K. 2); its poverty in England, 143; a misnomer, 163; in our own day has never had a single success, 164; its representatives in need of education, 168; they subordinate psychological interest to mere technique, 168 fol.; they believe it the duty of the dramatist to please the public, 169 fol.
Criticism, the function of, xxiv, 24 (K. 4, 5), 40 (K. 5), 45, 103, 105–6, 110–2, 114–5, 126, 136 (K. 2), 143, 162 (K. 4), 163–4: *N.*, 198(9), 246(4).
Cry of the Children, E. B. Browning's, 75: *N.*, 230(9).
Crystal Palace, the, 43.

Damascus, tiles of, xxi, 40 (K. 4), 72 (K. 1).
Daniel Press, the, *N.*, 215(25).
Dante, 65, 76–7: *N.*, 220(6).
Dante, the, in which Keats wrote his notes, 65.
Darmesteter, Mrs. Mary F. (Robinson), 80: *N.*, her works; W.'s opinion of her poems, 231 (18, V).
Darmont, Albert, 137.
Davray, Henry–D., *N.*, *Q.*, 214 (23); 257(2), 261(2).
Decamerone, Il, of Boccaccio, translation of, *N.*, 217(30).
Decay of Lying, The, Q., xi, xix, 2, 24, 64, 72, 88, 102, 122, 128, 136; xiv: *N.*, *Q.*, 201(3), 212(19), 232(21), 233(22), 247 (8, 12) fol., 248(13); 175(6), 178(25).
Decorative Art in America, xvii fol., 1, 3–15: *N.*, 178(16, 21–2, 24), 179(26, 32, 35); Notes for, 181–5; the first delivery of the lecture, 181(1); 203(12), 207 (5).
De Goncourt, Edmond, 98: *N.*, 244(16–7).

INDEX
277

De Goncourt, Jules, 98: *N.*, 244 (16).
Delaroche, Paul, 45: *N.*, 199 (12, I, II).
Delphi, 79: *N.*, 230(17) fol., 242(4).
Denver, Colorado, *N.*, 182(3).
De Profundis, Q., ix fol., 48, 88, 102: *N.*, Q., 203(13), 270(9); 175(1), 181(1), 214(23): in German, in French, 257(2); in Italian, Q., 264(4).
De Profundis. Aufzeichnungen und Briefe, Max Meyerfeld's translation, *N.*, 257(2).
De Profundis. Précédé de Lettres, etc., Henry–D. Davray's translation, *N.*, 214(23), 257(2).
Detroit, Michigan, *N.*, 183(9), 184(10).
Devonshire, Georgiana, Duchess of, 85: *N.*, her verses; Walpole's comment, 238(52).
Dial, The (London), *N.*, 219(4) fol., 220(6).
Dickens, Charles, 118 (K. 1).
Diplomacy, adapted from Sardou's *Dora*, 169.
Disraeli, Benjamin, Earl of Beaconsfield, his description of L. E. L., 85: *N.*, 238(50).
Divorçons, Sardou's, 141: *N.*, 258(7), 270(8).
Dora, Sardou's, 169: *N.*, 270(8).
Dorian, the grave, mode of verse, 80.
"*Dorian Gray*" *and its Critics*, xxiv, 101, 103–16: *N.*, Notes for, 245–9; 269(4).
Douglas, Lord Alfred, *N.*, Q., 226(18); 263(3, 4) fol.
Dramatic Art, the canons of, xxiv, 24 (K. 6), 32 (K. 2), 33, 36–7, 128 (K. 3).
Dramatic Critics and "An Ideal Husband," xxv, 161, 163–72: *N.*, Notes for, 269–70.
Dramatic Review, The, N., 205(1).
Dream, On a, Keats' sonnet, *N.*, 220(6).
Dress Reform (general), 43, 48 (K. 1, 2), 53: *N.*, 197(4), 207(5).
Dress Reform, for men, xv–xvii, xxii fol., 6–8, 53: *N.*, 183(8).
Dress Reform, for women, 7, 8, 52–3: *N.*, 183(6), 202(9, 10).
Dress Reform, More Radical Ideas Upon, Q., 48: *N.*, Q., 202(9).
Drummond, William, of Hawthornden, 83.
Dryden, John, 83.
Dublin University Magazine, The, N., 207(5).

Duchess of Padua, The, N., 253(4).
Dufferin, Lady Helen Selina, 85: *N.*, her lyrics, 238(53, I).
Du Maurier, George, *N.*, 176(10).
Dunciad, Pope's, 84: *N.*, Q., 235(32), 236(37, 40).
"Dusenbury, Hugo"—in *Puck*, *N.*, 177(14).

Easter Day, N., 241(2).
Eclectic Magazine, The, N., 175 (6), 179(29), 198(6).
Elizabeth of Bohemia, sister of Charles I, 83: *N.*, "The Queen of Hearts" in Wotton's poem, 234(31) fol.
Elizabeth of England, Q., 82–3: *N.*, her scholarship, translations, poems, quotation from her "sonnet"; her letters, 233 (27) fol.
Elizabethan Age, scenery of the, 29.
Elpinike, 89: *N.*, 242(5).
Emerson, *N.*, Q., 199(12, II).
Endymion (Keats), 56 (K. 2).
Endymion, Keats', 83: *N.*, 222 (12).
England, the home of lost ideas, 136 (K. 4); its narrowness in artistic judgment, 142; its establishment of Public Opinion, an attempt to organize the ignorance of the community, 146 (K. 3); where it is impossible to have a work of art performed, 147.
English Illustrated Magazine, The, N., 241(1).
English Poetesses, 71, 73–86: *N.*, Q., 208(9); Notes for, 229–39.
Epistle to Charles Cowden Clarke, Keats', *N.*, Q., 226(19).
Erōs, Sappho, the child of, 74.
Essays, Criticisms and Reviews, *N.*, 182(6), 229(2). See *Woman's World*.
Essays in Miniature, Agnes Repplier's, *N.*, 176(9).
Ethics and the Arts, the relation between, xxi, xxiii, xxiv, 40 (K. 4), 48 (K. 5), 102 (K. 1, 3), 103–5, 107–10, 112–3: *N.*, 246(4).
Ethics of Journalism, The, xxv, 153, 157–60: *N.*, Notes for, 265–7.
Eton, 98.
Every Day in the Year (1902), edited by James L. and Mary K. Ford, *N.*, 216(28).
"Exargasia, or the Gorgeous in Literature," Queen Elizabeth's "most sweet and sententious

278 INDEX

ditty," so termed by Putten-
ham, 82.
Exercise, the only possible, to
talk, not walk, 172.
Exodus, N., Q., 208(9).
Eyre, Sir Vincent, *N.,* 211(17).

Fame and Obscurity, the differ-
ence between, viii.
Fancy Ball, as the basis of Art,
52, 100: *N.,* 244(19).
Field, Kate, *N.,* 189(8).
Fifth Avenue, New York, 3, 8.
Fisherman and His Soul, The, N.,
Q., 212(21).
Fitznoodle in America—in *Puck,
N.,* 177(14).
Flaubert, Gustave, *N.,* 212(19).
Fletcher, 83.
Flockton, for the part of Prince
Paul in *Vera, N.,* 196(2).
Florence, Italy, 13, 27, 60, 76,
150: *N.,* 215(27), 230(12).
Forman, Mr. Harry Buxton, Q.,
68: *N.,* Q., 205(2) fol., 220(7),
222(13) fol., 224(15–7) fol.; 208
(10) fol., 215(25), 220(6).
Fortescue, Mrs. Marion T., W.
entertained by, *N.,* 188(3).
Fortnightly Review, The, xiii: *N.,*
176(8), 179(29), 198(6), 245(3).
See also *Pen, Pencil and Poi-
son, Poems in Prose, Preface
to the Picture of Dorian
Gray,* and *Soul of Man Under
Socialism.*
Franzos, Berta, *N.,* 246(6).
Freeman, Edward A., 82.
Freeman's Journal, The (Dublin),
N., 181(1), 202(9).
Freer, Mr. Charles L., of Detroit,
Mich., *N.,* 183(9), 184(10).
French criticism, 112.
French prose, compared to Eng-
lish. See *Prose.*
French Revolution, the, 3.
French song, the graceful forms
of old, 80.
Frères Zemganno, Les, by Ed-
mond de Goncourt, 98: *N.,*
244(17).
Froude, James Anthony, 81.
Fumagalli, Mario, *N.,* 264(4).
Fuseli, Henry, 94: *N.,* his life,
and art, 243(12) fol.
Fusiyama, Mount, 44: *N.,* 198(7).

Gainsborough, Thomas, 26.
Gamberale, L., *N.,* 257(2).
Garden of Erôs, The, Q., 56.
Garden of Florence, The, J. H.
Reynolds', Q., 67: *N.,* Q., 222
(11), 224(17); 222(12), 223(14).

Gathered (Scattered) Leaflets, N.,
265(2) fol.
Gaulke, Johannes, *N.,* 246(3).
Gaulois, The, 142, 147: *N.,*
261(1).
Gay, John, *N.,* 235(35).
Gazette, The Saturday Evening
(Boston), *N.,* its attacks on W.,
N., 190(10) fol.
Gazettes. See *Pall Mall Gazette*
and *St. James Gazette,* and
above.
Genoa, 60: *N.,* 213(23), 241(2).
Gentle Art of Making Enemies,
Whistler's, Q., x: *N.,* 198(11)
fol., 199(12, I, II), 243(9);
175(2), 190(9), 197(1, 2),
198(6). See *"Ten O'Clock."*
Gentleman's Magazine, The, N.,
226(20).
Gibbon, Edward, Q., 85.
Gide, André, Q., xxix: *N.,* Q.,
246(6); 261(2).
Gifford, William, 85: *N.,* Q.,
237(44).
Gil Blas, 90.
Gilbert, William Schwenck, xv:
N., 176(12), 188(6).
Giorgione, Basil—in *The Colonel,
N.,* 177(13).
"Girl Graduate," her letter on
dress reform, *N.,* 202(10).
Girometti's medallion of Keats,
N., 215(25).
Globe, The Boston Daily, N., Q.,
189(9), 190(10); 187(2).
Glover, J. M., *N.,* 259(11).
Goethe, Q., 102 (K. 4).
Golden Gleams of Thought
(1881), edited by Rev. S. P.
Linn, *N.,* 216(28).
"Golden Screen, The," by Whist-
ler, *N.,* 201(4).
Golden Treasury, Palgrave's, *N.,*
Q., 235(31).
Gonsowska, Hew., *N.,* 264(4).
Goring, Lord—in *An Ideal Hus-
band,* 168.
Gosse, Edmund, 83.
Gounod, Charles, 141: *N.,* 258(5).
Graces, the flower of the, 74.
Grande Revue, La, N., 226(18),
241(1), 257(2), 261(2).
Grant, General, *N.,* 189(8).
Grave of Keots, The, N., bibl.,
Q.i.f., 216(28) fol.; 230(8).
Grave of Shelley, The, N., Q.,
211(19), 212(21); 241(2).
Gray, Dorian—in *The Picture of
Dorian Gray,* 108.
Gray, Dorian, The Picture of.
See *Picture of Dorian Gray,
The.*

INDEX

279

Gray, John, 132–3: *N.*, 255(5).

Grazebrook, Hester—in *An Unequal Match*, 25–6; her dresses, 27; 29: *N.*, 193(2). See *Langtry* and *Mrs. Langtry*.

Greece, Ancient, its literature, art, language, dress, customs, etc., 7, 12, 25–7, 30, 48 (K. 1, 5), 49, 53, 74–6, 89, 92, 98, 100, 139, 147, 150: *N.*, 193(4, 5), 197(5), 202(11), 229(5, 6), 230 (8, 13, 17) fol., 234(27), 241 (2, 3) fol., 242(4–6). See *Parthenon*.

Greve, Felix Paul, *N.*, 246(3).

Grierson, Constantia, 85: *N.*, her scholarship; elegant verses, 239(55).

Grosvenor Gallery, 51.

Grosvenor Gallery, The, a critique, *N.*, 207(5).

Guido Reni, 60: *N.*, 213(23).

Hallward, Basil—in *The Picture of Dorian Gray*, 108.

Hamilton-King, Harriet E., 80: *N.*, her works, 231(18, II).

Hamlet, *N.*, 206(3).

Hampstead, 97: *N.*, 208(10), 215(25), 221(9).

Handicraftsmen, encouragement for, xvii, 4–6, 9, 13: *N.*, 207(5).

Happy Prince, The, *N.*, Q., 211 (19).

The Happy Prince and Other Tales, Q., 64; x: *N.*, 211(19).

Harper's Bazar, *N.*, 182(7); 178 (14).

Harper's Weekly, *N.*, 182(4); 178(14), 189(9).

Hartford, Conn., *N.*, 182(3).

Harvard students, their treatment of W., xvi: *N.*, 188(7).

Hawtrey, Charles, *N.*, 259(11) fol.

Haydon, his pen and ink sketch of Keats, 60: *N.*, his life mask of Keats, 215(25) and 219(3); "Christ's Entry into Jerusalem," 215(26).

Haywood, Eliza, 84: *N.*, her novels and poems; Pope's satire, 236(37).

Hazlitt's lectures, Keats at, 60: *N.*, 225(18).

Hebrew literature, 139.

Helen of Troy, 26: *N.*, 193(4).

Hellas, Sappho, the pride of, 74.

Hellenism, an oasis of, a good circus, 98.

Hemans, Felicia, 85: *N.*, 239(56).

Herald, Chicago, *N.*, its attack on W., Q., 190(10).

Herald, Halifax Morning, *N.*, Q., 193(4).

Herald, New York, Q., viii, xx: *N.*, Q., 177(12), 242(7); 179 (27), 184(10), 187(2), 189(7), 270(7).

Hérodiade, Massenet's, 141, 147: *N.*, 258(4).

Herodotus (2 vols.), the copy of, which W. used and annotated during his course at Oxford, *N.*, 216(28).

Heu Miserande Puer, a sonnet, Q.i.f., 61: *N.*, its gradual growth; subsequent appearance as *The Grave of Keats;* collated with same, 216(28) fol.; 241(2).

Hilton, William, his portraits of Keats, *N.*, 215(25).

Hitzen vase, a, 40 (K. 4).

Hokusai, *N.*, 198(7).

Holmes, Oliver Wendell, *N.*, 189(8).

Homer, 74.

Honour School, The, 107: *N.*, 247(11).

Horne, Richard Hengist, 77: *N.*, 230(15–6), 247(9).

Horwood, A. J., Q., 67–8: *N.*, Q., 223(14) fol.; 220(7).

Houghton, Lord (R. M. Milnes), Q., 58; 66–9: *N.*, Q., 209(13) fol., 225(18); 211(18); his life, 221(8); MSS. of Keats, 222 (9); 222(10), 224(14, 17) fol.

House of Pomegranates, A (the book), x, 123; its illustrators and their specific contributions, 124; *The Speaker's* description of the cover; W.'s view of its artistic beauty; what it suggests to W., 125–6: *N.*, Q., 212(21), 255(4); full text of title-page; description by the Chiswick Press, 253(3); 254(5).

"*House of Pomegranates, A*," 121, 123–26: *N.*, Notes for, 253–4.

Howe, Julia Ward, *N.*, 189(8); entertains W. on his Boston trip; defends him in print; extracts from her letter to *Boston Daily Globe;* entertains W. at Lawton's Valley during his July visit to Newport, 189(9).

Hunt, Leigh, *N.*, Q., 225(18); 213 (22), 222(12).

Ideal Husband, An, Q., 24, 102; 163; the critics at sea over its significance; its psychological

280 INDEX

import; the bracelet incident not borrowed from Sardou, 168: *N., W.*'s presentation copy to Charles Shannon, 253(4); the first night; bibl., 269(2).
Illustrated London News, The, N., 263(3), 270(7).
Importance of Being Earnest, The, Q., 102: *N., W.*'s presentation copy to "the wonderful Sphinx," 212(19); its possible cover designer, 253(4).
Impression de Voyage, N., 241(2).
Impressions, W.'s several, parodied, *N.,* 177(14).
Impressions of America, N., Q., 185(13, 17), 243(7).
Impressionist Painting, by Wynford Dewhurst, *N.,* 184(10).
In a Balcony, Browning's, 130.
In Memoriam. O. W., Franz Blei's, *N.,* 175(4); translated into English by Percival Pollard, 246(6); 261(2).
Incomparable and Ingenious History of Mr. W. H., The, N., 254(5).
"Indian Civilian, An," 119: *N.,* 251(2).
Individualism, *W.*'s ideas regarding, xxix (K. 1), 18 (K. 7), 32 (K. 3), 40 (K. 2, 5), 48 (K. 4), 115, 124–5, 132–3, 136 (K. 3) 146 (K. 1), 147, 151–2, 160, 162 (K. 1, 3), 169–70: *N.,* 246 (4), 249(19).
Individuality and personality, the chief characteristics of the masterpieces of our literature, 80; individuality, in art, 88 (K. 2, 5); in acting, 130–1, 169–70.
Ingelow, Jean, 80: *N.,* her works; *W.*'s comment on her *Chess King,* 231(18, VI).
Intentions, xiii, xiv, xviii: *N.,* 175(6), 251(3); translated into French by J.–Joseph Renaud, 226(18), 257(2). See also *The Critic as Artist, Parts I* and *II, The Decay of Lying, Pen, Pencil, and Poison,* and *The Truth of Masks.*
Interview with Oscar Wilde (New York World), Q., 32, 122.
Interviews, with W., Q., viii, xx, xxix (K. 2), 32, 122, 138–43, 163–72; xxiv, xxv: *N.,* Q., 198(10), 242(7) fol., 246(6); 176(11), 184(13), 195(1), 226 (18), 259(10). See *Anecdotes.*
Introduction to *Decorative Art in*

America, vii, ix–xxvii: *N.,* Notes for, 175–80, 203(12), 207(5).
Introductory Keynotes. See *Keynotes.*
Ireland, 142, 148, 155–6: *N.,* 181 (1), 202(9), 207(5), 216(28), 235(34), 238(53), 239(55), 241 (2), 259(9), 265(2) fol., 266 (5) fol.
Irish Monthly, The, N., 207(5), 216(28), 241(2).
Irish Winner of the Newdigate, An, by the Editor of *The Irish Monthly, N.,* 241(2).
Irving, Sir Henry, 142: *N.,* his portrait by Whistler, 201(4).
Isabella, with reference to Keats' poem of that name, *N.,* 217(28).
Isabella, Keats', *N.,* Q., 217(30); 222(12).
Isabella, Story of, Boccaccio's, translated by John Payne, *N.,* Q., 217(30).
Israel, The Children of, 57.
Italia, N., 241(2).

Japan, 44, 51: *N.,* 193(5), 198(7).
"Japanese Girls on the Terrace," by Whistler, *N.,* 201(4).
Jewelry, modern, 13.
Joaquin Miller, the Good Samaritan, xxv, 17, 19–22: *N.,* 178 (19); Notes for, 187–91.
Johnson, Esther (Swift's "Stella"), 84: *N.,* 237(43).
Johnson, Robert Underwood, *N.,* Q., 209(12).
Johnson, Samuel, 84: *N.,* 237(44).
Jonson, Ben, 83: *N.,* Q., 234(30).
Jorba, J. Pérez, *N.,* 264(4).
Journalism, *W.*'s remarks on; its attacks on W., viii; xv–xviii, xxiv, xxv, 18 (K. 2–4), 19, 21–2, 81, 103–16, 118 (K. 1), 130, 146 (K. 1, 3), 151, 154 (K. 1, 2), 157–60, 170: *N.,* 177 (14) fol., 189(9) fol., 190(10) fol., 191(11), 196(1), 201(2), 242(7) fol., 248(17) fol., 263 (3), 265(2) fol., 266(5) fol.
Judæa, 72 (K. 1).
Judas Maccabæus, Rubinstein's, 141: *N.,* 258(6).

Kansas City, *N.,* 182(3).
Keats, George, 65, 69: *N.,* his life, 219(4) fol.; 227(22).
Keats, George, Memoir of, by J. F. Clarke, *N.,* Q., 219(4) fol.; 220(6).
Keats, Mrs. George, 69: *N.,* 219(4).
Keats, John, 3, 56 (K. 1, 2); his

INDEX

281

burial-place; inscription on his tomb; the cemetery described by Lord Houghton and Shelley, 58; his love of flowers, with citations; the nature of his tomb; his medallion-profile; the beauty of his countenance as represented by Severn and Haydon; the Priest of Beauty; compared to St. Sebastian, 59–60; W.'s sonnet to him, 61; his delicate sense of colour-harmonies shown in the *Sonnet on Blue;* original MS. of this in the possession of Mrs. Speed, 65; the gradual growth of this sonnet noted, 66; this growth shown by quotation i.f. and collation, 67–9; colour of his eyes; his sonnet to his brother, George, Q., 69; his remark Q., with reference to Katherine Philips, 83; read Mrs. Tighe's *Psyche* with pleasure, 85: *N.,* his love letters to Fanny Brawne published, 205(2) fol. (see *Forman* and *Colvin*); love letters sold at auction, 206(3); his grave, with references to illustrations and descriptions of same, 208(10) fol.; his dying request to Severn, 209(11); poems in his honour, 209(12); remarks of Houghton and Shelley on the cemetery, Q.i.f., 209–10(13–4); his love of flowers, with citations, 210(15); The Keats-Shelley Memorial at Rome, 210(16); the committee of 1875, 211(17); his many portraits; the artists and articles concerning the same, 214(25) fol. (see *Keats, pictures of*); Haydon's life mask, etc., 215(25–6); W.'s revised sonnet to him, Q.i.f., 216(28) fol.; his *Isabella;* its source, 217(30); his resemblance to certain American relatives, recently living, 219(3); his relations with his brother George, 219(4); his notes on Milton; admiration for Dante, 220(6); his *Sonnet on Blue,* Q.i.f., from the facsimile, 220(7) fol. (see *Sonnet on Blue*); relations with Charles A. Brown, 221(9) fol.; with John Hamilton Reynolds, 222(12); his personal appearance: colour of his eyes and hair, 225(18) fol. (see *Keats' appearance*); his relations with Charles Cowden Clarke, 226(19); with Joseph Severn, 226(21);

his reference to Mrs. Tighe, 239(54). Allusions to his poems, prose, and letters, with quotations, sources and bibliographical matter, occur, *N.,* 205–227 *passim.*
Keats' appearance, according to: Mrs. Procter, 59–60 (Note), 69; Mrs. George Keats, C. C. Clarke and Severn, 69: *N.,* Mrs. Procter, C. C. Clarke and Leigh Hunt, 225(18); Severn, 226(18).
Keats, pictures of by: Severn and Haydon, 60 (Note); Severn, 69: *N.,* Warrington Wood, 211(17); Severn, Haydon, Hilton, Girometti; bust by Anne Whitney, 214–5(25–6); Severn, 226(21).
Keats' *Endymion.* See *Endymion.*
Keats' *Epistle to C. C. Clarke.* See *Epistle.*
Keats' *Isabella.* See *Isabella.*
(*Keats*) *George, To my Brother,* Keats' Sonnet, Q., 69: *N.,* 227(22).
Keats' *Lamia.* See *Lamia.*
Keats' letter, a, to James Rice (Feb. 16, 1820), *N.,* Q., 210(15).
Keats' *Sonnet on Blue.* See *Sonnet on Blue.*
Keats, John, Letters of, to *Fanny Brawne* (1878), edited by H. Buxton Forman, *N.,* 205(2) fol.
Keats, John, Letters of (1891), edited by Sidney Colvin, *N.,* 206(2).
Keats, John, Letters of (1895), edited by H. Buxton Forman, *N.,* Q., 205(2) fol., 206(3).
Keats, John, Letters and Poems of (1883), edited by John Gilmer Speed, *N.,* 220(5).
Keats, John, Life, Letters and Literary Remains of (1848), by Lord Houghton, Q., 58–9, 59–60 (Note), 67, 69; 66: *N.,* Q., 209(13) fol., 225(18); 211(18), 221(8), 222(9, 10), 224(14, 17).
Keats, John, Odes Sonnets & Lyrics of, printed by the Daniel Press, *N.,* portrait in, 215(25).
Keats, John, Poetical Works and Other Writings of, edited by H. Buxton Forman, London, 1883, *N.,* Q., 224(15, 17) fol.; 205(2) fol., 208(10) fol., 215 (25); Glasgow, 1901, Q., 224 (16); 220(6).
Keats, John, Poetry and Prose by. A Book of Fresh Verses, etc. (1890), edited by H. Buxton Forman, *N.,* Q., 220(7), 214(25) fol.

282 INDEX

Keats and Severn, The Graves of, N., Q., 219(3), 225(18) fol.; 218(10).
Keats in Hampstead, N., 208(10), 215(25).
Keats, Last Days of, Joseph Severn's Account of the, Q., 59: N., Q., 209(11).
Keats, Life of, by Sidney Colvin, N., Q., 206(2), 223(13).
Keats, Portraits of, etc., by William Sharp, N., Q., 215(26); 214(25) fol.
Keats' Sonnet on Blue, 63, 65–69: N., 182(3), 211(18), 215(25); Notes for, 219–228.
Keats, Tomb of. See Tomb of Keats.
Keats, Fragment on, Shelley's, N., Q.i.f., 209(12). See also Grave of Keats, Keats' Love Letters (below), and Name Writ in Water.
Keats' Love Letters, On the Recent Sale by Auction of, a sonnet, Q.i.f., 56: N., hibl. of 205(1); date and account of sale by auction 206(3). See also Fanny Browne.
Keats-Shelley Memorial, the proposed; its supporters and its object, 210(16) fol.
Kelly, J. E., his etching of W., N., 181(1).
Kendall, May, 80: N., her works, 231(18, VII).
Kendrick, Charles, his caricatures of W., N., 178(14).
Keynotes, Introductory, viii, xxix, xxx, 2, 18, 24, 32, 40, 48, 56, 64, 72, 88, 102, 118, 122, 128, 136, 146, 150, 154, 162, 174, 272.
Kiefer, Dr., N., 264(4).
King Henry VIII, N., Q., 209(12).
King Lear, 90.
Kipling, Rudyard, criticism of, 118 (K. 1), 119–20.
Koolapoor, The Rajah of, bust of, 60: N., 215(27).
Kottabos, N., 214(24), 216(28).

L. E. L. See Landon.
L. E. L., Christina Rossetti's, N., Q., 238(50).
Labouchere, Henry, owner and editor of Truth, viii.
Lachmann, Hedwig, N., 264(4).
Lady Alroy, N., 212(19).
Lady's Pictorial, The, N., Q., 226(18).
Lady Windermere's Fan, 168: N., 253(4); burlesqued, 259(11); first night, 269(3); hibl. 270(6).

La Jeunesse, Ernest, N., 261(2).
Lamb, Edward, as Prince Paul in Vera, N., 196(1).
Lamia, Keats', N., 223(14).
Landon, Letitia Elizabeth (L. E. L.), 85: N., her verses, etc., 238(50).
Lang, Andrew, 81.
"Lange Leizen—of the Six Marks, Die," Whistler's, N., 201(4).
Langtry, Mrs., her beauty analyzed, 25; the charm of her acting, 26; her beauty as an influence on the art of Albert Moore, Leighton, Whistler, etc.; her dresses in the part of Hester Grazebrook, 27: N., her remarks as to the model for Bunthorne in England, 177(12); her American début, 193(2); Wilde's comment on her beauty, 193(4); the fire which prevented her début as originally planned, 194(7); her trip on the Hudson, 242(7).
Lēda, Helen, the daughter of, 26.
Le Gallienne, Richard, N., 176(9).
Leighton, Frederick, Lord, 27: N., 194(6).
Leland, James Godfrey, 15: N., 185(15).
L'Ermitage, N., 246(6).
Lesbos, Sappho, the singer, 75: N., 183(9–10) fol.
Letters, W.'s unpublished, Q., xxvi, 32: N., Q., 178(15), 190 (10), 195(1), 196(2); 180(41).
Lexicographer, the great, Samuel Johnson, 84.
Leyland, Frederick R., patron of Whistler; his "Peacock Room," N., 183(9–10) fol.
Life, N., 178(14), 270(7).
Lippincott's Magazine, 113: N., 245(3), 248(17).
Literæ Humaniores, 107: N., 247 (11).
Literature, the rights of, 115; difference between it and journalism, 154 (K. 1).
Literature and Dogma, Arnold's, N., 247(8).
Literature and Painting, the relation between, xxi, 40 (K. 4), 48 (K. 5).
Literary and Other Notes, Q., 136: N., Q., 229(2), 230(13), 231(18, VI), 232(18, IX, XII, 21), 235(35), 263(1); 182(6), 233(25. See asterisk), 235(32).
Literary Notes, Some, Q., 122: N., Q., 231(18, VIII) fol., 233(24), 237(46), 254(6).

INDEX

283

"Little White Girl, The," by Whistler, *N.*, 183(9).
Lives of the Cæsars, of Suetonius, 107.
"London Editor, A," 113–4: *N.*, his letter, Q.i.f., 248(17) fol.
London Models, 87, 89–100: *N.*, Q., 201(2), 202(6, 7), 214(24); 202(8), 207(5), 217(29); Notes for, 241–4.
Longfellow, Henry Wadsworth, *N.*, 189(8).
Lord Arthur Savile's Crime and Other Stories, N., 212(19).
Lord Byron and Some of his Contemporaries, Leigh Hunt's, *N.*, Q., 225(18).
Lord Chamberlain, the, his censorship of *Salomé,* 137–143.
Lotus Leaves, Q., xxx.
Louis Quatorze furniture, the gilded abyss of, *N.*, 194(8).
Louisville, Kentucky, 65: *N.*, 182(3), 219(2–4).

Madonna Mia, N., Q., 214(24).
Maeterlinck, Maurice, 141.
Magdalen College, xxx: *N.*, 247 (11).
Magdalen Walks, Q., xxx.
Mahaffy, Professor John P., Q., 89: *N.*, his writings, 241(2).
Mallarmé, Stéphane, *N.*, 199(11).
Man and the Actor, Richard Mansfield's, *N.*, Q., 260(12).
Monette Salomon, by E. and J. de Goncourt, 98: *N.*, 244(16).
Mansfield, Richard, *N.*, Q., 260 (12).
Mary, Queen of Scots, 82: *N.*, Queen Elizabeth's "sonnet" on, Q., 234(27).
Massenet, Jules, 141, 147: *N.*, 258(4).
"Matchless Orinda, The," Katherine Philips, 83: *N.*, 235(34).
Maturin, Rev. Charles Robert, *N.*, 214(23).
McClellan, General and Mrs., *N.*, 189(8).
McClure, Rev. William J., *N.*, 265(2).
Mediocrities, only, progress, etc., 160.
Melodrama, modern English, 128 (K. 3).
"Melmoth, Sebastian." See "*Sebastian Melmoth.*"
Melmoth the Wanderer, Charles R. Maturin's, *N.*, 214(23).
Meltzer, *N.*, 259(10).
Mercure de France, N., 261(2).
Meredith, George, as a warning,

18: *N.*, his style and art, 232 (21) fol.
Meyerfeld, Doctor Max., *N.*, 257(2).
Meynell (Thompson), Alice, 80: *N.*, her poems, 232(18, XI).
Michael Angelo, 13, 79.
Miller, Cincinnatus Heine (Joaquin), his letter to W., 19–20; W.'s reply, 20–22: *N.*, biography of, 187(1); meets W., 187(3) fol.; his visits to London, 188(4); 191 (Note).
Millet, Jean François, 26.
Milton, 65, 84: *N.*, 220(6).
Milton, Keats' notes on, *N.*, 220(6).
Milnes, Richard Monckton. See *Houghton.*
Milwaukee, Wisconsin, *N.*, 182(3).
Mimes, Marcel Schwob's, *N.*, presentation copy to W., 258(8).
Miners, Western, dress of, 8 fol.: *N.*, W. caricatured in the dress of, 182(7) fol.; W. adopts their head-gear, 183(8).
Miranda—in *The Tempest,* 132.
Mirandola, 150.
Mission of Art in the Nineteenth Century, The, 65.
Mitylene, *N.*, 217(28), 230(8).
Models, professional, 51–2; a modern invention, 89; none in America; Italian the best; the French possess quickness of intellectual sympathy; the English form a class by themselves; are without tradition, 90; usually lack interest in art, 91; will pose for anything; intellectually Philistines, 92; their habits; their tariff, 93; their dull season; the veteran of grand style, 94; the Academy model, the "apotheosis of anatomy"; the Oriental models, who have lovely costumes; the Italian youth; the English lad, who never sits at all, 95; street *gamins* who object to posing; privileges of the English, 96; influence on the English school of painting; cause of artificiality in modern art; their advantages and disadvantages, 99; should be painted as of the modern age, or not at all, 100: *N.*, 202(6, 7).
Modern Actor, The, John Gray's lecture, 132.
Montagu, Lady Mary Wortley, 84: *N.*, her verses, letters, etc., 236(39).
Monte Testaccio, 60: *N.*, 212(20).

284 INDEX

Moore Albert, 27, 48 (K. 5): N.,
  his art, 193(5).
Morality, an attitude, 102 (K. 2);
  the social code of, 166 fol.
More, Hannah, 85: N., her plays
  and verses; reference to W.'s
  review, 237(46).
Morpeth, Mary, 83.
Morris, Clara, Miss, N., 189(8);
  W.'s two letters to Carte, as
  regards her taking the part of
  Vera, 196(2).
Morris, William, N., 207 (Remark).
Morrison, Lewis, as the Czarevitch in Vera, N., 196(1).
Morse, W. F., N., sometime manager of W.'s lecture tour in
  America; W.'s letter to him
  from Omaha, 190(10); from
  Boston; his suggestion to W.
  as to copyright of Vera, 195(1).
Mr. Kipling and the Anglo-Indians, 117, 119–20: N., Notes
  for, 251.
Mr. Pater's Last Volume, Q., xii,
  174: N., Q., 232(19–20), 233
  (23); 176(7).
Mr. Whistler's "Ten O'Clock,"
  39, 41–46: N., 175(2), 179(31–
  3), 180(36); Notes for, 197–200.
Mrs. Grundy, that amusing old
  lady, 103.
Mrs. Langtry as Hester Grase-
  brook, 23, 25–30: N., 180(40);
  Notes for, 193–4.
Mrs. Langtry on the Hudson, N.,
  242(7).
Much Ado About Nothing, 108.
Mulock, Dinah Maria, 80: N., her
  poems; reference to W.'s review, 232(18, X).
Munkittrick, Mr. R. K., his parodies of W.'s Impressions, N.,
  177(14).
Muses, the, 72 (K. 3), 74, 79,
  130.
Museums, xvii, 9, 11.

Name Writ in Water, The, R. U.
  Johnson's, N., Q., 209(12).
Narcissus, 22: N., 191(11), 177
  (14).
Narcissus in Camden. A Classical
  Dialogue, Helen G. Cone's, N.,
  177(14).
Nast, Thomas, N., 178(14); his
  caricatures of W., 182(4, 7)
  fol.
Nation, The (New York), N.,
  181(2).
Neologisms, W.'s aversion to, 114:
  N., 249(18).

Nesbit (Bland), Edith, 80: N.,
  her works; W.'s review of
  Leaves of Life, 231(18, VIII)
  fol.
Newcastle, Margaret, Duchess of,
  83: N., her writings; Pope's
  comment, 235(32).
Newdigate Prize, The, Oxford,
  N., 217(29), 247(11).
New Haven, Ct., N., 182(3).
New Orleans Morning Star, N.,
  266(2).
Newport, Rhode Island, N., 183
  (8); W. lectures at Casino;
  visits Mrs. Howe; receives
  many courtesies, 189(9).
Niagara, 90: N., W.'s several
  comments on same, 242(7) fol.
Nightingale and the Rose, The,
  Q., 64.
Nile, the glories of old, 60.
Nincompoopiana, xiv: N., 176(10).
Nineteenth Century, The, xiii, 119:
  N., 175(3, 6, 7), 179(28), 229(4),
  251(3). See also The Critic, as
  Artist, Parts I and II, the De-
  cay of Lying, Shakespeare and
  Stage Costume, The True Func-
  tion and Value of Criticism, and
  The Truth of Masks.
Nocturnal Reverie, The Countess
  of Winchilsea's, 83; Words-
  worth's remark, 83–4; W.'s ob-
  jection, N., 235(35).
Norman, Henry, N., 263(3).
Norton, Hon. Caroline Elizabeth,
  85: N., her poems, 238(53, II).
Note on Some Modern Poets, A,
  Q., 72, 118: N., Q., 231(18, V);
  232(18, X).

Obelisks, Egyptian, at Rome, 57:
  N., their names; their positions
  defined, 208(8).
O'Connor, Mr. T. P., 157–60.
Ode to Solitude, Mrs. Chapone's,
  85.
Ode to the Snowdrop, Mrs. Mary
  Robinson's, 85: N., 239(57).
Ode to the West Wind, Shelley's,
  N., 212(21).
Odysseus, 150.
Omaha, Nebraska, N., 181(1), 182
  (3), 190(10).
Opera Comique, London, N., 176
  (12).
Ophelia, N., 206(3).
Oregon, 19: N., 187(1).
O'Reilly, John Boyle, N., 189(8).
Orientalism, its rejection of real-
  ism in art, 2 (K. 2).
Oroonoko, Aphra Behn's, Swin-
  burne's remark on, N., 235(33).

INDEX

285

Oscar Wilde. See *Wilde*.
"OW!", *New York World's* signature for its parodies of W.'s poems, *N.*, 177(14).
Oxford, 83, 98, 107, 130: *N.*, 197(2), 215(25), 216(28), 217 (29), 247(11), 268(3). See *Magdolen*.

Painter, the, his choice of subjects, 139. See under *Art*.
Painter, To the, W.'s reply to Whistler, *N.*, 199(12, II).
Painters and Painting, Cyclopedia of, edited by J. D. Champlin, Jr., *N.*, *Q.*, 243(12) fol.
Painting, The History of Modern, by Richard Muther, *N.*, *Q.*, 193(5); 184(10),·194(6).
Pall Mall Budget, 157–60: *N.*, 182(6), 183(8), 184(10), 197 (1), 201(1), 257(1), 265(1), 266(4, 5) fol.
Pall Mall Gazette, 157–60: *N.*, 182(6), 183(8), 197(1, 4), 201 (1), 202(10), 257(1), 265(1), 266(4, 5) fol.
Palmer, Albert M., the theatre manager, *N.*, 195(1).
Pan, Goat-foot, 150.
Pantechnicon, 53.
Paradise Lost, Milton's, 84: *N.*, 220(6).
Paris, 112, 123, 126, 131, 137–8, 141–3, 147, 151 fol.: *N.*, 182(2), 211(19), 230(14), 245(3), 247 (10), 257(2), 261(1, 2), 269(5), 270(6). See *Dovray, Gide, La Jeunesse, Renaud, Sardou, Schwob*, etc.
Paris, the Abode of Artists, xxv, 145, 147–8: *N.*, 259(9); Notes for, 261.
Parma, 10: *N.*, 184(11).
Parodies, of W.'s poems, xv: *N.*, 176(10), 177(14) fol.
Parody, W.'s remark on, *N.*, *Q.*, 178(15).
Parthenon, the, 22, 25, 45, 53: *N.*, 198(7), 241(3).
Pater, Walter, his prose, as form, 81: *N.*, as music; as mosaic, 232(20).
Pater's Last Volume, Mr. See *Mr. Pater, etc.*
Patience, W. S. Gilbert's, xv: *N.*, 176(12) fol., 188(7).
Paul, John, *Q.*, xvii; xvi: *N.*, 178(20).
Pavia, Isidore Leo, *N.*, 264(4).
"Peacock Room," Whistler's, 10: *N.*, described; formerly in the house of F. R. Leyland; now in

house of C. L. Freer, Detroit; references to accounts and illustrations of same, 183(9, 10) fol.
Peekskill, N. Y., *N.*, 189(8).
Pembroke, Mary Herbert, Countess of, 82: *N.*, her works 234(28).
Pen, Pencil, and Poison, *Q.*, 88: *N.*, *Q.*, 244(12).
Pennington, Arthur, *N.*, illustrator of *London Models;* his portrait of Wilde, 241(1).
People I Have Met, by Mary Watson, *N.*, 184(13).
People's Library, Ogilvie's, *N.*, 182(2, II).
"Perdita," Mrs. Mary Robinson, 85: *N.*, 239(57).
Perikles, 89.
Petronius Arbiter, 106–7: *N.*, 247 (10).
Pfeiffer, Emily Jane, 80: *N.*, her works, 231(18, I).
Phèdre, Racine's, *N.*, 263(1).
Phèdre, a sonnet, *N.*, 263(1). See also *Sonnet to Sarah Bernhardt*, and same in Index.
Pheidias, 89: *N.*, his art and fame, 241(3) fol.
Philadelphia, Penn., 15: *N.*, 182 (3), 185(14, 15).
Philaster, Beaumont and Fletcher's, *N.*, *Q.*, 209(12).
Philips, Katherine, 83: *N.*, her verses; a play, 235(34).
Phrases and Philosophies for the use of the Young, *Q.*, 24, 102, 272.
Phrases, catch, used by W., xii, 14–5, 20, 22, 25, 36, 45, 50, 52, 54, 57, 60–1, 72 (K. 3), 74, 80–1, 91, 95, 100, 108, 115, 131, 142, 148, 170: *N.*, 175(7) fol., 184, (12–3) fol., 185(17), 188(6), 191 (11), 193(3, 4), 198(9, 10), 201(2, 3), 202(6, 7), 203(13), 208(9), 211(19) fol., 212(21), 214(24), 216(28), 217(29), 232 (20–1), 233(24), 243(7, 8, 10–1), 244(13, 18–9), 246(4), 247(12) fol., 248(13), 249(19), 255(4), 269(4), 270(9). See *Parthenon*.
Piacenza, Donna Giovanna, Abbess of San Paolo, *N.*, 184(11).
Piazza di Spagna, 51: *N.*, 209 (12), 226(21).
Picture of Dorian Gray, The, *Q.*, 24, 146 103, 105; its chief personages *are* puppies; peculiarities of syntax; erudition, 106; its characters non-existent; its moral, 107–8; the moral the only

286 INDEX

error in the book, 109; too crowded with sensational detail; too paradoxical in style—these, its two great defects 111; its publishers, 113; the story an interesting problem, not a "novelette," 114; 115–6: *N.*, W.'s other replies to his critics, 245(1); bibl., in English, 245 (3) fol.; in French, German, Italian and Swedish, 246(3); the novel, the result of a wager, 246(6); its advertisement by Messrs. Ward & Lock; "London Editor's" comment, 248(17) fol.

Picture of Dorian Gray, The, Preface to, Q., xii, xviii, 102, 125, 128, 162: *N.*, 176(8), 178(23); sometimes termed *The Credo* or *The Dogmas*, 245(3).

Pilot, Boston, N., 266(2).

Plagiarism, the accusation of, as regards *The Shamrock*, 157; explanation of the assistant editor of *The Weekly Sun*, 158–9: *N.*, 265(1, 2) fol., 266(3–5).

Plato, 72 (K. 1, 2), 77.

Play, a, its actable value nothing to do with its value as a work of art, 129; its spectator in need of a most perfect mood of receptivity, 136 (K. 2); its relation to the stage purely accidental, 171.

Playgoers' Club, 129.

Poe, Edgar Allan, 45: *N.*, 198(11).

Poems in Prose (The Artist), Q., 56.

Poet, the, as a spectator of all time and all existence, 72 (K. 1).

Poet and the Puppets, The, a travesty by Charles Brookfield, 143: *N.*, 259(11) fol.

Poetry, English, its menace, 72 (K. 4).

Poetry, the joy of, 56 (K. 3), 64 (K. 2, 3); its field, 140; the source of bad poetry, 154 (K. 3).

Poets and the Poetry of the Century, The, edited by Alfred H. Miles, *N.*, 205(1).

Poets and Puppets—and Censors, N., 255(2), 258(3).

Poets' Praise, The (1894), collected by Estelle Davenport Adams, *N.*, 216(28).

Polygnotus, 89: *N.*, his life and art, 242(4).

Pope, Alexander, 84, 86: *N.*, Q., 235(32, 35), 236(37, 40).

Porta San Paolo, 57: *N.*, 207(6).

Post, The Washington, N., 190 (10) fol.

"Postlethwaite, Jellaby," xiv: *N.*, 176(10).

Pre-Raphaelites, the school of the, 3, 27, 48 (K. 5).

Prescott, Marie, W.'s expressed confidence in her acting, 33; 34–7 *passim*: *N.*, purchases *Vera*, 195(1); her losses; her letter of protest published in two New York papers; acts in the title-rôle, 196(1).

Prétextes, André Gide's, Q., xxix: . *N.*, Q., 246(6); 261(2). See *In Memoriam*.

Primrose, Diana, 83.

Prince Regent (George IV), 85: *N.*, 239(57).

Princes' Hall, 41.

"Princesse du Pays de la Porcelaine, La," Whistler's, *N.*, 183 (9), 184(10), 201(4).

Probyn, May, 80: *N.*, her works; W.'s opinion of her art, 232 (18, IX).

Processo e l'estetica di Oscar Wilde, Il, by L. Gamberale, *N.*, Q., 257(2).

Procter, Mrs., on Keats, Q., 59–60 (Note), 69: *N.*, Q., 225(18); 212(19).

Prose, English, compared with French; its few masters; a field for women, 81; hope that they will apply themselves to it more than to poetry, 86; the importance of artistic effect, 106: *N.*, criticisms of the work of certain masters, mostly contemporary, 232(19–21) fol., 233 (22–3); woman's unstudied felicity of phrase, 233(24).

Protestant Cemetery, the Old, at Rome, 58: *N.*, 208(10), 209 (13) fol., 210(16) fol., 227(21).

Protestant Cemetery, the New, at Rome, *N.*, 208(10), 213(22).

Psyche, Mrs. Tighe's, 85: *N.*, 239 (54).

Public Industrial Art School, The, Philadelphia, 15, *N.*, 185(14).

Puck, 54.

Puck, its cartoons and parodies of W., xv: *N.*, 177(14).

Punch, xiv: *N.*, 176(10), 177(13), 259(9), 270(7).

Puppet and Playwright, N., 255(2).

Puppets, the stage a frame furnished with a set of, 129; living actors or moving, 130; the advantages in, 131: *N.*, 255(4).

INDEX
287

Puppets and Actors, N., 255(1), 258(3).
Puttenham, George, Q., 82: *N.*, Q., 234(27) fol.
Pyramid of Cestius, the, 57–9: *N.*, 207(6, 7) fol., 211(19).
Pythia, the, 79: *N.*, 231(17).

Queen, The Lady's Newspaper, N., 229(1).

Racine, Jean, 147 fol.: *N.*, 261(5), 263(1).
Racine, Wisconsin, *N.*, 182(3).
Radcliffe, Ann, 85: *N.*, her novels, *N.*, 238(51).
Ravenna, N., Q., 217(29); 241(2), 247(11).
Reading Goal, *N.*, 212(19), 213 (23) fol. See *Ballad*.
Realism, detrimental to art in literature, 102 (K. 6), 108; its danger, 118 (K. 2); the sign of an unimaginative mind, 167: *N.*, 247(12) fol.; as a method, a failure, 248(13).
Realism in Painting and in Drama, N., 194(10).
Recollections of Writers by Charles and Mary Cowden Clarke, Q., 69: *N.*, Q., 225(18); 226(19, 20).
Reinach, Edwige, *N.*, 264(4).
Reine de Saba, La, by Gounod, 141: *N.*, 258(5).
Relation of Dress to Art, The, Q., xxiii; 47, 49–54: *N.*, Q., 243(8, 11), 244(18–9); Notes for, 201–3; 179(31–2), 180(37), 244 (15).
Relation of the Actor to the Play, The, xxiv, 127, 129–33: *N.*, Notes for, 255; 260(12).
Religion, as a subject for dramatic treatment, 138, 140–1, 147–8.
Rembrandt, 49.
Remus, the sepulchre, 57.
Renaissance, The English, Lecture on, Q., xxii, 2, 18, 32, 40, 64, 72, 136; *New York Sun's* comment, xv; "Ruskin and Water," xvi; 3: *N.*, Q., 182(5), 184(12), 188(6); 179(32); first delivery of the lecture; bibl. of same, 181(2) fol.; the Western tour, 182(3); at Rochester, 187(2); at St. Louis, 188(5); at Boston, 188(7); at Brooklyn, 189(7); 207(5).
Renan, Joseph E., 115.
Renaud, J.–Joseph, *N.*, Q., 226 (18), 241(1), 257(2), 261(2).

Repplier, Agnes, *N.*, 176(9).
Republican, The Springfield, N., its editorials on W., 191(10).
Restoration, the, 83.
Reynolds, John Hamilton, Q., 67: *N.*, Q., 222(11), 224(17); his life and relations to Keats, 222 (12); 223(14).
Reynolds, Sir Joshua, Q., 49; 26.
Revista d'Italia, N., 257(2).
Rheinisch-Westfälischen Zeitung, N., 246(6).
Rhyme, as a spiritual element, 72 (K. 3).
Ricketts, Charles, 124: *N.*, 205 (1), 211(19); an illustrator of *A House of Pomegranates*, 253(3); his connection with the Vale Press; illustrator and cover designer of several of W.'s books, 254(5).
Rise of Historical Criticism, The, N., 246(4).
Robert Elsmere, Mrs. Humphry Ward's, *N.*, 247(8).
Robertson, Johnson Forbes, for the part of Czarevitch in *Vera*, *N.*, 196(2).
Robinson, Mary. See *Darmesteter*.
Robinson, Mrs. Mary ("Perdita"), 85: *N.*, 239(57).
Rochester, New York, 19: *N.*, 182(3), 187(2), 188(7).
Rodd, Sir Rennell, *N.*, 179(30), 210(16).
Rodoshevski, Baroness, translator of *Salomé N.*, 264(4).
Rodríguez, B., *N.*, 264(4).
Rome, 57–61 *passim*, 74, 79: *N.*, 207(6, 7) fol., 208(8, 10), 209 (12–3) fol., 210(16), 211(17, 19), 212(20–1), 213(22), 216 (28) fol., 226(21) fol., 241(2).
Rome Unvisited, N., 241(2).
Roosevelt, President Theodore, *N.*, 210(16).
Rose Leaf and Apple Leaf, Rennell Rodd's, described, *N.*, 179 (30).
Rose Leaf and Apple Leaf: L'Envoi, Q., xxi, 40, 48, 64, 88: *N.*, "Privately Printed"; reprinted by Thomas B. Mosher, 179(30), 182(2, IV); 207(5).
Ross, Robert, *N.*, W.'s letters to, Q., 212(19), 214(23); repudiates translation of *The Satyricon*, 247(10); W.'s letter to him as regards *Salomé*, 257(2).
Rossetti, Christina, considered by Swinburne to be the peer of E. B. Browning, with her New Year hymn by far the noblest

288 INDEX

of sacred poems in our language; her subtle choice of words, rich imagery, etc., admitted by W.; her position, however, merely that of a very delightful artist in poetry, 73; lacking a music sufficiently passionate and profound, etc., 74: *N.*, Swinburne on *The Advent*, 229(3); Swinburne's dedications and elegy, 229(4); her poem on L. E. L., Q., 238(50).
Rossetti, Dante Gabriel, Q., 80; 142, 170: *N.*, Q., 229(3); 214 (23).
Royal College of Music, the, 123.
Rubens, *N.*, 194(10).
Rubinstein, Anton, 141: *N.*, 258(6).
Rudyard Kipling and the Anglo-Indians, 117, 119–20: *N.*, Notes for, 251.
Ruskin, John, xxi; his style, 81: *N.*, his eloquence, 233(23).
Russell, Lady Rachel, 84: *N.*, her letters, 236(36).
Russia, Nihilistic, 34.

Saint-Saëns, Camille, 147: *N.*, 261(3).
Sallust (De Catalinae Conjuratione et de Bello Jugurthino), the copy of, which W. used and annotated on interleaves, during his course at Oxford, *N.*, 216(28).
Salomé—the play—in French, its presentation prohibited in London, 137; Sarah Bernhardt charmed by it, 138; not written for her; in manuscript six months before she saw it; every rehearsal a source of pleasure to W., 139; its suppression an insult to the stage, 140; Sarah Bernhardt on having it read, immediately decided on the title-rôle, 142; in rehearsal for three weeks; costumes and everything prepared; decision to have *première* in Paris, 143; 147; W. looks forward to Paris production, 151: *N.*, the Paris *première* delayed; finally produced; its furore in Germany; production in Italy; privately in London; semi-privately in New York, 257(2) fol.; used as libretto by Richard Strauss, 264(4). See also below.
Salomé—the book—in French, Q., 24; W.'s intention to publish, 140; how it came to be written

in French; W.'s desire to touch a new instrument (the French language); written in Paris some six months before intended production, 141; reviewed in *The Times* (London), 151; was in no sense written for Sarah Bernhardt, 152: *N.*, E. Gómez Carrillo's statement that it was written for Sarah Bernhardt, 259(10); reference to reviews in *The Times;* also by Henry Norman and Lord Alfred Douglas, 263(3); first edition; the editions of Douglas' translation into English, 263(4); the three German translations; the Swedish, Spanish, Polish, Russian, and Italian translations, 264(4); new editions announced, 264 (Note).
Salomé, dancing, 139: *N.*, 259(10).
Salomé, illustrations for, *N.*, Beardsley, 263(4); Marcus Behmer, L. Valera, and in the Polish edition, 264(4).
"Salomé,, de Wilde, El Origen de la, by E. Gómez Carrillo, *N.*, Q., 259(10).
Salon, Paris, the, *N.*, 184(10).
Salvator Rosa, *N.*, 194(10), 238 (51).
Samson et Dalila, Saint-Saëns', 147: *N.*, 261(3).
San Francisco, California, 14: *N.*, 182(3), 184(13) fol., 264(4).
San Miniato, N., 241(2).
San Paolo, Camera di, at Parma, its decorations, a history and description of, *N.*, 184(11).
Sappho, to the antique world a pillar of flame, to us a pillar of shadow; "The Poetess," 74; more flawless an artist than Mrs. Browning; never had Love such a singer, 75; 85: *N.*, 208(9), 217(28), 229(5); her works, 229(6); her native home, 230(8).
Sarah Bernhardt and Salomé, 149, 151–2: *N.*, Notes for 263–4.
Sardou, Victorien, 141, 169: *N.*, 258(7), 270(8).
Satire, on Wilde, xiv, xv: *N.*, 176(10, 12), 177(13–4) fol., 182(4, 7) fol., 188(6), 190(10) fol., 191(11), 258(9) fol., 259 (11) fol.
Satire, W.'s remarks on, 18 (K. 1): *N.*, 188(6).
Saturday Review, The, xxvii: *N.*, 180(42), 255(2), 258(3), 260 (11), 270(7).

INDEX
289

Satyricon, The, of Petronius, 107: *N.,* a translation attributed to W.; repudiated by Ross, 247 (10).
Saunders' Irish Daily News, N., 207(5).
Scene-painting and stage properties, modern, 28–9: *N.,* 194(8–10).
Schwob, Marcel, *N.,* his assistance to Wilde in *Salomé,* 257(2); his works, 258(8). See also *Mimes.*
Scots Observer, The, N., 245(1).
Scott, Sir Walter, *Q.,* 84: *N., Q.,* 237(47); 238(49).
Sculptor, his choice of subjects, 139 fol.
Sculpture, modern, 6, 7, 12.
Seaside Lihrary, Munro's, *N.,* 181(2, I).
Seasons, Thomson's, 84.
"Sehastian Melmoth" (Oscar Wilde), *N.,* theory as to the origin of his *nom de plume,* 213(23) fol.; affixed to an English translation of *The Satyricon,* issued in Paris, 247(10). See *The Satyricon.*
Self-Reliance, Essay on, Emerson's, *N., Q.,* 199(12, II).
Severn, Joseph, *Q.,* 58–9; 60, 69: *N., Q.,* 209(11), 210(13), 225 (18) fol.; his grave, 208(10); 215(25), 222(9); his life; his friendship for Keats, 226(21) fol.
Severn's Account of the Last Days of Keats. See *Keats.*
Severn's Portraits of Keats, 60, 69: *N.,* 215(25), 226(21).
Sévigné, Mme. de, *N.,* 233(24).
Seward, Anna, 85: *N.,* her elegiac verses, etc.; poems edited by Scott, 238(49).
Shakespeare, 58, 76, 85, 90–1, 98–9, 108, 132: *N., Q.,* 209(12); 206(3), 255(3).
Shakespeare and Stage Costume, N., 175(3). See also *The Truth of Masks.*
Shamrock, The, by Helena Callanan, Q.i.f., 155–6; xxv, 157, 159–60: *N.,* its author, history etc., 265(2) fol.; 266(5) fol.
Shannon, Charles, 124: *N.,* as illustrator, 253(3); as coverdesigner of several of W.'s hooks, 253(4). See also *An Ideal Husband.*
Sharp, William, *N., Q.,* 215(26); 214(25) fol.
Sharp, Mrs. William, *N.,* 233(25).
Shelley, Percy Bysshe, *Q.,* 40 (K.

1), 58 fol.; his heart said to be buried in the Protestant cemetery, 60; 129: *N.,* 208(10); his
. *Fragment on Keats,* Q.i.f., 209 (12); *Q.,* 210(13–4); the proposed memorial, 210(16); W.'s sonnet on his grave, *Q.,* 211 (19), 212(21); his death hy drowning, 212(22); his cremation; his heart—where huried? inscription on his tomb, 213(22).
Shelley's *Adonais.* See *Adonais.*
Shelley's *Cenci.* See *Cenci.*
Shelley's *Fragment on Keats.* See *Keats.*
Shelley, Percy Bysshe, *Poetical Works of,* edited by H. Buxton Forman, *N.,* 213(22).
Shelley, *Recollections of,* Trelawny's, *N., Q.,* 213(22).
Shelley, *Life of,* by John Addington Symonds, *N., Q.,* 213(22).
Sherard, Rohert Harborough, *N., Q.,* 216(28), 249(18), 257(2), 258(8), 261(2).
Sherwood, Mrs. Rohert H., *N.,* 189(8).
Sihyl, 78–9.
Sidney Freemon, The, N., 266(2).
Sidney, Sir Philip, 82: *N.,* 234 (28, 30).
Singer, Mr. H. W., *Q.,* xxii fol.; xxiii: *N.,* 179(34), 184(10).
Silverpoints, John Gray's, *N.,* 255(5).
Sistine Chapel, the, 79.
Sketch, N., 269(1).
Smithers, Leonard, W.'s letter to, *Q.,* xxvi: *N.,* 180(41).
Sonnet on Approaching Italy, N., 241(2).
Sonnet on Blue, Keats', *Q.,* hy W. in a lecture at Louisville, 65; given to W. hy Mrs. Speed in MS.; an example of gradual growth, 66; Q.i.f., from Lord Houghton's version; text collated with Mr. Horwood's version in *The Athenæum,* 67; H. B. Forman's comment on the latter; W.'s doubt as to genuineness of sixth line of that version; he calls his own MS. the first draft, 67–9: *N.,* facsimile reproduction in *The Hobby Horse;* Forman's comment; facsimile, Q.i.f., with all variations, 220(7) fol.; A. J. Horwood's version; his article and sonnet, Q.i.f., 223(14) fol.; Forman's remarks on both versions, 224(15–6); Forman's punctuation of the sonnet, 224

290 INDEX

(17); Forman's reading collated with both Houghton and Horwood texts in capitalization and punctuation; remark on further variants, 225(17).
Sonnet on Dark Eyes, J. H. Reynolds', last two lines of, Q., 67: *N.*, sestet, Q., 222(11); Q., 224(17); 223(14).
Sonnet Written in Holy Week at Genoa, *N.*, 241(2).
Sonnets from the Portuguese, E. B. Browning's, 75: *N.*, 230(10).
Sotheby, Messrs., the London auctioneers, *N.*, 206(3).
Soul of Man Under Socialism, The, Q., xx, xxiii, xxix, 2, 18, 48, 136, 146, 154, 162: *N.*, Q., 201(2), 233(21), 249(19); 179 (29, 32), 180(39).
South Kensington Museum, The, 9.
Spain, 34.
Speaker, The, Q., 124–5; 123: *N.*, 176(7, 9); 253(1, 2), 254(7). See *A Chinese Sage*, "*A House of Pomegranates*," and *Mr. Pater's Last Volume*.
Spectator, The, *N.*, 258(9) fol., 260(11).
Speed, Mrs. Emma Keats, 65–6: *N.*, her resemblance to Keats, 219(3). See also *Sonnet on Blue*.
Speed, Mr. John Gilmer, *N.*, 220(5).
Spenser, 58: *N.*, 234(28–9).
Sphinx, the, 60: *N.*, its fascination for Wilde; his many references to it, 211(19) fol.
Sphinx, The, Q., with remarks as to publication, 211(19); illustrated by Charles Ricketts, 254(5); dedicated to Marcel Schwob, 258(8).
Sphinx Without a Secret, The, *N.*, 212(19). See *Lady Alroy*.
Spirit Lamp, The, edited by Lord Alfred Douglas, *N.*, 263(3).
Springfield, Mass., *N.*, 191(10).
St. James Gazette, The, Q., 104–7, 110–5; 103: *N.*, Q., 248 (17); 245(1, 2), 246(7), 248 (14, 16–7).
St. John, the Baptist, 140.
St. John, *N.*, Q., 206(4) fol.
St. Louis, Missouri, 20: *N.*, 182(3), 188(5).
St. Matthew, *N.*, Q., 206(4).
St. Patrick, 155–6.
St. Paul, Minnesota, *N.*, 182(3), 196(2).
St. Sebastian, 60–1: *N.*, 213(23) fol., 216(28).

Stage, the English, its future, 171.
"*Stale Joke, A*," *N.*, 189(9).
"Stella," Swift's. See *Esther Johnson*.
Sterne, Laurence, Q., 167.
Stevenson, Robert Louis, 81: *N.*, his delightful prose, 233(22).
Stoddart, J. M., *N.*, 179(30).
Strafford, Browning's, 130.
Strauss, Richard, *N.*, 264(4).
Studies in Prose and Verse, Arthur Symons', Q., xi: *N.*, 175(4).
Style, the very condition of any art, 102 (K. 4).
Suetonius, 106–7.
Sullivan, Sir Arthur Seymour, *N.*, 176(12).
Sun, New York, Q., xvi: *N.*, 178(17–8), 181(2), 188(7), 189 (7), 196(1), 258(3), 265(1, 2) fol., 266(3, 4), 270(7).
Sun, Weekly (London), Q., 157–60: *N.*, Q., 266(5) fol.; 265(2) fol., 266(3).
"Swan of Lichfield, The." See *Anna Seward*.
Swinburne, Algernon Charles, Q., xxiii, 73, 77; xxii, 129: *N.*, Q., 197(6) fol., 235(33); 229(3, 4).
Swift, Jonathan, 84: *N.*, 236 (42) fol., 237(43), 239(55).
Switzerland, wood carving in, 12–3.
Symonds, John Addington, *N.*, Q., 213(22); 208(10).
Symons, Arthur, Q., xi: *N.*, 175(4).
"Symphony in White, No. 3," Whistler's, *N.*, 183(9).
"Symphony in White, No. 4," Whistler's, 10: *N.*, 183(9).
Syracuse, 25.

Tartuffe, 148.
Taylor, Tom, *N.*, 193(2).
Telegraph, The Daily (London), Q., 129–30, 132: *N.*, 255(1).
Tempest, Shakespeare's, 132.
Tenderness in Tite Street, Whistler's, *N.*, Q.i.f., 199(12, I); W.'s reply, Q.i.f., 199(12, II).
Ten Moments with a Poet, *N.*, 176(11).
"*Ten O'Clock*," Whistler's, Q., xxi, 49; xxii, 41–46, 49–51, 54: *N.*, Q., 197(5), 198(7, 8), 202 (11–12) fol., 197(2).
Thackeray, William Makepeace, 106.
Thames, River, 98.
Theatre, The (London), *N.*, Q., 267(6); 260(11), 270(7).

INDEX   291

Theatres, American (New York), Abbey's New Park, *N.*, 177 (13), 194(7); Berkeley Lyceum, *N.*, 258(2); Lyceum (Old), *N.*, 270(7); Madison Square, 29: *N.*, 194(9); Standard, *N.*, 176 (12), 188(7); Wallack's, *N.*, 181(1), 193(2), 194(7); Academy of Music (Brooklyn), *N.*, 189(7).

Theatres, English (London), Bijou, *N.*, 257(2); Comedy, *N.*, 259(11); Haymarket, *N.*, 269 (2, 3); Lyceum, *N.*, 194(10); Prince of Wales, *N.*, 177(13); St. James, *N.*, 269(3).

Theatres, German (Berlin), Neue Theater, *N.*, 257(2), 264(4).

Theocritus, 84.

Thirteen Club, Letter to the, Q., 102.

Thomson, James, 84.

Thrale, Hester L. (Piozzi), 84: *N.*, her writings; Gifford's satire, 237(44).

Three Critics: Mr. Howells, Mr. Moore, and Mr. Wilde, G. R. Carpenter's, *N.*, 176(9).

Tighe, Mary, 85: *N.*, her poems, 239(54).

Time (London), *N.*, 216(28).

Times (London), 119–20, 151–2: *N.*, Q., 206(3), 263(3); 251 (1, 2), 259(10), 260(11), 263 (2), 270(7).

Times, New York, Q., 18:.*N.*, Q., 206(3), 243(7); 176(11), 195 (1) fol., 270(7).

Tite Street, 51, 104, 113, 116; *N.*, 199(12).

Titian, 29: *N.*, 194(10).

Tolstoi, Count Leo, 107.

Tomb of Keats, The, 55, 57–61: *N.*, Q., 244(13); Notes for, 205–17; 227(21).

Tomson (Mrs.), Graham R., 80: *N.*, her works, 231(18, IV).

Tosca, La, by Sardou, 169: *N.*, 270(8).

Tragedie of Mariam, the Faire Queene of Jewry, A, by Elizabeth Carew, 83: *N.*, 234(29).

Transcript, Boston Evening, *N.*, Q., 188(7) fol., 189(9), 191 (11); 187(2), 190(10) fol.

Trelawny, Edward John, *N.*, Q., 213(22); 222(9).

Tribune, New-York Daily, Q., xvii; xvi: *N.*, Q., 198(10), 226 (18); 178(20), 181(2), 189(9), 195(1), 269(1), 270(7).

Troy, 72 (K. 1), 89: *N.*, 193(4).

True Function and Value of Criticism, The. Concluded. N., 175(7), 251(3). See *The Critic as Artist. Part II.*

Truth (London), *N.*, 190(9).

Truth of Masks, The, Q., x fol., 24: *N.*, Q., 194(8), 201(2); 175(3), 194(10).

Turner, J. M. W., *N.*, 201(3).

"T. W. H." Episode, The, 21–2: *N.*, 189(9) fol.

Unequal Match, An, by Tom Taylor, *N.*, 193(2).

Urbs Sacra Æterna, N., 241(2).

Valera, L., *N.*, 264(4).

"Vanessa," Swift's, 84. See below.

Vanhomrigh, Esther (Swift's "Vanessa"), 84: *N.*, her relations with Swift, 236(42) fol.

Velasquez, 28, 43: *N.*, 197(5).

Vera, or the Nihilists, its keynote and aim, 33–4: *N.*, when written; its production withdrawn in England; reasons for this; offered to several American managers; privately printed in America (1882); produced in New York by Miss Marie Prescott, who played the title-rôle; damned by the critics; withdrawn as a failure after one week's run; royalties received by W.; the cast; "Privately printed" in England, 195(1) fol.; the cast which Wilde first attempted to secure, 196(2).

"Vera" and the Drama, xxiv, 31, 33–7: *N.*, Q., 193(3); Notes for 195–6.

Via Ostiensis, 57: *N.*, 207(6, 7).

Vision of Poets, E. B. Browning's, 76: *N.*, 230(11).

Wainewright, Thomas Griffiths, *N.*, 244(12).

Wallack, Lester, 28: *N.*, 177(13), 194(7), 195(1).

Waller, Edmund, Q., 84: *N.*, Q., 236(38).

Wandsworth, *N.*, 185(13, 17).

Ward, Mrs. Humphry, *N.*, 247(8).

Ward, Lock & Co., Messrs., 113: *N.*, 245(3), 249(17).

Washington, D. C., *N.*, 182(3), 190(10) fol., 195(1).

Wasted Days, N., Q., 214(24).

Watson, William, *N.*, 258(9) fol.

Webster, Augusta, 80: *N.*, her works, 231(18, III).

West, Benjamin, 45: *N.*, 199 (12, I, II).

292   INDEX

Wharton, Anne, Marchioness of, 84: *N.*, her verses; Edmund Waller's praise, 236(38).

Whistler, James McNeill, xxi, xxii, 10, 27-8, 41-46 *passim*, 48 (K. 5), 49-51, 54, 91: *N.*, 175(2), 177 (12), 179(31-4), 180(36-7), 183 (9, 10) fol., 190(9), 197(1-3, 5, 6) fol., 198(7, 8, 11) fol., 199(12), 201(1, 4, 5) fol., 202 (11-2) fol., 243(9). See also *The Gentle Art of Making Enemies*, "Peacock Room," "*Ten O'Clock*," and *Tenderness in Tite Street*, and below.

Whistler's *Gentle Art of Making Enemies.* See *Gentle Art.*

Whistler's "*Ten O'Clock.*" See "*Ten O'Clock.*"

Whistler's *Tenderness in Tite Street.* See *Tenderness.*

Whistler v. Ruskin: Art and Art Critics, N., Q., 243(9).

Whistler as I Knew Him, by Mortimer Menpes, *N.*, 184(10).

Whistler, James McNeill, hy H. W. Singer, Q., xxii fol.: *N.*, 179(34), 184(10).

Whistler, James McNeill, Recollections and Impressions of, by A. J. Eddy, *N.*, 184(10).

Whistler, James McNeill, The Art of, by T. R. Way and G. R. Dennis, *N.*, Q., 183(9), 201(5); 184(10).

Whistler's Lecture on Art, Mr., by Algernon C. Swinhurne, Q., xxiii; xxii: *N.*, Q., 197(6) fol.

Whistler, Mr., N., Q., 197(3).

Whistler's "Ten O'Clock," Mr. See *Mr. Whistler.*

"White Girl, The," by Whistler, *N.*, 183(9).

Whitman, Walt, *N.*, 177(14).

Whitney, Anne, her bust of Keats, *N.*, 215(25).

Why either Claude or Titian? N., 194(10).

Wilde, Oscar (Fingal O'Flahertie Wills), born October 16, 1854, died November 30, 1900; The Epicurean, the *flâneur*, ix fol.; poet, wit and dramatist; The Protean; the great paradox, x; "an artist in attitudes"; his character analyzed by Arthur Symons, xi; his assumption of various rôles, xii; his most brilliant mood found in *Intentions*, xiii; his practical side as a teacher; satirized in Punch, xiv; ridiculed by Gilbert and Burnand; first trip to America

(1882); his first lecture in New York; his reception; his dress, xv; his treatment by the Press; by the public and by the Harvard students, xvi; his Western tour; his second lecture in New York, xvii; its reception by the public and the Press; its relation to Decorative Art, xviii fol.; his definition of Decorative Art; his teachings, xix; opinion of American Art (1883); of the improvement in house furnishing (1891), xx; his relation to Whistler; to Ruskin, xxi; Mr. H. W. Singer's strictures, xxii, xxiii; his hope for a national, a universal acceptance of Art; his insistance on liberty for the artist, xxiii; the true function of criticism, xxiv; his egotism; its sometime justification; his affectations, xxv; his child-like nature, his enthusiasm and lack of reserve; his resentment at the world's attitude; his gradual change from idealism to cynicism, xxvi fol.; dreamer and wit; Pater's comment; a verbal colourist, for whom Art formed the dominant note, xxvii; his decided views on Decorative Art (see *Decorative Art in America* and *Art, Decorative*); on the painter's art (see *Mr. Whistler's "Ten O'Clock," The Relation of Dress to Art, London Models, Art, Pictorial*, its *Conditions*, etc.); on Art in a hroader sense, in its relation to literature, painting, sculpture, acting, etc. (see *Art—general*); on book illustration (see *A House of Pomegranates* and *Art, Illustrative*); on criticism, its field, its function, its rights (see *Mr. Whistler's "Ten O'Clock," "Dorian Gray"* and its *Critics, A House of Pomegranates, Dramatic Critics and "An Ideal Husband,"* and *Criticism*); on the drama, the stage and acting (see *Mrs. Langtry as Hester Grazebrook, "Vera" and the Drama, The Relation of the Actor to the Play, The Censure and "Salomé," Dramatic Critics and "An Ideal Husband,"* the *Actor*, the *Drama* and the *Stage*); on literature, poetry and prose (see *The Tomb of Keats, Keats' Sonnet on Blue, English Poetesses*,

INDEX   293

"*Dorian Gray*" *and its Critics, Mr. Kipling and the Anglo-Indians, The Ethics of Journalism, Dramatic Critics and "An Ideal Husband," Literature, Poetry* and *Prose*); on journalism, its uses and abuses (see *Joaquin Miller, the Good Samaritan, "Dorian Gray" and its Critics, The Ethics of Journalism* and *Journalism*); on ethics in relation to art and literature (see "*Dorian Gray*" *and its Critics*, and *Ethics*); on the religious drama (see *The Censure and "Salomé*," and *Paris, the Abode of Artists*); on government censorship (see "*Dorian Gray*" *and its Critics, The Censure and "Salomé," Paris, The Abode of Artists*, and *Censorship*); on individualism, individuality and personality in the arts (see under those headings); on dress reform for men, women and children (see *Decorative Art in America, The Relation of Dress to Art*, and *Dress Reform*); on realism in the arts (see *Decorative Art in America*, "*Dorian Gray*" *and its Critics, A House of Pomegranates* and *Realism*); his beliefs condensed and crystallized into the formulæ of the New Æsthetics (see under that heading); presented in their most concise and epigrammatic form in the introductory keynotes (see *Keynotes*); his repetition of a pleasing word, phrase, or thought (see *Phrases, catch*); his fine "word sense," *N.*, 207(4), 208(9); his scholarship and care in revision, *N.*, 216(28); his tours of Italy (1876-7); of Greece with Professor Mahaffy (1877), *N.*, 241(2); the winner of the Newdigate Prize Poem and other honours at Oxford, *N.*, 217(29), 247(11); his three periods from 1876 to 1891, *N.*, 207(Remark); his second trip to America for the production of *Vera* (1883), *N.*, 195(1); the colour of his eyes, *N.*, 226(18); the butt of caricature and satire (see under those headings); his poems parodied (see *Parodies*); his remarks on America; on Niagara, San Francisco, the Atlantic

Ocean (see *Art, American*, and under those headings); his claim that he was not English but Irish, 142, 148; his love of Paris, 147: *N.*, 261(2); of the Sphinx, *N.*, 211(19) fol.; his hatred of neologisms, 114: *N.*, 249(18); his connection or dealings with Charles Godfrey Leland, Mrs. Julia Ward Howe, R. D'Oyly Carte, Colonel Morse, Joaquin Miller, Mrs. Langtry, Miss Marie Prescott, Miss Clara Morris, James McNeill Whistler, Mme. Sarah Bernhardt, Mr. T. P. O'Connor, Charles Ricketts, Charles Shannon, Aubrey Beardsley, Marcel Schwob, Robert Ross, Robert Harborough Sherard, André Gide, Ernest La Jeunesse, etc., etc. (see under those names); his admiration for or comments on Keats, E. B. Browning, Christina Rossetti, George Meredith, Walter Pater, Ruskin, Carlyle, Rudyard Kipling, Robert Louis Stevenson and the numerous English poetesses; Whistler, Albert Moore, Corot, Millet, Velasquez, etc., etc. (see *English Poetesses* and under the names given); his self-pity after his release from Reading Gaol and adoption of the name "Sebastian Melmoth," *N.*, 213(23) fol.; his poems, plays, novels, fairy tales, prose poems, letters, etc. (see under titles of same).
Wilde, Oscar, unpublished letters of. See *Letters*.
Wilde, Oscar, The Best of. See *Best of Oscar Wilde.*
Wilde, Oscar, The Plays of, N., 216(28), 269(2, 5), 270(6). For individual plays, see under their own titles.
Wilde, Oscar, The Poems of, N., 181(2) fol., 205(1), 214(24), 216(28), 254(5), 263(1). For individual poems see under their own titles.
Wilde, Oscar, in Prétextes, by André Gide, Q., xxix: *N., Q.*, 246(6).
Wilde, Oscar. A Study, translated from *Prétextes*, by Stuart Mason, 246(6).
Wilde, Oscar, Author of "Ravenna," To, a sonnet by Augustus M. Moore, *N.*, 241(2).
Wilde, Oscar, et son œuvre, by J.—Joseph Renaud, *N., Q.*, 226 (18), 241(1), 257(2), 261(2).

294   INDEX

Wilde, Oscar, Il processo e l'estetica di, by L. Gamberale, *N.*, Q., 257(2).
Wilde, Oscar. In Memoriam. See *In Memoriam. O. W.*
Wilde, Oscar. The Story of an Unhappy Friendship, by Robert Harborough Sherard, *N.*, Q., 216(28), 249(18), 257(2); 261 (2).
Wilde, Interviews with. See *Interviews.*
Wilde's, Oscar, Arrival, N., Q., 226(18).
Wilde's, Oscar, Mr., Bad Case, N., 245(1).
Wilde's, Oscar, Mr., Defence, N., 248(14, 16).
Wilde's, Oscar, Prototypes, N., Q., 191(11).
Wilde, Oscar, Returns, N., Q., 243(7).
Winchilsea, Anne Finch, Countess of, 83: *N.*, her poems; Pope's debt to her; Wordsworth's statement, 235(35).
Windsor Forest, Pope's, 84.
Winter's Tale, 85.
Woman of No Importance, A, 168: *N.*, Q., 211(19); 196(2), 253(4); the first night, 269(3); bibl.; translations in German and Italian, *N.*, 269(5).
Woman's Dress, Letter on, Q., 48: *N.*, Q., 202(10).
Woman's Journal, The, N., Q., 189(9).
Woman's World, The, 72, 118,

122, 136: *N.*, 179(32), 182(6), 229(2), 230(13), 231(18, IV–VI, VIII) fol., 232(18, IX, X, XII, 21), 233(24–5. See asterisk), 235(32, 35), 237(46), 254(6), 263(1).
Women, as the writers of poetry, 73–86; as the writers of prose, 80–1, 86: *N.*, 233(24).
Women's Voices, edited by Mrs. William Sharp, *N.*, 233(25).
Wood, Warrington, *N.*, 212(18).
Woodhouse MSS. of Keats, *N.*, 223(13).
Wordsworth, 83; Q., 84: *N.*, 222 (12), 236(35).
World, The (London), Q., x: *N.*, Q., 199(12, I, II); 175(2), 212 (19), 216(28), 263(1).
World, New York, Q., 32, 122: *N.*, Q., 226(18), 243(7); 177(14), 178(15), 181(2), 183(8), 188 (7), 189(7), 190(10), 193(1), 194(10), 195(1), 259(10), 270 (7).
Wotton, Lord Henry—in *The Picture of Dorian Gray*, 106, 108.
Wotton, Sir Henry Wotton, *N.*, Q., 235(31).
Writer, the, his choice of subject-matter, 140.
Wroth, Lady Mary, 83: *N.*, 234 (30).

Ye Soul Agonies in Ye Life of Oscar Wilde, illustrated by Charles Kendrick, *N.*, 178(14).

Made in the USA
Charleston, SC
21 February 2016